God's Radical Love in *Missio Dei*

God's Radical Love in *Missio Dei*

Focused on Missiology for Jewish Mission

EDWARD KIM

WIPF & STOCK · Eugene, Oregon

GOD'S RADICAL LOVE IN *MISSIO DEI*
Missiology for Jewish Mission

Copyright © 2024 Edward Kim. All rights reserved. Except for brief quotations in critical publications or reviews, no part of this book may be reproduced in any manner without prior written permission from the publisher. Write: Permissions, Wipf and Stock Publishers, 199 W. 8th Ave., Suite 3, Eugene, OR 97401.

Wipf & Stock
An Imprint of Wipf and Stock Publishers
199 W. 8th Ave., Suite 3
Eugene, OR 97401

www.wipfandstock.com

PAPERBACK ISBN: 978-1-6667-5689-0
HARDCOVER ISBN: 978-1-6667-5690-6
EBOOK ISBN: 978-1-6667-5691-3

VERSION NUMBER 123024

Scripture quotations marked ESV are taken from the ESV® Bible (The Holy Bible, English Standard Version®) are copyright © 2001 by Crossway, a publishing ministry of Good News Publishers. Used by permission. All rights reserved.

Scripture quotations marked KJV are from the King James (or Authorized) Version.

Scripture quotations marked NIV are taken from the Holy Bible, New International Version®, NIV®. Copyright © 1973, 1978, 1984, 2011 by Biblica, Inc.® Used by permission of Zondervan. All rights reserved worldwide.

For the Lord, my Father in heaven, who initiated this research

For my Messianic Jewish fellows in Israel, who are building the kingdom of God until Yeshua comes back

Your kingdom come, your will be done, on earth as it is in heaven.

—Matt 6:10

Contents

Illustrations | xi
Tables | xii
Preface | xiii
Acknowledgments | xv
Abbreviations | xvii
Glossary | xix
Prologue | xxi

CHAPTER ONE | 1

1. Introduction | 1
2. Purpose Statement | 4
3. Research Hypothesis | 4
4. Research Rationale | 5
5. Research Questions | 8

CHAPTER TWO: Literature Review | 10

1. Introduction | 10
2. Beginnings of *Missio Dei* | *11*
3. Martin Luther's Understanding of *Missio Dei* | *14*
4. Theology of *Missio Dei* after 1970 | 17
5. *Missio Dei* in the OT | 21
6. Conclusion | 30

CHAPTER THREE: Philological Study of God's Love | 32

1. Introduction | 32
2. Defining God's Motivation for *Missio Dei* | *34*
3. Philological Study of Hebrew Words for God's Love | 38
   3.1. A Study of נחם | 38

Contents

3.2. A Study of רחם | 43
3.3. A Study of חסד | 47
   3.3.1. Review of Previous Studies on חסד | 48
      3.3.1.1. Nelson Glueck's Understanding of חסד | 48
      3.3.1.2. Katharine Doob Sakenfeld | 50
      3.3.1.3. Other Studies on חסד before Gordon R. Clark | 52
      3.3.1.4. Gordon Clark | 52
      3.3.1.5. Menahem Qadari's Categorization of the Usage of חסד | 54
      3.3.1.6. What Is Missing in Previous Studies on חסד | 58
3.4. A Study of אמת | 61
3.5. A Study of חנן | 64
   3.5.1. Context and Usage | 64
   3.5.2. Etymology | 65
   3.5.3. Meaning | 66
4. Findings from the Studies of Hebrew Words of God's Love | 67
5. Conclusion | 70

Chapter Four: The Radical Love of God and *B'rith* (ברית) | 72

1. Etymology of *B'rith* | 72
2. Meaning of *B'rith* | 76
3. God's Radical Love and *B'rith* | 78
4. *B'rith*, Election, and *Missio Dei* | 80
5. Conclusion | 84

Chapter Five: Understanding *Missio Dei* through Christology and Pneumatology in Light of John 3:16 | 85

1. Introduction | 85
2. God's Radical Love as the Foundation of Christology | 86
3. κένωσις | 87
   3.1. Theological Study of κένωσις | 87
   3.2. Exegetical Study of κένωσις | 92
   3.3. κένωσις in the OT | 93
     Isaiah 7:1–17 | 96
     Psalm 113:6 | 97
     Isaiah 53 | 98
   3.4. Conclusion of the Exegetical Study of κένωσις in the OT | 101
4. The Holy Spirit and God's Radical Love | 104
   4.1. Exegetical Study of the OT on the Work of the Holy Spirit with God's Radical Love | 105

4.1.1. Creation and Preservation | 107
   4.1.2. Giving Knowledge of God and Scripture | 110
      4.1.3. Sanctification, Transformation (Healing), and Salvation | 112
      4.1.4. Κήρυγμα and Prophecy | 114
   4.2. The Holy Spirit's Ministry in the OT and NT: The Discrepancy | 117
   4.3. Conclusion | 118

CHAPTER SIX: Missiological Interpretation of God's Radical Love and a New Definition of *Missio Dei* | 120

1. Introduction | 120
2. Defining *Missio Dei* in the Light of God's Radical Love | 122

CHAPTER SEVEN: Missiological Application of God's Radical Love and *Missio Dei* in the Messianic Jewish Context in Israel | 124

1. *Missio Dei* in the Jewish Context | 125
   1.1. A Mini Survey among Israeli Messianic Jewish Leaders | 125
   1.2. A Short History of the Research on Jewish Mission in Israel | 127
2. Framing a Target for *Missio Dei* | 130
   2.1. Ethnicity of Jewish People in Israel | 130
      2.1.1. A Long History Short | 130
   2.2. Ethnicity, Identity, and Community | 132
      2.2.1. Ethnicity | 132
   2.3. Social and Cultural Identity among Israeli Jews | 138
      2.3.1. Ultra-Orthodox | 140
      2.3.2. National Religious | 141
      2.3.3. Sephardic | 142
      2.3.4. Russian | 143
      2.3.5. Secular | 143
3. How to Carry Out *Missio Dei* in Israel | 145
   3.1. Evaluating the Possibility | 145
      3.1.1. Indigenization and Contextualization | 145
      3.1.2 Tools for Carrying Out Missio Dei in Israel | 147
   3.2. What to Do | 147
   3.3. What Is Cultural Synthesization? | 148
   3.4. Components of Cultural Synthesization | 151
      3.4.1. Cultural Common Ground | 151
      3.4.2. Thin and Thick Culture | 152
      3.4.3. Supra-Cultural, Countercultural, and Cross-Cultural | 155
      3.4.4. Globalization | 157

Contents

 3.4.5. Peter Berger's World-Making Theory | 161
 3.5. Assembling the Cultural Synthesization Components | 165

CHAPTER EIGHT: Conclusion | 170

Further Need of Research | 174
Appendix | 177
Bibliography | 187

Illustrations (in Appendix)

Fig. 1. Social Group Relation (Closeness-Distance) Map | 178

Fig 2. The Importance of the God of Israel's Torah | 179

Fig. 3. Berger's Globalization Model | 185

Fig. 4. The Goal of Globalization through Radical Cultural Synthesization of the Gospel | 185

Fig. 5. Radical Cultural Synthesization of the Gospel | 186

Fig. 6. Berger's Theory of Making a Society | 186

Tables (in Appendix)

Table 1. Greek Words Used for Translations of God's Radical Love | 178

Table 2. Collective Identity in Israel | 181

Table 3. Jewish Identity at the Beginning of the Twenty-First Century | 182

Table 4. Formulations of Modern Jewish Identity | 184

Preface

A COUPLE OF DECADES ago, I began to travel around the Negev and Aravah Deserts in Israel. While I spent time in the desert, I wondered how God felt as the Father toward his people, the Israelites, when they were wandering in the desert for forty years without understanding the reason—their sin. Many of them had tried to give up their journey with God from the very beginning. The more I traveled in those deserts, the more clearly I could feel God's emotion for his rebellious children, but I could not express it in any words. I'd gotten a burning passion to know God's heart as the Father toward his children. I went down to the desert as much as possible, just to better understand the Father's heart. This passion has been crystallized through my research. The more I studied the Father's heart, the more clearly I could hear his deep breath with great compassion and love, but also with great agony.

I don't think that I could have learned of the Father's heart if I hadn't taken Dr. D. K. Schulz's class, *Missio Dei*. This class led me to make a 180-degree turn in faith and in theology. Therefore, I appreciate Dr. Schulz for teaching me so many things, and I feel that I owe him a great debt in theology. The *missio Dei* has revived my first love for mission among Jewish people, and among all people who need Jesus. I want to thank you, Dr. Schulz, for providing me with patient advice and guidance throughout the research process. Thank you for your unwavering support.

Acknowledgments

First, I would like to express my sincere gratitude to my advisor, Dr. Detlev Klaus Schulz, for his patience, motivation, immense knowledge, and continuous support of my PhD study and related research. His guidance has helped me throughout the entire duration of the research and writing of this book. I cannot imagine having a better advisor and mentor for my study.

Besides my advisor, I would like to thank the rest of my thesis committee, Dr. Charles Gieschen and Dr. Wayne Allen, not only for their insightful comments and encouragement but also for the hard questions that gave me incentive to widen my research from various perspectives.

My sincere thanks also go to Rev. Robert Smith, who helped me to gain access to any sources I needed, whether I was in school or in Germany. Last but not least, I would like to thank my wife and daughters for supporting me spiritually and technically throughout the writing of this thesis and in my life in general.

Abbreviations

ABD   *Anchor Bible Dictionary.* Edited by David Noel Freedman. 6 vols. New York: Doubleday, 1992

AnOr   Analecta Orientalia

BDB   Brown, Francis, et al. *A Hebrew and English Lexicon of the Old Testament.* Peabody, MA: Hendrickson, 2015

CMJ   Church's Mission among Jewish People

DBL   *A Dictionary of Biblical Languages: Aramaic; Old Testament.* By James A. Swanson. Oak Harbor, WA: Faithlife, 1997. Electronic ed.

EB   *Encyclopaedia Biblica: Thesaurus Rerum Biblicarum Alphabetico Ordine Digestus.* [In Hebrew.] Edited by Bialik Institute. Jerusalem: Bialik Institute, 1950

EM   *Encyclopedia Miqrah.* [In Hebrew.] Edited by Bialik Institute. 9 vols. Jerusalem: Bialik Institute, 1952–82

FC   "Formula of Concord." In *Concordia: The Lutheran Confession*, edited by P. T. McKain, translated by W. H. T. Dau, 637–906. St. Louis: Concordia, 2009

ICR   *A Calvin Treasury: Selections from the "Institutes of the Christian Religion."* By John Calvin. Edited by William F. Keesecker. New York: Harper, 1961

IMC   International Missionary Council

Int   *Interpretation*

JE   *Jewish Encyclopedia.* Edited by Isidore Singer et al. New York: Funk and Wagnalls, 1906

Abbreviations

LC	"Large Catechism." In *Concordia: The Lutheran Confessions; A Reader's Edition of the Book of Concord*, edited by Paul T. McCain and Gene Edward Veith Jr., 475–636. Pocket ed. St. Louis: Concordia, 2007
LCJE	Lausanne Consultation for Jewish Evangelism
LCL	Loeb Classical Library
LW	*Luther's Works*. By Martin Luther. 55 vols. St. Louis: Concordia, 1955–86
NCB	*A New Concordance of the Old Testament: Using the Hebraic and Aramaic Text*. [In Hebrew.] By Abraham Even-Shushan. Vol. 1. Jerusalem: Kireyat Sefer, 1980.
NT	New Testament
OT	Old Testament
SAAB	*State Archives of Assyria Bulletin*
SD	Solid Declaration of the Formula of Concord
TDNT	*Theological Dictionary of the New Testament*. Edited by Gerhard Kittel and Gerhard Friedrich. Translated by Geoffrey W. Bromiley. 10 vols. Grand Rapids: Eerdmans, 1964–76
TDOT	*Theological Dictionary of the Old Testament*. Edited by G. Johannes Botterweck and Helmer Ringgren. Translated by John T. Willis et al. 8 vols. Grand Rapids: Eerdmans, 1974–2006
TWOT	*Theological Wordbook of the Old Testament*. Edited by R. Laird Harris et al. Chicago: Moody, 1999
WA	*Luthers Werke: Kristische Gesamtausgabe*. By Martin Luther. 65 vols. Weimar: Böhlau, 1883–1993
WSC	Westminster Shorter Catechism

Glossary

Aliyah (עליה): The Aliyah is a Jewish immigrant movement. It officially started in 1882 under the influence of Zionism and the persecution of Jewish people in Russia following the assassination of the Russian tzar Alexander II in 1881, because a rumor had spread that a Jew had assassinated the tzar. However, there were always a handful of Jewish groups moving to Israel throughout Israel's history following the Roman occupation.[1] After the independence of Israel in 1948, according to the Israeli Laws of Return, more than four million Jews have returned home, and Aliyah continues even today.

Messianic Jew or *Hebrew Christian*: Since Christians believe in the God of Israel, Messianic Jews are different than Muslim Christians. Messianic Jews are Jewish people who believe in Yeshua (Jesus) as the Jewish Messiah prophesied in the OT. However, their theology is not so different from any mainline conservative Christian theology except in relation to the identity of Israel, the Jewish people, and the understanding of sacraments.

    The author was raised in the Korean Wesleyan tradition but has been heavily influenced by Messianic Judaism since 1991. Since then, the author's theology has been deeply rooted in Messianic Judaism. However, there is currently no concrete systematic theology of Messianic Judaism, because every Messianic Jewish group has a different theological training and background. One has charismatic-oriented theology, another has Anabaptist, and another has Calvinistic. People can find literally all kinds of denominational doctrines in Israel, including Baptist, Wesleyan, and even Lutheran. However, there is still no denominational doctrine among Messianic Jews. Nevertheless, all Messianic Jews reject replacement theology,

---

1. AJC, "5 Facts," fact 1.

Glossary

which denies the biblical identity of Israel as one who is chosen and has ברית with God, and which also teaches that God is done with Israel, and the church has replaced Israel by becoming the spiritual Israel. They all believe that God's election is not a particularity but a role as the light of the gentiles. They all believe that their Jewishness is a crucial issue so that they can witness Jesus to their people. They all believe that all are sinners in front of God, and the ברית is not the way to bring the salvation of Israel, but only Jesus is. They believe that the current state of Israel is identical with the biblical Israel, which presents God's faithfulness of his ברית לעולם, and that God continues to work for Israel.

Messianic Jews have a unique understanding of sacraments. Passover is given to Jewish people, and Jesus had just performed the Jewish tradition of the Passover for the Last Supper. His blood and body have been prophesized and hidden in the Passover meal (Seder), and Jesus has revealed the secret of the third cup (the cup of salvation) and afikomen (the hidden bread), which means the blood of the lamb of the Passover (1 Cor 5:7) and the body of the Christ.

Religion (דת): Messianic Jews and most Jewish people understand religion as a social system that humans have created. They do not believe that God has created any religion. A religion is optional for humans because it is made by humans, and it is not mandatory. Any individual can choose any religion they like. However, Messianic Jews believe that God wants a relationship with humanity, not a religion. This relationship is more like that between a father and a son. There is no choice in this, because God is the only Creator of all humanity. As we do not have any choice of our parents, humans do not have choice of their Creator either. All must understand that only the Father has created us in the universe. It is not a choice but a realization. However, the relationship has been broken because of sin, and his children do not know who their Father is. Accepting God as our Father through Jesus is mandatory for all humanity, according to Messianic Jewish belief.

Prologue

MISSIO DEI WAS A burning theme in missiology at the end of the twentieth century and the beginning of the twenty-first century. The author's initial assumption was that research on *missio Dei* has been mostly limited to the NT area. Furthermore, while John 3:16 is a key verse of *missio Dei*, it has been widely neglected in missiology until today. Additionally, the theme of God's love in John 3:16 has barely been noticed as God's motivation for *missio Dei*. If the meaning of God's love in John 3:16 is found in light of the OT, the meaning of *missio Dei* for churches and Christians becomes much clearer.

Based on these assumptions, the hypothesis of this research follows: *John 3:16 reveals that, motivated by his radical (רחם, חסד, אמת) and self-giving love,* missio Dei *is the triune God's eternal salvific action and plan to bring humanity to eternity, which is fully from his free will as the Creator.*

In light of *missio Dei*, the following questions arise:

1. How does God's love in John 3:16 justify God's motivation for *missio Dei* as the work of the triune God in the OT?
2. What does God really plan to achieve in *missio Dei* through "the begotten Son" and the Holy Spirit?
3. How should the Messianic Jewish congregations (Jewish Christian churches) in Israel respond to and participate in *missio Dei*?

No modern languages in the world can deliver the correct meanings of God's Radical Love (רחם, חסד, אמת). Even the Greek word *agape* does not contain the full meaning of God's Radical Love. Likewise, no love in the universe is comparable. Therefore, this research suggests using God's Radical Love with capital letters. It is a supra-cultural, transcultural, and countercultural love, because God's Radical Love is universal.

Prologue

The meaning of God's Radical Love has been defined through the philological study of the Hebrew terms in the OT, and this complete understanding of his love forms a new definition for *missio Dei*. This study will show how John 3:16 reveals *missio Dei* as the triune God's salvific activities in the world.

Based on this new definition and perspective of *missio Dei*, a way to apply the concept of *missio Dei* among churches and Christians in the cultural context of the twenty-first century is suggested. Since God's Radical Love is universal, so too can be the witness of Christians. By using a cultural common ground, the gospel can be injected into new cultures, and then the radical synthesization of culture into the gospel will be processed by the work of *Parakleton*.

Chapter One

1. Introduction

THIS STUDY IS INITIATED by one premise: John 3:16 might be a summary of the entire Bible about *missio Dei*, and οὕτως in the verse explains God's Radical Love throughout the OT.[1]

What is *missio Dei*? The definition of *missio Dei* was formulated in the twentieth century, and there has been a great effort to clarify this mission since the beginning of the twentieth century. The conference of the International Missionary Council (IMC) in Willingen, Germany, in 1952 was the first attempt to clarify the *missio Dei* concept and to answer the question "What is *missio Dei*?"[2] The answer was: the mission begins with God! Vicedom defines *missio Dei*, explaining,

> God sends His Son; Father and Son send the Holy Ghost. Here God makes Himself not only the One sent, but at the same time the Content of the sending, without dissolving through this Trinity of revelation the equality of the essence of the divine Persons.[3]

Defining mission as *missio Dei* in missiology stirred up debates in the late twentieth and beginning of the twenty-first centuries. This debate on *missio Dei* as a novelty surprises the author, because Jesus had already provided a clear and simple description of *missio Dei*: "For God so loved the world, that he gave his only Son, that whoever believes in him should not perish but have eternal life" (John 3:16 ESV). How can this verse help provide more understanding on *missio Dei*? This verse, in fact, is not only the summary of the entire Bible but is also the blueprint of God's mission

1. The explanation for capital letters will be in ch. 3.
2. Goodall, *Missions under the Cross*, 238; cf. Thomas, *Classic Texts in Mission*, 103–4.
3. Vicedom, *Mission of God*, 18.

throughout human history. Some missiologists took this verse as the foundation of God's mission and also understood God's love as that foundation.[4] As a matter of fact, the entire OT demonstrates God's Radical Love as the motivation for his mission.[5] Furthermore, his love is the core of the entire Johannine literature.

Unfortunately, the Johannine understanding of God's love in the context of *missio Dei* has been largely ignored by theologians and missiologists, much as the meaning of God's love in the OT in the same context has been overlooked. If John 3:16 is the blueprint of *missio Dei*, then the verse must be able to reveal the meaning of love in *missio Dei* and its connection to the OT. The author has not yet found a single study on God's love in relation to the OT that sheds light on John 3:16. No single manuscript exists on the meaning of God's love in the aforementioned verse and its relation to *missio Dei* either. Even Luther and Calvin did not clarify the term "so loved" in the context of the OT.[6] Connecting the theology of God's love in John 3:16 to the OT paradigm is an important and necessary task, because the verse can be used as a key to unlock the meaning of *missio Dei* in the entire Bible for all Christians and churches in the twenty-first century.

As Klaus Detlev Schulz describes in his book *Mission on the Cross*, *missio Dei* is the action of the triune God: "The *missio Dei* term reflects the mission of the triune God, *missio Trinitatis*."[7] God's mission has always been the work of God, the Father, the Son, and the Holy Spirit. Thus, God's motivation for the mission is deeply rooted in the Father's heart of love, and is performed outwardly by the Son and the Holy Spirit. However, the current understanding of *missio Dei* among missiologists is mostly based on the NT. It is unclear if the OT and its concept of "love" inform "agape" in the NT, and this is also not clear to laypersons among Christians and to churches, because the *missio Trinitatis* is rarely preached from the pulpit of most churches in Israel or globally.

Therefore, understanding *missio Dei* in light of the OT is greatly needed for missiological studies today. Indeed, many studies of *missio Dei* with various themes such as *Heilsgeschichte*, the work of the Holy Spirit, ecclesiology, and eschatology have been completed since the introduction of the *missio Dei* concept in Willingen in 1952. The theology of *Heilsgeschichte*

---

4. See Bosch, *Transforming Mission*, 208–9; Schulz, *Mission from the Cross*, 97.
5. The next section will investigate God's love as a Radical Love.
6. See *LW* 22:351–74; Calvin, *Gospel According to John*, 122–24.
7. Schulz, *Mission from the Cross*, 88.

has clarified God's salvific action throughout human history. Nevertheless, much more study is required on *missio Dei* in relation to the OT because, it seems, mission theologians have focused mostly on the theology of the NT to shape the theology of *missio Dei*.[8] God's salvific action has been defined thus by theologians or missiologists mostly from the NT, following a promise and fulfillment scheme.[9] Thus, the issue of God's motivation itself for *missio Dei* in the OT context has been left mostly untouched. Furthermore, *missio Dei* presents an undiscovered frontier of theology. Luther framed God's work by formulating theology proper, based on Trinitarian theology and including God's kenotic love (as a part of Christology) in the OT (see ch. 4).[10]

In addition, God's mission in the OT reveals more information about his motivation for his mission, a key element to understanding *missio Dei*.[11] Without understanding this motivation, *missio Dei* cannot be defined, because any action without a motivation leaves the *missio Dei* discussion incomplete.

One critical issue to consider in this research is the understanding of God's love in the theology of the Trinity. The Johannine Gospel reveals much about the triune God, and John 3:16 has already named God and the Son and God's love as part of the inner Trinity, as Schulz has mentioned.[12] Therefore, it is important to understand God's love as the motivation for *missio Dei* not only from the NT perspective but also from that of the OT.[13] Therefore, this book will take John 3:16 as the master key with which to unlock the following:

- The definition of *missio Dei* through the motivation (of God's Radical Love) in the OT

---

8. The Great Commission in Matt 28:19–20 is the initial inspiration of the church missions in the early stage of gentile missions. See Schnabel, *Early Christian Mission*, 1:348–467. It was the beginning of missions. Then, Christian missions were expanded to spread the gospel of Jesus based on the NT. Therefore, NT theology is the initial foundation of Christian mission. Furthermore, there are a few issues of New Testament theology that have somehow been ignored, such as how the Father's attributes shed light on Christology. See Thompson, *God of the Gospel*, 1–15; Dahl, *Jesus the Christ*, 153–63.

9. Cullmann, *Christ and Time*; Becker, *Self-Giving God*; N. T. Wright, *New Testament*.

10. WA 40:327; theology proper is theology of the Father in the Trinity, which is also called patrology.

11. Glasser with Van Engen et al., *Announcing the Kingdom*, 28.

12. Schulz, *Mission from the Cross*, 88.

13. Schulz, *Mission from the Cross*, 88.

- The action of *missio Trinitatis* (Father, Son, and the Holy Spirit) in the current situation of Israel, based on God's Radical Love in the OT context.

These issues will lay a foundation for this research to conceptualize the OT paradigm of *missio Dei* in the context of Israel. The motivation for *missio Dei* is always crucial for understanding the mission of God and for setting each Christian mission. The better we understand God's motivation for *missio Dei*, the clearer the goals and actions of our missions can become.

2. Purpose Statement

The purpose of this study is to more fully express *missio Dei* by defining God's motivation for the mission based on the missional exposition of John 3:16 in light of the OT paradigm, and to create a road map for the missional actions of Messianic Jews (Jewish Christians) in Israel in the twenty-first century. John 3:16 provides the blueprint of *missio Dei*. Therefore, it is essential to define God's motivation for *missio Dei* based on John 3:16. Consequently, revisiting the concept of *missio Dei* must lead to the OT to define the meaning of God's love, because John 3:16 has clearly identified God's love as the motivation for *missio Dei*. This book will examine the full aspect of *missio Dei* and God's love in the OT and the NT. It will also demonstrate how Christians in the twenty-first century should carry out their missions with the concept of *missio Dei* when faced with the tremendous social obstacles and various challenges in Jewish society in Israel today.

3. Research Hypothesis

The foundation of this book's hypothesis is the assumption that John 3:16 acts as a master key for the exposition of God's motivation for his mission toward humankind, due to the fact that John 3:16 offers the full picture of *missio Dei* and explains the love of God as the motivation for that mission. However, the OT also reveals God's love. Thus, the philological study of the meaning of God's love will uncover the full picture of *missio Dei* in the OT. In this exposition, God's love in John 3:16 will serve as the key to the entire research of this book as we proceed to the NT. Based on these assumptions, the hypothesis of this research is this: *John 3:16 reveals that, motivated by his radical (אמת, חסד, רחם) and self-giving love, the* missio Dei *is the Triune*

Chapter One

God's eternal salvific action and plan to bring humanity to eternity, which is fully from his free will as the Creator.

4. Research Rationale

Throughout the history of the development of *missio Dei* theology, since its beginnings in Willingen and from Karl Hartenstein, the statement of God's mission in John 3:16 in connection to the paradigm of *missio Dei* in the OT has been largely ignored. The traditional concept of *missio Dei* is that God is a missionary God, and he has sent the church to participate in his mission of reconciling the world to himself. When the 1952 conference in Willingen introduced the term *missio Dei*, it was clear that the term was rooted in Trinitarian theology. David Bosch summarizes the significance and the impact of the proposal at Willingen:

> Mission was understood as being derived from the very nature of God. It was thus put in the context of the doctrine of the Trinity, not of ecclesiology or soteriology. The classical doctrine on the *missio Dei* as God the Father sending the Son, and God the Father and the Son sending the Spirit was expanded to include yet another "movement": Father, Son, and Holy Spirit sending the church into the world. As far as missionary thinking was concerned, this linking with the doctrine of the Trinity constituted an important innovation. Willingen's image of mission was mission as participating in the sending of God.[14]

The introduction of the *missio Dei* concept into the image of mission was truly revolutionary at that time, and it brought a shift in the mission paradigm. The concept of *missio Dei* enjoyed ecumenical attention and acceptance not only by Protestant groups but also by other church bodies, such as Catholic and Orthodox churches.[15] However, there soon came a disagreement over the Willingen definition of the term. The term's creators at Willingen desired the understanding of *missio Dei* to follow a conservative line, but that did not happen.[16] The term *missio Dei* today is used primarily among ecumenical groups, and as the ecumenical groups follow a liberal agenda, so does the theology of *missio Dei*.

---

14. Bosch, *Transforming Mission*, 390.
15. Bosch, *Transforming Mission*, 391.
16. Bosch, *Transforming Mission*, 391.

At the center of this modification was J. C. Hoekendijk. He rejected the ecclesial-centered mission from the very beginning of his attendance at the Willingen conference in 1952. At the time, he was not accepted by many; however, a decade later, his idea became popular in many ecumenical mission groups. His view was that Christ is the primary subject of evangelism, and the primary goal of mission is nothing more than bringing shalom.[17] Whether Hoekendijk intended to or not, he laid a foundation for the liberal concept of *missio Dei* for ecumenical groups. That shifted the concept of *missio Dei* from the Bible to the humanistic mission and focused on bringing social peace as the major goal of the Christian mission. Through Hoekendijk's missiological influence, North American and Western European churches have shifted their mission focus from the redemption of Jesus to humanistic work to help people and to bring social justice.[18] This understanding of *missio Dei* is in complete discord with John 3:16. Unfortunately, many European and American churches left the traditional definition of *missio Dei* through Hoekendijk's mission theology.

After Willingen, the liberal theological approach toward *missio Dei* faced several rejections by scholars, among them Rosin, Berentsen, and Krusche.[19] Rosin declared *missio Dei* as "the Trojan horse through which the (unassimilated) 'American' vision was fetched into the well-guarded walls of the ecumenical theology of mission."[20] Berentsen criticized the generalization of God's mission and talked instead of a distinction between *missio Dei generalis* and *missio Dei specialis*,[21] as did Werner Krusche, according to Engelsviken:

> He criticizes, on the basis of the scriptures, both the understanding of the church and the world that is found in the ecumenical documents. He opposes the thesis that, "Through the death and resurrection of Jesus Christ all men already belong to the new mankind, even if they are not aware of it." Thereby he rejects the universalism that is inherent in a view that sees all of world history as a history of redemption. It does not come to grips with the biblical reality of divine judgement and the necessity of faith, baptism and conversion. The world is a lost and fallen world "in which God initiated the redeeming counteraction by sending His Son, who,

17. Hoekendijk, *Church Inside Out*, 21.
18. Beyerhaus, *Missions*, 43–49.
19. Engelsviken, "*Missio Dei*," 489.
20. Rosin, *Missio Dei*, 25.
21. Engelsviken, "*Missio Dei*," 489.

with His death and resurrection, broke through the law of death which was ruling and ruining this world, and who gives life in the form of freedom from the compulsion to self-assertion and self-justification." Krusche argued that, "Only God's saving acts in the world should be described as missionary. The *missio Dei* must be comprehended in a precise way as the sending of the Son into the world for its salvation and as the sending of the Church into the world with the saving Gospel."[22]

Since Willingen's proposal of *missio Dei* in 1952, one common theme among theologians and missiologists in both conservative and ecumenical circles has been the primary focus on God's actions, whether *missio Dei* is understood as salvific in the traditional sense or if it now implies humanization or the proclamation of shalom to the world. However, in these discussions, it is rare to find any work on God's motivation for the mission based on an exposition of the OT or on a missional exegesis of John 3:16. John 3:16 is very popular, since all children in Sunday school memorize the verse. Nevertheless, the verse has never gotten much attention from missiologists, particularly in connection with the mission paradigm in the OT.

Perhaps Luther had a better understanding of John 3:16 than modern missiologists do. Luther understood that John 3:16 was describing the deity and humanity of Jesus. The verse also declares the mission of Jesus to destroy death and the devil, and to transfer humanity "from the devil's realm to the kingdom of God" through the Father's love.[23] Luther did not use any missional terminology in his preaching of John 3:16, but he did cover a full range of *missio Dei* theology. In particular, Luther noticed the Father's love as the key element of mission:

> Christ says: "God so loved the world." This is an inexpressibly beautiful message; that God, the heavenly Father, had compassion on us and in His mercy and pity gave us His Son. Add to this the fact that we did not deserve it but that it was done, not in view of any piety or merit in us but out of sheer grace. And to whom was this grace shown? To "the world," that is, to those who were condemned and lost.[24]

In Luther's view, God's love is the fundamental foundation of his mission to the lost in the world. However, Luther did not go further in

22. Engelsviken, "*Missio Dei*," 489–90.
23. *LW* 22:355.
24. *LW* 22:373.

clarifying the theological foundation of John 3:16 in the context of the OT. At this point, the author's study can contribute to missiology and shed light on *missio Dei* through the missional hermeneutic of using John 3:16 as a stepping stone into the OT's portrait of God's love.

5. Research Questions

The grand question of this research is: How does John 3:16 reveal God's motivation for *missio Dei* in the context of the OT? Or, phrased another way: How does the OT shed light on John 3:16? Three research questions follow:

1. How does God's love as revealed in John 3:16 justify God's motivation for *missio Dei* as the work of the triune God in the OT?

    a. Why is God doing what he is doing in this world, according to John 3:16?

    b. What is God's motivation for *missio Dei* according to John 3:16?

    c. How does the OT identify God's love as his motivation for *missio Dei*?

    d. What is the philological meaning of God's love (אמת, רחם, חסד, חנן) in the OT?

    e. How does the concept of God's Radical Love (אמת, רחם, חסד, חנן) in the OT define the ontological, immanent, and economic Trinity?

2. What does God plan to achieve in his *missio Dei* through "the begotten Son" and the Holy Spirit?

    a. What is God doing with his Radical Love in this world?

    b. How does John 3:16 disclose God's kenotic love through Jesus as the fundamental foundation of *missio Dei*?

    c. How does God's kenotic love define *missio Dei*?

    d. What is the ultimate destination of God's kenotic love?

    e. How was God's Radical Love in his mission revealed by the action of the Holy Spirit?

    f. How does God's kenotic love reveal the immanent and economic Trinitarian action of his mission?

3. How should Messianic Jewish congregations (Jewish Christian churches) in Israel respond to and participate in *missio Dei*?

    a. What is the understanding of the local Messianic Jewish congregational leaders of *missio Dei*?

    b. What is the theological and missiological foundation of God carrying out his mission for Messianic Jews in Israel?

    c. What is the definition of "countercultural" and "transcultural" mission? And what is the difference between those concepts and "cross-cultural" mission?

    d. What are the benefits and problems of the cross-cultural mission concept in the Jewish mission context in the twenty-first century?

    e. How can one define the culture of Israeli society in the twenty-first century?

    f. How can the concept of countercultural, transcultural, and supracultural mission be applied in the context of twenty-first-century Israel?

    g. How can local Messianic congregations' leaders learn about *missio Dei*, and how could it shape their understanding of mission?

Chapter Two

Literature Review

1. Introduction

Countless articles and books have been published on *missio Dei* since Karl Barth supposedly ignited a fire for the topic at the Brandenburg Missionary Conference in 1932. It has become a law in modern missiology to define *missio Dei* as *the* principle of mission. Since then, there have been various trials to give the concept clearer form and to apply it more effectively to the mission field. Therefore, discussions of the issue cover quite a wide range of areas in missiology, such as how *missio Dei* relates to each doctrine or to every ethnic group. Nevertheless, few researchers and writings on *missio Dei* speak of God's initial motivation for the mission. Most researchers have identified God's love as the foundation of *missio Dei*, but it is hard to find any missiological writing that has articulated what the true attributes of God's love are and how these attributes function as *missio Dei*'s foundation.

Furthermore, many missiological writings on *missio Dei* have quoted John 3:16, but few have treated the verse as key to perceiving *missio Dei*. John 3:16 is rarely taken as the grand plan of the entire *missio Dei*, and no missional exegesis on the verse as it relates to the OT context exists. Therefore, this literature review will focus on *missio Dei* in the context of God's love in John 3:16 and its relation to the OT.

2. Beginnings of *Missio Dei*

It has become cliché to mention that Karl Barth initiated the missiological concept of *missio Dei* in 1932, as it is noted in almost every missiological textbook or article published from the last half of the twentieth century until today. However, the idea can actually be attributed to the theologian Karl Hartenstein. Hartenstein's theology always focused on mission, used theology as a tool for delivery of the gospel message, and defined the role of the church in the mission. It is not often mentioned among missiologists that his theology of *missio Dei* is based on God's love, through the suffering of Christ. Christof Sauer writes,

> Leiden ist einer der drei Schlüsselbegriffe *missio, unio, passio*, in der Theologie Karl Hartensteins. Das Leiden (*passio*) gehört neben der Mission (*missio*) und der Einheit (*unio*) zu den Zeichen der Kirche in der Zeit zwischen Himmelfahrt und Wiederkunft Christi und zieht sich wie ein roter Faden durch seine Theologie.[1]
>
> Suffering is one of the three key concepts of *missio, unio, passio* in the theology of Karl Hartenstein. Suffering (*passio*), in addition to mission (*missio*) and unity (*unio*), is one of the signs of the church in the time between the ascension and the second coming of Christ and stretches like a thread through his theology.

This is the theological point at which Karl Hartenstein initiates *missio Dei*. Through his declaration of *missio Dei*, Hartenstein laid a new foundation for Christian mission for the twentieth century. The basic concepts of Hartenstein's *missio Dei* are God's creation of the universe, human sin, God's mission of sending the Son for salvation, God's salvific work through the Holy Spirit, and reconciliation through the Son. These elements of *missio Dei* present two fundamental conceptions of *missio Dei*: as Trinitarian and as *Heilsgeschichte*. These two conceptions have become the theological foundation of *missio Dei*.

Conceptualization of *missio Dei* was further developed at the IMC in Willingen in 1952. Norman Goodall wrote a report of the conference, identifying two key issues. The first is that the Godhead of the Trinity functions in mission. According to the report of the IMC at Willingen in 1952, the second is that "God's redeeming love" is the foundation of *missio Dei*.[2] God sent his Son and the Holy Spirit to humanity because of "God's redeeming

---

1. Sauer, "Bedeutung von Leiden," 96.
2. Goodall, *Missions under the Cross*, 189.

love."³ Therefore, the three most important keywords from the report of the IMC at Willingen are *God*, *love*, and *sending*.

This concept of "God sending in love" in relation to *missio Dei* was fully articulated in Georg Vicedom's book *Mission of God*. Vicedom holds onto the full concept of *missio Dei* from the perspective of the IMC in Willingen in 1952 but goes even further and deeper. He emphasizes that mission is God's work from the beginning of creation to the end of the world. God is the sole-acting sovereign in his mission. "The mission is work that belongs to God."⁴ This is the initial definition of *missio Dei* by Vicedom. The most distinguished of his concepts of *missio Dei* is that God is the Sender and the Sent.⁵ Here, Vicedom develops the concept of Trinitarian theology in *missio Dei* further than Hartenstein. "God sends His Son, Father and Son send the Holy Spirit. Here God makes Himself not only the One sent, but also the content of the sending."⁶ Vicedom then reveals that the final goal of *missio Dei* is the salvation of all humanity. "The mission can be nothing else than the continuation of the saving activity of God through the publication of the deeds of salvation. This is its greatest authority and supreme commission."⁷ Vicedom's understanding of salvation is based on his understanding of the kingdom of God and the lordship of God. He defines the concept of *missio Dei* as the goal of the mission.

> It is my opinion that one can grasp God's activity with mankind as objectively under the heading "kingdom of God" as under "the *missio Dei*.... The goal of the *missio Dei is* to incorporate mankind in the Βασίλεια θεοῦ, and to convey to mankind the gift thereof.... Thus, the kingdom of God might be described as the goal of the *missio Dei*.⁸

For Vicedom, God has no purpose for *missio Dei* other than restoring the kingdom of God in his love. This is the reason why God has sent the Son who is the λόγος. Therefore, "the special *missio Dei* begins with Jesus Christ."⁹ Here it can be seen that Vicedom holds a Christocentric concept of *missio Dei*. For him, "beyond Jesus there is no further revelation of God....

3. Goodall, *Missions under the Cross*, 189.
4. Vicedom, *Mission of God*, 5.
5. Vicedom, *Mission of God*, 46.
6. Vicedom, *Mission of God*, 6.
7. Vicedom, *Mission of God*, 8.
8. Vicedom, *Mission of God*, 14.
9. Vicedom, *Mission of God*, 58.

Apart from this, the *missio Dei* in Jesus Christ, there can be no further sendings today."[10]

Vicedom brought several new insights to the concept of *missio Dei*. First, God is a sending God. God has sent Adam, Abraham, Moses, Israel, and the Son for *missio Dei*. Therefore, the mission is God's work. This concept has shifted the paradigm of *missio Dei*, clarifying *actio Dei* in a different perspective than the church-centered mission concept. For Vicedom, mission does not exist for the church, but the church exists to carry out *missio Dei*. *Missio Dei* is the only reason for the existence of the church, because God has sent the church to the world. "God's goal in dealing with men is the kingdom."[11]

Second, for Vicedom, salvation is not the final justification of *missio Dei*, but the kingdom of God is. Although the author doesn't agree with Vicedom's definition of kingdom of God,[12] the kingdom of God as the goal of *missio Dei* was a groundbreaking idea at his time, when the church had been focusing mainly on individual souls.

Third, God is both the Sender and the One who was sent. This concept shows that it is God who acts in the entire mission, because Jesus is God, who sent himself. As Hofmann describes, God was sent to the world by himself.[13] In coming to the world, he is emptying himself to be human: Jesus. The church was founded on this emptied God, Jesus, and exists as a tool for *missio Dei*. This concept is theologically connected with Johannes von Hofmann's theology of kenosis, which is Hofmann's main concept of *Heilsgeschichte*.[14]

Mission of God is a remarkable milestone of missiology in the twentieth century, because Vicedom laid the complete theological foundation for *missio Dei* for the first time in Christianity. Hartenstein sowed the seeds for the concept of *missio Dei*, and Vicedom made them grow, despite his

---

10. Vicedom, *Mission of God*, 53–54.

11. Vicedom, *Mission of God*, 22.

12. See Vicedom, *Mission of God*, 22–33. Vicedom's concept of the kingdom of God is based on amillennialism. The author can accept some theological parts of amillennialism, such as "Jesus reigns as the millennium has already begun with the churches." However, the author doesn't agree that this is the only kingdom of God. According to the OT and the NT, there are the earthly kingdom and the heavenly kingdom (Heb 11:13–16). In fact, Vicedom has mentioned that the kingdom of God cannot be in an earthly form, but his description of the kingdom of God is fully earthly, where Jesus reigns.

13. Becker, *Self-Giving God*, 136.

14. Becker, *Self-Giving God*, 22.

unclear portrayal of the attribute of God's love in *missio Dei*. Vicedom mentions the connection between *missio Dei* and God's love: "In His love, He always gives His kingdom to those who let themselves be led into it (Luke 12:32)."[15] However, Vicedom never clarifies the meaning of God's love in mission.

3. Martin Luther's Understanding of *Missio Dei*

Martin Luther spent his entire life studying and teaching how a person can be saved, but has never been officially named a "missiologist," despite all of his work to transform the world by the gospel of Jesus. Gustav Warneck's criticisms of Luther that the Reformer was never interested in missions became a famous source for nineteenth- and twentieth-century missiologists. However, many Lutheran missiologists and mission theologians have recently criticized Warneck's view of Luther's missions. James Scherer is one of the advocates of Luther's missional theology. He criticizes Warneck's view and that of Werner Elert, who also commented that Luther had no missional theology.

Scherer sees all of Luther's teachings as based on a missional concept. "For Luther, mission is always the work of the triune God—*missio Dei*—and its goal and outcome are the coming of the kingdom of God." Luther obviously never defined the meaning of missions, nor did he describe *missio Dei* in his life. However, he did use the terms *senden*, *Sendung*, or *Mittere* when speaking about spreading the gospel to all nations. According to Scherer, the keywords of Luther's mission are "the kingdom of God," "Jesus Christ," and "the Church." "It is always God's own mission that dominates Luther's thought, and the coming of the kingdom of God represents its final culmination."[16] The kingdom is the final destination of the mission of the church, as Vicedom mentions.

> God's kingdom comes to us in two ways: first, it comes here, in time, through the Word and faith, and secondly, in eternity, it comes through the final revelation. Now we pray for both of these, that it may come to those who are not yet in it, and that it may come by daily growth here and in eternal life hereafter to us who have attained it.[17]

15. Vicedom, *Mission of God*, 26.
16. Scherer, "Luther on Mission," 2.
17. LC; quoted in Scherer, "Luther on Mission," 2.

Literature Review

Victory for the kingdom will be won only through Jesus Christ on the cross. Scherer defines Luther's theology in his article as "the mission of the cross." Therefore, in terms of Luther's teaching, the concept of *missio Dei* is that our triune God's salvation work for the kingdom of God is done through Jesus Christ on the cross, and the church is the human instrument of *missio Dei*.

> God remains the author of the mission, but He uses a variety of instruments for His purpose. Priority belongs to the dynamic Word which is energized by the Holy Spirit, has power to encircle the earth and engender faith everywhere.[18]

One important point Scherer makes is Luther's "theocentric and eschatological dimension of the *missio Dei* in the Bible."[19] James Scherer believes that the *NT* confirms "Luther's starkly theocentric view." However, Scherer does not deny that Luther's theology is purely Christocentric. In conclusion, Scherer argues that, for Luther, mission is fully God's work. Based on his understanding of Luther's teaching, Scherer argues, "The *missio Dei* contrasts sharply with the humanistic missionary attitudes of later periods, is saturated in personal piety, and is vulnerable to the pressure of cultural imperialism and western expansion."[20]

Scherer's study on Luther's mission opened a new chapter of Luther's concept of *missio Dei*. Scherer clarified the eschatological perspective of Luther's mission and brought light to Luther's missional theology, which had been unexposed among missiologists until the early twenty-first century. Scherer also tried to define *missio Dei* in the light of Luther's theology. Nevertheless, Scherer does not provide the full picture of *missio Dei*. He understands Luther's unique missional concepts, such as the "theocentric concept of Luther's mission," but he does not articulate them fully in the context of *missio Dei*, nor does he explain what God's motivation is for *missio Dei* according to Luther's theology.

Study of Luther's missional thinking remained sporadic and inexhaustive until Ingemar Öberg published *Luther and the World Mission*. Öberg's based his thesis on "mission universalism."[21] The first premise of Öberg on Luther's limitations on mission is that Luther was a Reformer and that his

---

18. Scherer, "Luther on Mission," 7.
19. Scherer, "Luther on Mission," 5.
20. Scherer, "Luther on Mission," 7.
21. Öberg, *Luther and World Mission*, 9.

work was to reform the churches. Therefore, the historical context of the Reformation should be considered. This means that there were historical and social limitations for Luther in carrying out the modern concept of mission. Furthermore, the modern concept of the term *mission* did not exist in Luther's era. Öberg notes that Luther recognizes God's work in the church is completed through the word and sacraments. Organizing a movement was a secondary task. In this context, the church and mission through the Reformation have been embedded in Luther's theology. In Luther's terms, proclaiming the gospel to all the nations, including Jews and gentiles, is the work of the Father, Son, and Holy Spirit through the instruments of word and sacraments. Öberg notices the concept of *missio Dei* in Luther's theology as "God's work."

> Luther emphasized that mission is God's work (the *missio Dei*); therefore it needed no organized mission activity to the heathen. Instead, the Christianization of the non-Christian world would come about as Christians dispersed among the people were persecuted and as Christians in captivity or in business traveled in non-Christian lands.[22]

Öberg states that Luther's mission thinking is based on Trinitarian and Christocentric theology. This is not so surprising, since most pioneers of *missio Dei* theologians root their theology in Luther's Trinitarianism. In Luther's Trinitarian theology, God as the Creator and Preserver of life of all nations is the core concept.[23] God created and preserves the universe. In Luther's theology, the creation itself shows God's righteousness and love. Luther's christological exposition on the NT lays a foundation for the mission. The Christ-centered, universal salvation in his exposition later became the fundamental basis of *Heilsgeschichte*, although Luther never used this term.

Concluding Luther's understanding of *missio Dei*, according to Öberg, *missio Dei* is the triune God's own salvific action to restore his reign in the kingdom through Christ on the cross.

Furthermore, Luther's understanding of God as Father Almighty cannot be ignored in the concept of *missio Dei*; as Luther saw it, God the Father has given everything to human beings in his fatherly love.[24] There-

---

22. Öberg, *Luther and World Mission*, 3n2.
23. LC 1:17, in Kolb and Wengert, *Book of Concord*, 432.
24. LC 1:17, in Kolb and Wengert, *Book of Concord*, 432.

fore, Luther's understanding of Father Almighty somehow contains God's motivation for mission.[25]

Nevertheless, there is still some more room to study Luther's mission theology. First, despite the various publications on Luther's mission theology, it is unclear from missiological studies by Lutheran scholars whether or not Luther ever tried to connect John 3:16 to the OT context.[26]

Second, the attributes of Father Almighty from *racham, hesed,* and *emeth* (ואמת, חסד, רחם) provide another crucial element of Christology. Luther's work largely covers the Father's Radical Love of *racham, hesed,* and *emeth*.[27] Nevertheless, the author couldn't clarify Luther's understanding of רחם, חסד, ואמת in the English version of his writing.

Therefore, according to this author, a connection of Luther's mission theology to God's love in light of the OT will bring further understanding of God's motivation for *missio Dei* and will also help Christians learn how they can participate in *missio Dei*.

4. Theology of *Missio Dei* after 1970

One of the most significant publications on *missio Dei* after 1970 may have been John G. Flett's *The Witness of God*. Although Flett published his work in 2010, the author thinks that this book must be looked at before all others published after the late twentieth century, as it tackles the question of whether Flett can be credited for coining the term *missio Dei* instead of Karl Barth. In his book *The Witness of God: The Trinity, Missio Dei, Karl Barth, and the Nature of Christian Community*, Flett suggests a revised approach to *missio Dei* theology, arguing that mission is rooted in God's being and is not a question of secondary significance. He has suggested that an inadequate understanding of mission has severely impaired how we understand God.

Flett states, "*Missio Dei* is basic to a theological understanding of mission and dysfunctional to the point of being rejected by those supported by this foundation within the field."[28] Flett remains with the theological

---

25. LC 2:64: "For all in three articles, God himself has revealed and opened to us the most profound depth of his fatherly heart and his pure, unutterable love." See also Eph 3:18–19.

26. *LW* 22:350–70.

27. *LW* 24:156–58; 30:293–98; 43:28–30. There is much more description of God's love in *LW*.

28. Flett, *Witness of God*, 6.

tradition of *missio Dei* in Trinitarian theology, since his view is in full accordance with that of Karl Barth. For Flett, mission refers "to the activity of the Father in sending his Son and Spirit. God himself has acted and continues to act in redemptive mission."[29] Flett says that mission needs to be seen as a core part of theology, as it belongs to the very being of God. Flett notices that Barth himself was not really "a friend of mission," but what made Barth the origin of the theology of *missio Dei* was his "emphasis on divine agency, which did afford a necessary critical disjunction between missions and the colonialist enterprise."[30]

The most crucial problem in *missio Dei*'s foundation on Trinitarian theology is a separation of God's being from God's actions. This issue arises because Trinitarian theology uses the term *sending* "to connect God with the world, only focusing on a range of mediating entities external to who God is in and for himself."[31] The issue is that mission is understood as something that people *do*, not something that one is because of who God *is*. In closing, Flett points out the problem of *missio Dei* by criticizing the deficient concept of the Trinitarian basis, which is the perspective of the Western mindset and also the "God does everything" mindset in *missio Dei* theology. These perceptions must be examined cautiously in *missio Dei*.

Flett makes an extensive survey of *missio Dei* theology based on Karl Barth. Flett deals with the contemporary problem of *missio Dei* in the missiological world and draws a clearer picture of *missio Dei* based on Barth's Trinitarian and ecclesiastical theology. However, he does not find a different path than other Western missiologists on God's love and the *missio Dei* issue. He understands that God's love is the motivation for mission but does not explain why or how God's love functions in *missio Dei*. He writes, "The triune God is love, and love motivates the missionary to sink into the local context. Love simply cannot present itself to me other than through action!"[32] He paraphrases John 3:16 only once in his book. "The world loved by God is the object of his mission."[33]

Johannes Verkuyl defines God's mission as "the salvific activities of the Father, and the Holy Spirit throughout the world, geared to bringing the kingdom of God into existence." He also describes God's mission as God

---

29. Flett, *Witness of God*, 6.
30. Flett, *Witness of God*, 17.
31. Flett, *Witness of God*, 18.
32. Flett, *Witness of God*, 108–9.
33. Flett, *Witness of God*, 51.

being "actively engaged in the reestablishment of His liberating dominion over the cosmos and all humankind."[34] In this context, Verkuyl sets the goal of *missio Dei* as the restoration of the kingdom of God and his liberating domain of kingship.[35] It is clear that Verkuyl's understanding of *missio Dei* is based on Trinitarian theology. Verkuyl writes, "Missiology is the study of the salvation activities of the Father, Son, and the Holy Spirit throughout the world, geared to bringing the kingdom of God into existence."[36] Verkuyl sees that God's love is the core of the Christ's mission but, like others, doesn't explore further, using the term generally.

> Jesus Christ, and He alone, is the Light of the world. . . . It is surpassingly incandescent and can be outshone by no other light, whether in terms of the quantity or the quality of the leniency, the grace, the love that has been and shall be revealed in it. Jesus Christ is not a light but *the* Light.[37]

Klaus D. Schulz revisits the concept of *missio Dei* in the context of Lutheran theology in his book *Mission from the Cross: The Lutheran Theology of Mission*. Schulz begins the definition of *missio Dei* as *missio Trinitatis*: "The *missio Dei* term reflects the mission of the triune God."[38] Schulz takes *Heilsgeschichte* as the foundation of *missio Dei*, describing "God's intention to bring salvation through the proclamation of the Word in and through the Church."[39] He claims that "God uses His grace of creation (*gratia creatoris*)," sustaining the world in view of his *missio Dei* proper (the redeeming grace).[40] The cross of Christ is the core of God's redemptive action. Finally, Schulz provides a full definition of *missio Dei*.

> The *missio Dei* is the trinitarian redemptive and reconciling activity in history, motivated by God the Father's loving will for the entire world, grounded in the atoning work of Jesus Christ, and carried out by the Holy Spirit of Christ through the means of grace. God justifies man through the means of grace; delivers him from rebellion, sin, and death; subjects him under His kingly

---

34. Verkuyl, "Biblical Notion of Kingdom," 72.
35. Verkuyl, *Contemporary Missiology*, 197.
36. Verkuyl, *Contemporary Missiology*, 5.
37. Verkuyl, "Biblical Notion of Kingdom," 76.
38. Schulz, *Mission from the Cross*, 88.
39. Schulz, *Mission from the Cross*, 88.
40. Schulz, *Mission from the Cross*, 89.

reign; and leads him and the redeemed community toward the final goal in history.[41]

This definition covers most dimensions of *missio Dei*. The most stunning viewpoint of Schulz is his identification of God's motivation for *missio Dei*, which sets his work apart from that of other missiologists. This motivation is "the Father's loving will," a truth very crucial for understanding *missio Dei* in the OT context.

In fact, in the author's point of view, there is no clearer description of *missio Dei* in the Bible than John 3:16, which illustrates how *missio Dei* occurred through the Son because of God's love. Οὕτως γὰρ ἠγάπησεν ὁ θεὸς τὸν κόσμον explains that God gave his only begotten Son because οὕτως γὰρ ἠγάπησεν ὁ θεὸς τὸν κόσμον. In this Greek passage, οὕτως signifies how God manifested his love towards humanity throughout the Old Testament, emphasizing his continual and unconditional love for Israel, as encapsulated in Psalm 78. In fact, this is what the love of the Father is, which forms the main theological and missiological foundation of this book.

Nevertheless, the author believes that a bit more work remains to be done beyond defining *missio Dei* solely as "redemptive and reconciling activity in history." The author hopes that his research can cover the definition of *missio Dei* in the context of the OT and current missiological trends.

Most conservative mission theologians include the following five elements when defining *missio Dei*:

1. The Trinitarian mission through "sending"
2. A theology of *missio Dei* mostly rooted in *Heilsgeschichte*
3. God's salvific action through Christ
4. God's mission as Christocentric
5. The church as an instrument of *missio Dei*

These concepts are not new at all but are deeply rooted in the Reformers' theology. Some scholars like Newbigin or Bosch have tried to add different insights, but they do not stray far from the traditional understanding of *missio Dei*, which is Christocentric and based on the biblical theology of the NT. Nothing is wrong with this understanding, but perhaps it is not perfect enough to bring the full scope of what *missio Dei* really is, because the current *missio Dei* theology is mainly based on the NT. If one draws a

---

41. Schulz, *Mission from the Cross*, 97.

picture of *missio Dei* from both the NT and OT, it reveals a clearer view of the full image of *missio Dei*.

5. *Missio Dei* in the OT

Few theologians or missiologists have approached the concept of *missio Dei* from the OT context. The concept has mostly been developed from Jesus' redemptive work and the theology of the NT. David Bosch has greatly contributed to defining the mission paradigm in history, and sees God in the OT as he who acts, who promises, and who has elected Israel. Bosch identifies the election of Israel as for service for God. Nevertheless, the OT is not his strong area; Bosch failed to see that election and ברית have always been combined with the Hebrew term *olam*, ברית עולם (everlasting ברית) or חסד עולם (everlasting חסד). Furthermore, Bosch sees the missionary role of Israel as only a passive, centripetal mission agent, and failed to understand the meaning of the "God of Israel."

> Israel would, however, not actually go out to the nations. Neither would Israel expressly call the nations to faith in Yahweh. If they do come, it is because God is bringing them in. So, if there is a "missionary" in the Old Testament, it is God himself who will, as his eschatological deed par excellence, bring the nations to worship him there together with his covenant people.[42]

Bosch does not recognize the missionary work of Israel in Exodus in the desert, and skips the example of Jonah's missionary work.[43] Especially significantly, as a centrifugal and centripetal mission agent of God, the punishment of Israel also serves as God's pedagogical and missional work to reveal his intentions for the gentiles. This is the role of Israel as the "firstborn" child. Moreover, Bosch does not define God's motivation for *missio Dei*.

The greatest milestone of the OT theology of *missio Dei* may have been reached by Christopher Wright. Wright established a missional hermeneutic of the biblical narrative based on the theology of *missio Dei*. He recognizes that the Bible is all about God's mission. Wright tries to draw the grand picture of the Bible as a narrative of God's mission. Wright laid the firm foundation of *missio Dei* by exposing God's mission as rooted in the

---

42. Bosch, *Transforming Mission*, 19.
43. Bosch, *Transforming Mission*, 17.

authority of the Bible, which serves as the mission blueprint. Based on the authority of the Bible as the missional text, Wright argues that it is God's intention and action to make the whole creation know him. Knowing God is the initial goal of *missio Dei*. "If YHWH alone is the one true living God who made himself known in Israel and who wills to be known to the ends of the earth, then our mission can contemplate no better goal."[44] In all actions of God throughout the OT, God expressed his will for Israel and for all nations through Israel to know who God is. Israel did not necessarily have to speak out about God to all nations. The gentiles surrounding Israel watched what God was doing with Israel and learned who the God of Israel was. Wherever Israel was present, there was the God of Israel. Wright demonstrates how God uses Babylon to argue this viewpoint. God called Abram out of Babylon, promising that he would be the source of blessings for all nations. Then, God brought his descendants back to Babylon in captivity. Through the "mysterious purpose of God," Israel became captives of Babylon in order to find the fulfilment of God's promise.[45] This is what Wright calls "divine irony" in God's mission. Through this "divine irony," God reveals his love out of his judgment. Wright exposes this "divine irony" in a missional hermeneutic:

> Such teaching, conveyed by Jeremiah's letter, turned victims into visionaries. Israel not only had a hope for the future (in the famous words of vv. 11–14), they also had a mission in the present. Even in Babylon they could be a community of prayer and Shalom. As Ezekiel saw, YHWH was just as much alive and present in Babylon as in Jerusalem. His universal power and glory would be felt in judgment but would also protect and preserve his people through judgment for the sake of God's own name, and for the fulfillment of his wider purposes among the nations.[46]

Therefore, all of the actions of God in the OT, including judgment, are about God's will to let all people know who God is, and Israel was chosen to be a messenger of God to carry out the mission among all nations, regardless of their willingness or unwillingness. God revealed himself among all nations through Israel as Creator, Owner, Ruler, Judge, Lover, Savior, Leader, and Reconciler. Thus, God revealed himself in Jesus in the NT with all of the identities of God.

44. C. Wright, *Mission of God*, 71.
45. C. Wright, *Mission of God*, 100.
46. C. Wright, *Mission of God*, 100.

Wright explores, then, how God carries out *missio Dei* through his people. He finds one example in Abraham's blessings. Abrahamic blessings are connected to creation; they form God's missional gospel to all nations. Wright connects all of the narratives of the Bible through the story of God's revelation of his glory, which is fully based on the covenant and Trinitarian theology. Wright's perspective on God's mission in the OT has become a classic text for missiology. It opened a new chapter of understanding God's mission for humanity through Israel.

Nevertheless, it seems that a few missing parts remain in Wright's work. First, it is not clear how God can achieve his "ultimate universal goal" through Israel. Wright mentions God's love but never takes God's love as the initial foundation of "God's mission." He mentions only that God's love is "imperative," which should be carried out toward "neighbors and ourselves."[47] Significantly, he takes the goal of the mission from John Piper, who says that the goal of the church's mission is worship. He concludes, "*Ultimately* the goal was that God's people should know God and love him with wholehearted loyalty, worship, and obedience. It is a rich and pregnant model for mission."[48] Nevertheless, nowhere does he clarify the exact role and function of God's love in *missio Dei* and how it applies to humanity.

Second, Wright criticizes the concept of the term *missio Dei* as a "distorted theology that virtually excluded evangelism."[49] He explains:

> Mission flows from the inner dynamic movement of God in personal relationship. But in some circles the concept of *missio Dei* then became seriously weakened by the idea that it referred simply to God's involvement with the whole historical process, not to any specific work of the church.[50]

Unfortunately, Wright does not show how the theology of *missio Dei* was really "seriously weakened" at the end of the twentieth and the beginning of the twenty-first centuries.

Third, Wright speaks many times about God's "covenant" in the sense of Calvinistic theology. Since he is an OT scholar, he could clarify the difference between "covenant" and the Hebrew term ברית. If Wright explored the true meaning of ברית, he might reach a different conclusion of God's

---

47. C. Wright, *Mission of God*, 254.
48. C. Wright, *Mission of God*, 319; emphasis in original.
49. C. Wright, *Mission of God*, 63.
50. C. Wright, *Mission of God*, 63.

ברית with Abraham, because "covenant" is not a "translation" of ברית but a paraphrase.

Finally, Wright makes the same mistake as other scholars in interpreting God's blessing on Abraham in Gen 12:1–3. Wright translates Gen 12:3 as "All the families of the earth will be blessed though you." First, Wright could more closely examine the literal meaning of the Hebrew phrase וְנִבְרְכוּ בְךָ. What does it mean to be blessed in the Hebraic mentality? There are many issues to discuss on this subject. Although this term could be crucial for Wright's understanding of God's mission, he does not analyze it further. Based on the literal meaning of the Hebrew root word ברך,[51] it means all nations will come to kneel down in front of God. The Hebrew preposition ב has the meaning "through."[52] Therefore, the literal translation of Gen 12:3 could be: "All the families of the earth will submit to God through you." The true blessing of humanity comes only when one surrenders to God. Then, Wright could conclude that the "universal ultimate goal of God" is to lead all of humanity to submit to God in his new kingdom through the blood of Jesus. Concerning the use of John 3:16, Wright quotes the verse several times but never articulates it as the foundation of God's mission.

Walter Kaiser takes a unique path in examining God's mission in his book *Mission in the Old Testament: Israel as a Light to the Nations*.[53] Kaiser examines the role of Israel in *missio Dei* toward all nations. He sets a premise of the calling of Israel as the "priesthood" who "was to serve God and to minister to others" based on Gen 12:3 and Exod 19:4–6.[54] Kaiser sets Gen 12:3 as the beginning point of the mission, which is "a divine program to glorify himself by bringing salvation to all on planet Earth."[55] He also shapes his mission theology after Vicedom's "sending God" concept.[56] Kaiser argues that *missio Dei* was carried out through the "central figure of the Seed" of Abraham. He considers Gen 3:15 as the *protoevangelium* and demonstrates that Gen 12:1–3 is the first Great Commission mandate of the Bible.

---

51. "However, there may have been an association between kneeling and the receiving of a blessing" (John N. Oswalt, "בָּרַךְ," *TWOT* 132 [Strong's 285]). Cf. 2 Chr 6:13, also Arabic *baraka*, which shows the same range of meaning; see also "Brachah (ברך)," in Even-Shushan, *Milon Hahadash Le Ivrit*, 1:144; Ps 95:6; Gen 24:11.

52. "-ב," BDB 88.

53. Walter, *Mission in Old Testament*, 10.

54. Walter, *Mission in Old Testament*, 15.

55. Walter, *Mission in Old Testament*, 15.

56. Walter, *Mission in Old Testament*, 13.

Literature Review

Through this argument, Kaiser determines the universalism of *missio Dei*. He disputes the traditional understanding of God's election of Israel for *missio Dei*, the belief that God chose Israel to bring the message of salvation to the nations but that the Israelites failed the mission after the millennium's trials; as a result, God discarded them and chose "a new Israel" through the ministry of St. Paul. Kaiser challenges this traditional supersessionism by showing how the universalistic table of the seventy nations in Gen 10 were the very "families" who were to receive the blessing of Abraham's seed (Gen 12:3).[57]

Kaiser argues that Israel's mission was centrifugal, or outward-moving, in which Israel was to be active in sharing their faith—not centripetal, or inward-moving, where the people played a passive role.[58] However, he claims that Israel's centrifugal role in *missio Dei* should be understood in light of the universalism of salvation, because "God's mission was not exclusively Jewish in the OT."[59]

Kaiser's thesis is unique because of his approach to the role of Israel in *missio Dei*, which has been mostly ignored by the majority of doctrines. His insight on the role of Israel as "the light of the gentiles" in the context of the universalism of salvation, through Jesus who came from Israel, is a great contribution to the research of the theology of *missio Dei*. Furthermore, Kaiser's description of the role of Israel as a passive centrifugal mission agency is another stunning insight.

Despite such great insights in his book, Kaiser succumbed to some of the pitfalls of the Calvinistic understanding of *missio Dei* and to the mistake of dispensationalism. First, the problem in Calvinist theology's application to *missio Dei* is the theology of glorifying God himself as the final goal of *missio Dei*, which Kaiser laid out as his theological foundation. All salvation is for glorifying God. However, glorifying God is not the only motivation for *missio Dei*. Someone might use Isa 43:7 as a supporting verse for this claim, which is not adequate proof. The meaning of "glory" in Calvin's theology is unclear in the context of *missio Dei*. Most Calvinist theologians take the Hebrew word כבוד as the equivalent word of "glory," which causes a serious bias. In fact, the Hebrew words תפארת, הוד, גבורה have been translated as "glory, power, splendor, magnificence" in English. These words do not capture the full goal of *missio Dei*. If they do, how can these words

---

57. Walter, *Mission in Old Testament*, 24.
58. Walter, *Mission in Old Testament*, 39.
59. Walter, *Mission in Old Testament*, 52.

define what God is trying to achieve through such a complicated, time-consuming, and incredibly enduring task of *missio Dei* toward humanity? Does God really enact all of *missio Dei* only to "glorify himself"? God called his people to bring salvation for the glory of God according to Isa 43:7, but it doesn't say that this is the ultimate and final goal of *missio Dei*.

Furthermore, the major problem of dispensationalism is that it limits God's omnipotence. There is no biblical evidence that God works according to a finite time frame that he has set. It is true that God has chosen Israel as a messenger to all nations, but Israel does not need to function according to a certain timetable. Israel has been an everlasting בריתות conveyer from the beginning of history until the end comes, but there is no fixed timetable on how she should function. Israel has been, is, and will be the light of gentiles. There is no specific time period that God has set for Israel to function as the light of gentiles. Furthermore, Kaiser's interpretation of the Hebrew word עם (people) has dual usage in the Hebrew Bible. The word עם is usually used to determine the "people of Israel." To describe "gentiles," Scripture usually uses גויים rather than עם, although these two terms are interchangeable at times in the Hebrew text.

Third, Kaiser does not mention God's motivation for universal salvation through Israel. As a result, he does not clarify the main reason behind the election of Israel and her בריתות with God, and how they truly function in *missio Dei*. Israel was actually a passive centrifugal mission agent. However, if Kaiser recognized the meaning of בריתות and God's love in the Hebrew sense, he could see that Israel has both missional functions, centrifugal and centripetal, by being punished and by bringing judgment to gentiles (וּמְקַלֶּלְךָ אָאֹר [Gen 12:3]).

Finally, Kaiser misses this cardinal point: God always sent out Israel as captives to represent the God of Israel, and there were no gentiles among Christians in the early stage of Christianity. Jewish people like St. Peter or St. Paul were "sent" to gentiles by the Holy Spirit to witness to the God of Israel and salvation in Jesus.

A year after the publication of Kaiser's book, A. J. Köstenberger and P. T. O'Brien worked on a book of mission theology. They explored the mission of God throughout biblical history, from Genesis to Revelation. The greatest contributions of their book might be a clear picture of the

Literature Review

"missionary God,"[60] locating churches in the heart of God's mission for salvation, and dealing with the OT in a missiological perspective.[61]

In their book, Köstenberger and O'Brien approach *missio Dei* from the OT context. This study makes up only one chapter of their book but deals with the issue more thoroughly than most of the previous mission theology books. Nonetheless, Köstenberger and O'Brien's argument of the OT theology of mission is not different from that of previous mission theologians. They take the themes of universal salvation, supersessionism (Israel in Israel), conditional covenant, and the recovery of the nations (not Israel) after being rightly judged through God's mercy and grace. They also take a "spiritual interpretation" of the book of Jonah, arguing that the book represents "God's kindness" in extending the gospel to pagans.[62] In short, Köstenberger and O'Brien try to determine *missio Dei* for all nations in the OT by overlooking what God has really been doing with Israel. Kaiser at least attempts to figure out God's intentions in using Israel, but Köstenberger and O'Brien fail to understand the true function of punishment and judgment through the בריתות and election in *missio Dei*. For example, they identify the case of the golden calf in Exod 32–34 as evidence of Israel's failure as God's messenger.

> As a result, if the covenant promises to Abraham, which envisaged blessing overflowing to all the families of the earth, were to be fulfilled, it was clear that Yahweh himself must bring them to pass. Although His Intention was that Israel, by serving the world in holiness, should be the instrument in these gracious purposes, after the sin of the golden calf (Exod. 32–34) it became increasingly obvious that national Israel had failed disastrously in its God-given role, and the extension of the covenant blessings to the nations would come through an Israel within Israel. The concept of a remnant within the nation had already begun.[63]

If Köstenberger and O'Brien are right on this view, then a question arises: Did God finish being the God of Israel since then? Did God flush them out and take gentiles to also be "Israel in Israel" since then? Furthermore, how can God's words חסד לעולם (everlasting *hesed*) be translated in terms of Köstenberger and O'Brien's perspective? If God is omniscient, then

---

60. Köstenberger and O'Brien, *Salvation to the Ends*, 263.
61. Köstenberger and O'Brien, *Salvation to the Ends*, 266.
62. Köstenberger and O'Brien, *Salvation to the Ends*, 45.
63. Köstenberger and O'Brien, *Salvation to the Ends*, 37.

how did he not know that Israel would fail on their mission? Was being a messenger of salvation to all nations really what God chose Israel for? Jacob Jocz gives a clear answer to Köstenberger and O'Brien on this problem.

> The question arises, what happens when Israel breaks his promises and becomes faithless to the covenant? Does God cease to be Israel's God? This is the problem that the prophets had to puzzle out. It is at this point that the analogy between the despot and his subject breaks down, for YHWH remains the God of the covenant even in the face of Israel's faithlessness.... Does YHWH even so deal with Israel as Jehu dealt with his enemies? A crucial case is Israel's involvement in the worship of the golden calf in the wilderness. Here is an instance of a clear breach of loyalty, yet despite Israel's faithlessness, YHWH remains His people's protector and guide. This is the theological motif behind Ex. 32 and 33.... The more prevalent attitude, expressed in Hebrew piety, is that "he does not deal with us according to our sins, nor requite us according to our iniquity" (Ps. 103:10). The unconditional aspect of the covenant therefore is as indigenous to the Old Testament as is the conditional one.[64]

The grave misunderstanding of Köstenberger and O'Brien in their chapter of the book is that they completely miss God's motivation for *missio Dei*, which can be linked to חסד לעולם. The author will deal with this term later in the biblical exposition chapter.

A Catholic scholar, James C. Okoye, published an interesting book from the Catholic theological perspective called *Israel and the Nations: A Mission Theology of the Old Testament*. Okoye focuses primarily on what God did with Israel to articulate God's mission to gentiles. He raises two questions: "how and when Israel opened up its covenant with Yahweh to the gentiles" and "what the theological foundation for such a development might be." To answer the questions, Okoye sets the following premises:

> Israel was chosen as an eschatological milestone to represent the blueprint of *missio Dei*.... The creation was God's first action of redemption.[65]

> God is the missionary, who makes a way where there is no way.[66]

---

64. Jocz, *Covenant*, 27–29.
65. Okoye, *Israel and the Nations*, 34.
66. Okoye, *Israel and the Nations*, 54.

> Mission is all God's work in which we share. Paul would later say of God's action in Christ that "God was in Christ reconciling the world to Himself, not holding anyone's faults against them, but entrusting to us the message of reconciliation."[67]

> The twofold theme of proclamation in this psalm is Yahweh as creator and savior. . . . Mission proclaims the marvelous deeds of God on behalf of creation.[68]

Then, Okoye defines three motives of the mission based on the exposition of Isa 56:1–8 and 66:18–21: 1) shifting the focus from the nation to the individual; 2) calling the servants of God; and 3) proclaiming the universal worship of God on Zion.

Out of these premises, Okoye shapes four faces of Israel's missional action: 1) the universality of salvation and righteousness before God; 2) a believers' community in mission; 3) centrifugal witnessing; and 4) centripetal mission.

Israel stands on this missional identity as the "holy nation" and "kingdom of priests," "that is a nation that ministers to other nations on behalf of Yahweh."[69] Israel is God's messenger just by existing, and a servant just as she is. God used her as a messenger through wars, judgment, and captivity. Or rather, God sent Jonah as God's messenger to Israel's enemies to make them repent. This represents God's intention for universal salvation, and God's reign over the mount of Zion will be universal as well.

It is very interesting to see that Okoye takes a path a little different from that of most Protestant scholars: defining *missio Dei* through Israel. This choice makes him unique from others, because he articulates God's action from creation through the covenant in detail. He observes Israel's mission as a centrifugal and centripetal agent of God to all nations. Although he remains a Catholic theologian, he recognizes the uniqueness of God's election of Israel and the purpose of God's election, even partially.

Yet his argument misses what most Protestant missiologists have focused heavily on: the Trinitarian mission. Okoye's argument does not explain God's economy through the Father, Son, and Holy Spirit. Okoye explains God's mission through Israel in detail, but he remains obscure on what God is trying to achieve in *missio Dei* through Israel and his

---

67. Okoye, *Israel and the Nations*, 100.
68. Okoye, *Israel and the Nations*, 107.
69. Okoye, *Israel and the Nations*, 153.

motivation for doing so. Moreover, he is not interested in elaborating on the missional implications of his work: What can the church learn to do with Okoye's theory? His research is valuable for setting a new direction of the OT paradigm of the mission, especially regarding the role of Israel in God's mission, but does not fully explain why God is doing what he is doing with humanity.

6. Conclusion

Defining the meaning of *missio Dei*, especially in the OT context, is a task like assembling a huge puzzle cube. It is very true to say that the whole Bible is about *missio Dei*, as Arthur Glasser states.[70] No one will reject this basic understanding of the Bible. However, the Bible shows us many different aspects of *missio Dei*. Numerous scholars have tried to put them together to receive a complete and clear picture of *missio Dei*. Vicedom was the first person to draw a better picture of it by coining the meaning of *missio Dei* in missiology. Additionally, many other scholars have helped to assemble different parts of *missio Dei*, whether they agree with it or not. Even those negative critics of *missio Dei* helped missiologists to acknowledge its weakness. Over a half-century after Hartenstein's proposal on *missio Dei*, the concept has gained shape with increased understanding and has never faded beyond the curtain of history. The concept of *missio Dei* is still vital in missions, and many missiologists take it as a core of missions, as the author has reviewed in this chapter. This is because, despite its weaknesses, the *missio Dei* concept has presented the clearest picture of God's missional action and calling of Christians and churches for his mission since its inception in Willingen in 1952.

Despite such enormous work by scholars over such a long period, the author believes that there are still a few frailties in the theology of *missio Dei*.

1. First, the theology of *missio Dei* has mainly been initiated based on the theology of the NT. Therefore, the paradigm of *missio Dei* in the OT has been largely ignored.

2. No theologians or missiologists in Christian history have discussed God's fundamental motivation for *missio Dei* based on the context of the OT. Therefore, the theological conclusion of *missio Dei* has been

---

70. Glasser with Van Engen et al., *Announcing the Kingdom*, 17.

fragmented rather than comprehensive and totalistic, presenting Israel as a sample of the entire sinful humanity. It usually concludes with the universalism of salvation of all nations without explaining why God takes the actions he does.

3. The current Christocentric understanding of *missio Dei* is crucial, since Christ is the core of *missio Dei*. However, the Christocentric, Trinitarian theology of *missio Dei* is probably only partial or fragmentary because it does not present the full picture of God's love and its function in *missio Dei*.

4. The current theological understanding of *missio Dei* has been concentrated on "sending." However, sending the Son is not a motivation but a consequence of motivation. When the Father sent the Son, his motivation for sending initiated *missio Dei*. Sending cannot justify God's motivation for *missio Dei*. The motivation for God sending himself must be clarified.

5. Most missiological texts mention John 3:16 or use the phrase "God's love" from John 3:16. Nonetheless, none of the writings in missiology have taken John 3:16 as the primary text of *missio Dei* nor tried to understand it in light of the OT context.

This literature review has shown the need for further study of John 3:16 as a primary text in the context of *missio Dei*. Likewise, the review proves the need for further study of the theology of *missio Dei* based on the biblical foundation of the OT. Furthermore, these frailties of *missio Dei* theology until the twenty-first century will justify this study on God's motivation for *missio Dei*.

Chapter Three

Philological Study of God's Love

1. Introduction

IN THIS CHAPTER, THE study's first research question will be discussed: "How does God's love in John 3:16 justify God's motivation for *missio Dei* as the work of the triune God in the OT?" In other words, it is the question of God's motivation for *missio Dei*: How does John 3:16 define the fundamental motivation for *missio Dei* through God's love, and can the OT shed more light on understanding that love? This question was derived from John 3:16, "For God so loved the world." To answer the question, John 3:16 was used as a key to unlock the mystery of *missio Dei*, because God's love is the core of Jesus' teaching. John 3:16 describes clearly that God's mission was initiated by his love, and in John 15:13, 17, Jesus describes that loving others is his greatest command. Saint Paul is not so different from Jesus on the understanding of God's love. In 1 Cor 13, he writes that he is nothing without love.

Nevertheless, a few obstacles arise in defining *missio Dei* in the light of God's love from John 3:16. The first is a linguistic barrier, and the second is a theological one. The linguistic barrier is understanding and interpreting Hebrew words in different languages. First of all, the English word *love* is just a general term and used only for an action but not for the attribute of God's love. Most biblical scholars, like Nelson Glueck or Katharine Doob Sakenfeld, have agreed that the Hebrew words for God's love do not have any equivalent words in other languages.[1]

---

1. Glueck, Hesed *in the Bible*, 58; see also Sakenfeld, *Studies in the Usage*, 19–21.

Philological Study of God's Love

The theological obstacle is very much connected to the theological definition of God's love in the context of *missio Dei* in the OT and the NT.[2] God's love in the NT has been revealed as God's self-giving love in incarnation. The love of God and kenosis will be discussed in chapter 4.

This chapter will focus on the etymological and exegetical understanding of God's love in Hebrew terms, mainly in the OT context. This study of the original language in the Hebrew Scriptures will form a theological foundation of *missio Dei*. Then, the theological issue of God's incarnation and kenotic love will be discussed in the next chapter.

As Sakenfeld has written, the road of translation of the Bible into different languages "winds circuitously and is full of dangers."[3] The major problem of understanding the concept of God's love is a language barrier. Language is the product of each local culture and worldview, which contains a lot of imbedded, unspoken meanings in a spoken language. Those meanings in one language cannot always be fully transferred to another, because a dictionary of each language cannot fully bridge the huge gap of all the connotations between two languages. This is the major problem and obstacle to understanding the concept of God's love in the Bible, because Hebrew expressions for God's love cannot be translated equivalently into a different language.

Furthermore, languages are used to borrow foreign terms from neighboring countries. This happened a lot in the ancient Middle East. However, the basic connotations usually remained, even if the meaning changed over time. Unfortunately, translations usually cannot bring out the meaning completely.

To clarify *missio Dei* based on God's love in John 3:16, it is essential to understand the concept of God's love in Hebrew words, because the verse defines ἀγάπη as the motivation for *missio Dei*: Οὕτως γὰρ ἠγάπησεν ὁ θεὸς τὸν κόσμον. The Greek word ἀγάπη is not exactly equivalent with the Hebrew words for God's love, חסד, רחמים, אמת either.[4] Therefore, this chapter

---

2. Phil 2:5–7; see also Ngien, *Suffering of God*; Fretheim, *Suffering of God*.

3. Sakenfeld, "Loyalty and Love," 190.

4. See Morris, *Testaments of Love*. In the NT, there are many cases in which ἀγάπη has been used for expressions of love between humans: "In the word ἀγαπᾶν the Greeks find nothing of the power or magic of ἐρᾶν and little of the warmth of φιλεῖν. Its etymology is uncertain, and its meaning is weak and variable. Often it means no more than 'to be satisfied with something' [ἀγαπᾶν: ἀρκεῖσθαί τινι καὶ μηδὲν πλέον ἐπιζητεῖν (Gottfried Quell and Ethelbert Stauffer, "Ἀγαπάω, Ἀγάπη, Ἀγαπητός," *TDNT* 1:36n76)]. Often it means 'to receive' or 'to greet' or 'to honor,' i.e., in terms of external attitude. It relates more to

will be dedicated to clarifying God's love in the Hebrew concept through exegetical and philological study of those Hebrew words.

2. Defining God's Motivation for *Missio Dei*

Any action of a human has a motivation. God's actions might also have a motivation, since human beings were created in God's image, with his soul. Motivation usually comes from an attribute and is exposed as an emotional expression. It is completely clear in the Bible that the motivation for *missio Dei* is God's love. God's emotional expression in the Bible always spills out of love. Therefore, without clarifying God's emotional expression of love, the study of God's love, which is חסד, רחם, אמת, will be only a superficial investigation, because חסד, רחמים, and אמת are God's fundamental attributes and God's ultimate expressions of the attributes. Based on this viewpoint, נחם can be the keyword for God's emotional expressions, which are the outcome of God's love (Ex 34:6).

To understand the Hebrew word נחם, it is probably best to begin from the story of creation. Human history, according to the Bible, begins with creation. Therefore, it is crucial to understand what God had in mind when he created κόσμος and set a human as the caretaker of his creation. It is certainly impossible to get into God's mind since we are just his creations, but we may infer it from Scripture. When we configure God's heart in the OT texts, God's heart is mainly expressed as a Father's heart. In fact, God as the Father in the OT has been pictured fifteen times, and God has been described twice as the Father of Israel (Deut 32:6; Isa 63:16).

הֲ־לַיהוָה תִּגְמְלוּ־זֹאת עַם נָבָל וְלֹא חָכָם הֲלוֹא־הוּא אָבִיךָ קָּנֶךָ הוּא עָשְׂךָ וַיְכֹנְנֶךָ׃

> Would the LORD pay your benefits like this, stupid and not wise people? Isn't He your Father who owns you, and made you, and supports you? (Deut 32:6)

God appears as the Creator in the book of Genesis, but he defines himself as the Father of Israel in the Song of Moses. As a matter of fact,

---

the inward attitude in its meaning of 'seeking after something,' or 'desiring someone or something'" (Quell and Stauffer, *TDNT* 1:36). "LXX mostly renders it ἀγαπᾶν, and only seldom and in a secular context φιλεῖν (10 times; φιλία 5 times for אַהֲבָה), ἐρᾶσθαι (twice) or φιλιάζειν (once)" (Quell and Stauffer, *TDNT* 1:22). However, it is interesting to see that ἀγαπᾶν is used mainly for אהב, רחם in the LXX.

Philological Study of God's Love

God's expression of his heart as the Father towards Israel and all humankind can be found in almost every chapter of the Bible. The Father's heart of the Creator is exposed in God's emotional expressions in Gen 1:10, כִּי טוֹב (That it is good [ESV]). On the first and second days of creation, this word is not used. But on the third day, God repeats this expression twice. On the first and second days, God is working on building the foundation of the earth from רקיעה (expanse or firmament). Then, God finally creates the heavens and the earth. Afterwards, he begins to create life on the earth. When God creates a life-form, it is "perfect." Everything is perfect! The Hebrew word טוב means "good." In the Jewish concept, however, טוב means that everything is perfectly in order (בסדר). God might have had the smile of a young father who just receives his first baby in his arms when he finished his third day of creation! Jacob Neusner explains the interpretation of Genesis Rabbah:

> The message throughout is clear. First, one must not speculate on matters not revealed in the Torah, a familiar theme. God reveals what God wants humanity to know. Second, the world is created for blessings, not for curse[s]. There is no evil creator, topped by a benevolent but unknown God. So, choosing the composition in these and other aspects forms part of the polemic of the compositors.[5]

Furthermore, the meaning of the Hebrew word טוב as "perfect" has been widely accepted by most of the rabbis throughout the history of Judaism.[6] Most Christians and Jews believe that God has a purpose for his every action, as he does for the creation. Therefore, it would be better to translate Gen 1:10, וַיַּרְא אֱלֹהִים כִּי־טוֹב, as "God saw that (his creations were) perfect," because his intention for creation was good and perfect, and the outcome was perfect. As the Father of the creation, God was fully satisfied about the perfection of his creation. Then, he gives all the creation to Adam to manage, control, and develop further. However, Adam and Havah (the woman) betray their Creator by breaking the commandment. Thus, as the perfection of the κόσμος is broken, so is God's heart. In Gen 3:9, God expresses his broken heart with one interrogative word: איכה (*Eicha*)? This word sounds like God cries out with his shattered heart due to the

---

5. Neusner, *Genesis Rabbah*, 2:23.

6. (בפסוק 5 נכתב: ... כי טוב" ציין לרביאה המעיד על שלמות ...) (רשב"ם בראשית רבה).
Author's translation: "In chapter 5, it is written . . . 'כי טוב.' This means that the creation was standing on perfection" (Rashbam, Gen. Rab. 1:31).

betrayal of his own creation. Why did God need to search where Adam and Havah were hiding? Didn't he know where they were? איכה has a very different connotation than איפה אתה (where are you). *TWOT* suggests that איכה is an interrogative term: "The interrogative adverb is sometimes used in requesting information (Gen 18:9; 22:7; 1 Sam 9:18), but more often no answer is expected. This is particularly true of poetic passages."[7] In Gen 3, God interrogates אישה and אדם, but not the snake. The snake receives only punishment, without interrogation.[8] Through the interrogation, God vents his shattered heart full of agony to humans through this single word. This is the only occasion on which God uses the word in the entire OT. The expression איכה might have a deep emotional connection to נחם because נחם might also be an expression that comes out of God's love and agony toward human beings. Luther has a similar understanding in Gen 3:15:

> Here grace and mercy begin to shine forth from the midst of the wrath which sin and disobedience aroused. Here in the midst of most serious threats the Father reveals His heart; this is not a father who is so angry that he would turn out his son because of his sin, but one who points to a deliverance, indeed one who promises victory against the enemy that deceived and conquered human nature.[9]

Thus, the expression of נחם might show us some clues toward God's motivation for *missio Dei*. First of all, נחם indicates that God's motivation for his mission is related to his love, because the expression is used for the first time when humans break their relationship with the Creator. Second, however, נחם is not the motive for *missio Dei*, but an expression of God's emotion, which can help us understand the real motivation for God's mission toward his creation. Third, נחם signals that God's true reason for his mission toward the entire creation might be from his love, which might be the love of a father as Prov 3:12 describes: כִּי אֶת אֲשֶׁר יֶאֱהַב יהוה יוֹכִיחַ וּכְאָב אֶת־בֵּן יִרְצֶה. As the verse presents, נחם is an expression of the Father's heart punishing his children with love and agony. This emotional expression of God's compassion and agony toward humanity might be the outcome of God's love—חסד, רחם, אמת—as the philological study of the word נחם will present in section 3.1.

---

7. Herbert Wolf, "איכה," *TWOT* 36 (Strong's 75).
8. Wolf, *TWOT* 36.
9. *LW* 1:189.

Philological Study of God's Love

Unfortunately, the true meaning of God's love in the context of the OT has been obscured in Western theology for a couple of reasons. First, no equivalent words for God's רחמים, חסד, and אמת exist in other languages.[10] Western theology is basically based on Greek and Latin translations of the Bible. *Love* in all translated languages is only "similar" to those Hebrew words, without the same connotations.

Furthermore, many Hebrew terms had different meanings in ancient times than they do now, especially those from borrowed lexicons of foreign languages such as Akkadian, Ugarit, Egyptian, Aramaic, or Arabic. Therefore, an etymological study of Hebrew terms for God's love can help to clarify the meaning of God's love.

Moreover, Western theology about God's love is not exactly identical to the ancient Judaic context, because Justin Martyr and his disciple Irenaeus contextualized St. Paul's Hebraic, Messianic Judaism into the Hellenistic worldview by using Neoplatonism.[11] This means that St. Paul's Hebraic, Messianic Judaism[12] was completely contextualized and incarnated in Neoplatonism by Justin Martyr and Irenaeus in the second century AD. As chapter 6 will describe, contextualization always has pros and cons. On one hand, by contextualizing St. Paul's Messianic Judaism to present Christianity through Neoplatonism to fit in the Hellenistic worldview, Justin Martyr did a great work. On the other hand, he had to give up many Hebrew cultural contexts and meanings from the Hebrew Scripture. Daniel Boyarin describes this issue.

> Later Justin could boldly claim, "whatever has been spoken aright by any man belongs to us Christians." There are two ways of taking this. From one perspective Justin might be described as generous in his appraisal of non-Christian cultures since he was not dismissing them out of hand. But from another perspective, which is probably nearer to the truth, he could be seen as attempting to place Christianity on the intellectual and cultural map without much real interest in a theological assessment of other cultures.[13]

10. See the following philological studies of each of the Hebrew words in this chapter.

11. Briggman, *Irenaeus of Lyons*, 12, 27; see also Soulen, *God of Israel*; and Boyarin, "Justin Martyr Invents Judaism," 427, 460.

12. Among current Messianic Jews in the world, it is widely considered that the first believers in Jesus were Messianic Jews because they were Jewish and believed in their Jewish Messiah, Jesus. See Rudolph and Willitts, *Introduction to Messianic Judaism*, 302–25.

13. Boyarin, "Justin Martyr Invents Judaism," 460.

Consequently, it is no wonder to find that Western theologians always have some missing parts in their interpretations of the Scriptures. It is the same with the meaning of God's love in the OT context. Unfortunately, no absolutely perfect solution exists to get through these two hindrances in theology and exegesis. Therefore, this study will try to bridge the linguistic and theological gaps between the Hebrew Judaic meaning and the Western Neoplatonic comprehension of God's love as much as it can.

3. Philological Study of Hebrew Words for God's Love

3.1. A Study of נחם

The Hebrew word *nacham* (נחם) does not present an attribute of God's love in the OT; rather, the Hebrew words נחם and התעצב in Gen 6:6 show emotional expressions of God's love and express God's heart as the Father of all creation. In this verse, התעצב is just a double descriptive term of נחם, to stress the expression.

וַיִּנָּחֶם יְהוָה כִּי־עָשָׂה אֶת־הָאָדָם בָּאָרֶץ וַיִּתְעַצֵּב אֶל־לִבּוֹ׃

God has deeply sighed in agony because He made man on earth,
and His heart became upset.

After איכה in Gen 3:9, נחם is God's next emotional expression in the Bible. Most of the translations of this verse in various languages have not conveyed the original meaning of נחם. BDB or other Hebrew lexicons translate this word as "regret," "have compassion," "be consoled for."[14] There is mostly no problem with this translation of the word נחם in other contexts.[15] Genesis 6:6 is the first passage that reveals God's emotion literally in the OT. For the most part, the translations of 6:6 in other languages do not convey the symbiotic emotional expression of the Father, which is mixed with God's agony over the humans' betrayal and, at the same time, God's love, which is God's fundamental attribute. Furthermore, didn't God know that people would fall into evil lives? God is omniscient, so he knows everything that could happen. Then how could he "regret" making people? Therefore, most foreign language translations of the verse do not make sense in the

---

14. "נחם," BDB 636–37.
15. Exod 3:17; Jer 20:16.

context of God's omniscience. Rather, נחם should be understood in a parallel context to איכה in Gen 3:9. It is an extreme expression of the broken heart of the Father toward his children. Therefore, the translation of "be consoled for" can somehow make sense, although it doesn't fully capture the original meaning.

The etymology of נחם will clarify its original meaning at the time when Genesis was written. *TWOT* states that נחם originated from Ugaritic.[16] In Ugarit, ניחם has the same meaning and is used many times as a part of the name מנחים. However, the beginning of the word can be traced far back to Old Akkadian. I. J. Gelb describes the root word *nḥm*. The infinitive of the root word is *nuāḥum*, "to be restful."[17] Then, the word appeared in the Amarna text with a variety of forms of *ia-an-ḥa-mi*, which has the root of *nḥm* with the same meaning of Ugarit. Interestingly, in the form of a name, both Akkadian and Ugarit have a similar form: *ynḥm* or *mnḥm*.[18] However, in Aramaic, the letter form and meaning have changed. First of all, there is no Aramaic word that is fully equivalent to the three-letter root, נחם. However, in the author's opinion, חמה in Aramaic possibly shares the same root with *nḥm* in Old Akkadian. In Semitic languages, borrowing vocabularies from different languages has caused many problems in tracing their origins, as Paul Mankowski has described in his monograph. This occurs because each language often swapped prefix or suffix letters in the process of borrowing. Mankowski explains:

> The reality is complicated by the consideration that the judgment that a lexical item in Akkadian and another in Hebrew reflect the same Semitic word is often not a datum but a demonstrandum. For example, if BH אתיק ("passage") and Akkadian *etequ* ("to cross") reflect the same root (cTQ), then one can confidently conclude that the Hebrew was borrowed from Akkadian, since the native BH reflex of PSc is ע, and the א would indicate the vocalic onset.[19]

Through time, the borrowed vocabularies kept changing their forms, depending on each language structure. As Mankowski has mentioned above, we often see an exchange between א and ע in the first letter of the root between Semitic languages, and we also see one between חמא in Hebrew and חמה in Aramaic. Furthermore, we can often find an interchange

---

16. Marvin R. Wilson, "נחם," *TWOT* 570 (Strong's 1344).
17. I. J. Gelb, cited in Gordon, *Ugaritic Textbook*, 189.
18. Richard Hess, "Amarna Personal Names," in Gordon, *Ugaritic Textbook*, 223.
19. Mankowski, *Akkadian Loanwords*, 5.

between ה and י in the first letter of the root between Semitic languages. *Ia-an-ha-mi* in Akkadian and *ynḥm* is one of those cases.[20] In particular, there have often been mistakes of transcribing from tablets, which caused changes of letters. These cases have often caused confusion and a mix-up of meanings between languages. *Maddattu* and *nadānu* in Akkadian is one of those cases. The Hebrew word נתן is certainly borrowed from Old Akkadian, which means "give."[21] However, the original Akkadian word for "give" was *maddattu*, but it changed form and swapped the meaning of the two vocabularies in the process of borrowing.[22]

The author assumes that this phenomenon of exchanging letters and mixing up the meanings of vocabularies in the process of borrowing languages happened to the Hebrew word נחם too. *TWOT* explains:

> The origin of the root seems to reflect the idea of "breathing deeply," hence the physical display of one's feelings, usually sorrow, compassion, or comfort. The root occurs in Ugaritic (see "to console" in UT 19: no. 1230) and is found in OT proper names such as Nehemiah, Nahum, and Menehem. The LXX renders *nḥm* by both *metanoeō* and *metamelomai*. The KJV translates the Niphal of *nḥm* "repent" thirty-eight times. The majority of these instances refer to God's repentance, not man's.[23]

Therefore, an Old Akkadian word *yḥmn* (rage) may share a similar connotation with נחם, and *nḥm* might be borrowed by Ugarit and then Aramaic, and then transferred to Hebrew. However, there is no proof of whether both words have the same root in origin. Both have a similar form of letters. It is very interesting to see that נחם in the Bible is used mainly in *piel* form when it is used for God's emotion, which is probably influenced by *yḥmn* in Akkadian and Ugarit. It has been mixed up between the two words and fixed in Aramaic as חמה, which means "in anger, fury."[24] Yona Sabar explains that חמה/חמא in Neo-Aramiac means "curse, poison, or sickness to someone."[25] *Vḥm* or *nḥm* might have begun as an expression of a deep sigh as "the physical display of one's feelings, usually sorrow and anger with compassion." However, the sounds of sighs have different connotations: the

20. Mankowski, *Akkadian Loanwords*, 5.
21. Mankowski, *Akkadian Loanwords*, 5.
22. Goldenberg, *Semitic Languages*, 70.
23. Wilson, *TWOT* 570.
24. "חמה," *DBL* §2779.
25. Sabar, *Jewish Neo-Aramaic Dictionary*, 63.

sound of relief and the sound of anger. This connotation can be related to one of God's characters, אל קנא (Exod 34:14). God's jealousy and anger are fundamentally based on his חסד, רחמים, and אמת. Jealousy is a kind of the Father's anger that comes out of frustration with his children's failure of faithfulness.

Therefore, נחם in the *piel* form could share both implications. This might be the reason why נחם has been used in two totally opposite meanings: comfort and regret. In Gen 24:67: וַיִּנָּחֵם יִצְחָק אַחֲרֵי אִמּוֹ (And Israel sighed deeply after his mother [passed away]).

One of the prominent linguistic phenomena in the borrowing process among Semitic languages, and in creating new vocabulary even in modern-day Hebrew, is called חילופי למנ"ר, which means "exchanging למנ"ר."[26] In Hebrew and other Semitic languages, there were frequent exchanges of letters while a word was migrating to other languages or being created as a new word, like ש"זסע, בק"ר, or למנ"ר. The exchange of Hebrew letters among למנ"ר in words was common among Semitic languages. One example for this phenomenon can be found in Job 8:16–17.

רָטֹב הוּא לִפְנֵי־שָׁמֶשׁ וְעַל גַּנָּתוֹ יֹנַקְתּוֹ תֵצֵא: עַל־גַּל שָׁרָשָׁיו יְסֻבָּכוּ בֵּית אֲבָנִים יֶחֱזֶה:

> He is moisture before the sun, and his young shoots will grow on his garden. His roots are wrapped about the heap, he beholds the place of stones.

Here, there is an exchange between ל and נ in the word גל/גן. Most foreign language Bibles have translated these two words as "garden/spring." However, most Hebrew Bible scholars accept the consideration of this word as a phenomenon of the "exchange of למנ"ר" in Hebrew. This means that both words were supposed to be גן. Especially when the letters have the same guttural sound, like ר, ח, ה, it is very easy to mix them up in the transition. So, it seems like נחם may have had two different word roots in the beginning, from different language sources. The author guesses this is the reason why נחם contains two contrary meanings.

The translation of נחם, "repent" in English Bibles, is probably not even a very accurate word, but a better one cannot be found either. Perhaps there is only one action in the verb נחם (*naham*) with two opposing emotions. The first one is comfort, and the second is heartbroken agony. This נחם is a very typical emotional state of a father with an undutiful child. The verb

---

26. Qimron, *Biblical Hebrew*, 33–34.

occurs most famously in Isa 40:1, "Your God said, Console, O console my people" (נַחֲמוּ נַחֲמוּ עַמִּי יֹאמַר אֱלֹהֵיכֶם), and in Ps 23:4, "Because you are with me, those, your stick and staff, comfort me" (כִּי־אַתָּה עִמָּדִי שִׁבְטְךָ וּמִשְׁעַנְתֶּךָ הֵמָּה יְנַחֲמֻנִי).

Usually, according to Western theology, נחם in Gen 6:6 is not aligned with נחם in Isa 40:1. Nevertheless, if the ethnological context of נחם is considered, those two different emotional expressions are deeply connected with each other, because they are two different emotions in one action. In this context, Walter Maier has a better understanding of נחם if נחם is taken as a typical expression of a heartbroken father. Maier translates נחם in Gen 6:6 as "He grieved" or "He suffered grief,"[27] which is far better than "repent." The author thinks the translation of נחם as "sorry" is a too-Americanized expression that doesn't understand God's emotional situation: a broken heart. If we take נחם as an emotional expression of God's broken heart, Maier's translation can then fit, as he noticed on the *niphal* usage of נחם in other verses (1 Sam 15:11, 35; 2 Sam 24:16; 1 Chr 21:15; Jer 42:10).

Most of the foreign Bibles translate נחם in Isa 40:1 as "console," but נחם in this verse might have a dual expression of the meanings "compassion" and "console." When people feel relaxed or tormented, a deep sigh comes out unconsciously as an expression of their feeling. נחם, especially, expresses God's emotion. Therefore, it might be better to translate Isa 40:1 as the following: "Have a father's compassion for my people." Though this is not perfect English style, it would improve the understanding of God's emotion toward his people of Israel, which is a Father's broken heart and grieving compassion toward his children.

As a consequence, the usage of נחם in Gen 6:6 becomes very clear. On one hand, נחם is an expression of God's broken heart full of anger, fury, and agony from the bottom of his heart toward his creation. On the other hand, נחם is the outcome of God's compassion. In fact, איכה can be understood better when one understands the meaning of נחם, because איכה is just an emotional outpouring of God's נחם toward Adam and Eve. A case of the Father's broken heart can be found in the story of the prodigal son. Jesus explains the broken heart of God through the broken heart of the prodigal son's father. In fact, the parable of the prodigal son can be understood fully only when one recognizes that the story very much overlaps with Gen 3 and 6 in the sense of a father's emotion. Therefore, the author's own translation

---

27. Maier, "Does God 'Repent,'" 135.

of the verse Gen 6:6 can be supported by this conclusion: "God sighed deeply in agony for He made the people, and His heart became upset."

Most Bibles have translated God as the one responsible for the emotion in this verse, but in fact, God suffers from his own creation. It is God's agony that he has made the people, has taken care of them, and has been betrayed by them. All fathers in the world can understand this occasion. How much do those fathers rejoice when they hold the newborn babies in their arms? How much agony and suffering do they go through in bringing them up? In this context, we can understand how the word רחם is connected to נחם. Because of God's רחמים, God has to swallow the bitterness of נחם in his heart. Thus, the Hebrew term נחם is a crucial keyword to unlock the mystery of God's love in *missio Dei*, because נחם is an emotional expression that orchestrates God's love throughout the Bible. The expression of נחם continues in the NT through Jesus' cross as the presentation of God's חסד, רחמים, and אמת, which are the backbone of God's בריתות.

Therefore, the etymological study of רחם and נחם leads us to the etiology of *missio Dei* and gives us a profound comprehension of the reason for *missio Dei*. Clarification of God's motivation for *missio Dei* will sharpen the reason for Christian mission and will help to clarify its goal in the twenty-first century.

3.2. A Study of רחם

The Hebrew term רחם has been investigated widely among Semitic linguists and theologians for a century. *TDOT* and *TWOT* have explained that this word is common among Semitic languages but has various forms in each language. In Akkadian, we find *rêmu*. This word has two different meanings: compassion and the womb. According to *TDOT*, the word in a verb means "be devoted, love," and sometimes it was used with the meaning of "be benevolent, merciful."[28] Most of the Semitic languages have used this word in a way more related to "love and mercy" than to "womb." In fact, M. Dahood mentions in his short note on *riḥḥam* of Ugarit that "the relatively large number of denominative verbs in Ugaritic [were] derived from names of parts of the body."[29]

TDOT also explains the translation cases of LXX. In the case of the *pa'al* stem, רָחֵם, it was translated to *agapán*. For the *piel* stem, רִחֵם, it used

[28]. Johannes F. Diehl, "רחם," *TDOT* 13:438.
[29]. Dahood, "Denominative Riḥḥam," 204.

ἐλέειν. However, there are various forms of the translation of רחם in the LXX. It is interesting to find that it has also been translated to *oikteírein*.[30] *TDOT* explains that a noun form of רַחַם is represented twenty-eight times by *oiktirmós* and seven times by *éleos*. In the Bible, רחם appears forty-nine times, and forty-two times in the *piel*. The crucial issue here is that the subject of רחם in *piel* form is often אלהים. In these cases, the word is mostly translated as *oiktirmós* in the LXX.

These Greek words bring different connotations of God's love in the Hellenistic perspective. The Greek word ἐλέειν comes from ἔλεος, which means "compassion, pity." However, it has the connotations of "pain, lament, commotion" rather than of "compassion."[31] Furthermore, οἰκτιρμός is another Greek word that has been used the most, along with ἐλέειν and αγαπάω for רחם in the LXX. οἰκτιρμός is from οἰκτός, which means "lamentation, compassion, pity." One of the derivatives of the word is οἰκτιστος, "loving pity the most."[32] Robert Beekes explains that its denominative verb οἰκτρός means "to pity, commiserate, bewail," which is similar to other derivatives.[33] There are many other Greek words that were used to translate רחם, but the plural form of רחם was always translated with ἔλεος or οἰκτιρμός.

The significant discrepancy between Greek and Hebrew words here is the connotation of love. In fact, the connotations of רחם and ἔλεος, οἰκτιρμός are not exactly identical. This is because, first of all, the Greek words were borrowed from secular vocabularies to apply to God's word. Second, the most popular Greek word for love is probably αγαπάω. However, according to *TDNT*, it has seldom been used to translate God's love (רחם) in the LXX.[34] The original meaning of the αγαπάω in the prebiblical text was "to be satisfied with something," which is far from the meaning of God's love.[35] In fact, αγαπάω has mostly been used to translate אהב in the Bible, and אהב was never used to determine the attribute of God's love in the Hebrew text. Rather, it was used to express an action of God's love or love among people. This connotation of love has a little gap from the Hebrew word רחם, and this chapter will reveal the translation gap between Greek and Hebrew.

---

30. Ulrich Dahmen, "רחם," *TDOT* 13:439.
31. Beekes with Van Beek, "ἔλεος," *Etymological Dictionary of Greek*, 1:407.
32. Beekes with Van Beek, "οἰκτιρμός," *Etymological Dictionary of Greek*, 2:1056.
33. Beekes with Van Beek, *Etymological Dictionary of Greek*, 2:1056.
34. Quell and Stauffer, *TDNT* 1:36.
35. Quell and Stauffer, *TDNT* 1:36.

Philological Study of God's Love

There is another interesting Hebrew word, רחים (pl.: ריחיים), which means a stone hand mill or quern. Another meaning of רחים is a grindstone. It is in the *pa'il* form of ריחיים. רחם was probably deprived from the Ugarit word רחמ and also transferred to the Arabic ריחא. A quern in Akkadian and Aramaic is different than in Hebrew. It is *erittu* in Akkadian and *eru* in Aramaic.[36] Therefore, רחיים might be derived from Ugarit. However, רחים (loving) in Aramaic is רחימת, or רחימא too. Thus, רחים is more connected in Hebrew and Aramaic. We can find an example of רחים as a millstone in Isa 47:2: קְחִי רֵחַיִם וְטַחֲנִי קָמַח (You will take a millstone, and will grind flour).

It is very interesting to see how Jewish rabbis used רחים in medieval times. The meaning of רחים suddenly changed to "loving" from this period. Most of the Talmudic Hebrew use רחים as "loving" or "friendly." A famous Israeli Hebrew poet, Abraham Regelson, has written a Zionist poem that every Israeli has memorized: רחימה בלשונות, חקוקות אותיותיך בתבנית עולמי (Carved letters in the everlasting mold, and love speaking).[37] However, Regelson has used רחים in two different meanings. One is "loving," and the other is "grinding," reflecting the origins of the word. Therefore, what we can see is that the understanding of the term רחם is not just אהבה or חסד. Regelson's usage of רחים was from medieval rabbinic literature. The meaning of רחים means an enduring love.

רחיים was one of the most significant tools for life in the ancient Middle East. Karel van der Toorn mentions that hand mills were widely used in the OT time.[38] Every morning a village woke up with the sound of a millstone grinding to prepare fresh לחם. This is a very typical woman's job. Fred Wight describes,

> This sound of the grinding is not exactly musical, and yet many love to go to sleep under it. In the mind of those who live in the East this sound is associated with home, and comfort, and plenty. The women are the ones who engage in this task, and they begin it early in the morning, and it often requires half a day to complete.[39]

When Jeremiah foretold judgment upon Israel for her sins in Jer 25:10, he spoke concerning what GOD would take from her:

---

36. Even-Shushan, "רחם," *Milon Hahadash Le Ivrit*, 3:1271.

37. "Engraved Are Thy Letters" [in Hebrew], by Abraham Regelson. Published with permission of the rights holders. See https://benyehuda.org/read/3861#%D7%90.

38. Karel van der Toorn, "Millstone," *ABD* 1:831–33.

39. Wight, *Manners and Customs*, 22.

וְהַאֲבַדְתִּ֣י מֵהֶ֗ם ק֤וֹל שָׂשׂוֹן֙ וְק֣וֹל שִׂמְחָ֔ה ק֥וֹל חָתָ֖ן וְק֣וֹל כַּלָּ֑ה ק֥וֹל רֵחַ֖יִם וְא֥וֹר נֵֽר׃

> I will make lose them the voice of joy, the voice of gladness, the voice of the bridegroom, and the voice of the bride, the sound of the millstones, and the light of the candle.

Thus, the sound of these hand mills is an indication of life and activity, and the absence of them would be a sign of utter desolation, because there would be no food to grind anymore. Therefore, the grinding sound of women means prosperity and rejoicing in the life with which God has provided them. This is an expression of God's רחם toward his children. At the same time, however, רחים requires the hard work of women to acquire their happiness and satisfaction in the meal.

Therefore, רחיים symbolizes God's hard work and enduring love toward his people. Moreover, when they grind wheat to bake לפה or נען (Middle Eastern tortilla), all of the women gather to chat. In Judaism, loving requires the hard task of bearing pain until "it is ground up." Exodus 34:6 reveals this attribute of God, who is gracious and merciful but also has a broken heart:

וַיַּעֲבֹ֨ר יְהוָ֥ה ׀ עַל־פָּנָיו֮ וַיִּקְרָא֒ יְהוָ֣ה ׀ יְהוָ֔ה אֵ֥ל רַח֖וּם וְחַנּ֑וּן אֶ֥רֶךְ אַפַּ֖יִם וְרַב־חֶ֥סֶד וֶאֱמֶֽת

> The LORD passed before him and proclaimed, "The LORD, the LORD, a God merciful and gracious, slow to anger, and abounding in steadfast love and faithfulness." (ESV)

In the viewpoint of the author, רחם is a figurative term of God's unconditional love that symbolizes his enduring love full of compassion toward his creation, like a woman who carries a baby in her womb. *TDOT* supports this understanding: "In any case, it is clear that the nouns רֶחֶם/ רָחַם/רַחֲמָא are connected etymologically with the Ugaritic and Moabic רחם and probably also with the Phoenician רחם, womb."[40] Thus, רחם might be a rhetorical expression of God's unconditional love (ἀγάπη) with a painful endurance, which is pictured in a woman who carries a baby in her womb (רחם). It is a great joy to get a lovely baby, but that requires a great labor at the same time. We can find several such cases in the OT. Isaiah 49:15 compares God's love to a pregnant woman. The verse says that God's love is even greater than a woman's love for her baby in her womb: הֲתִשְׁכַּ֤ח אִשָּׁה֙ עוּלָ֔הּ מֵרַחֵ֖ם בֶּן־בִּטְנָ֑הּ גַּם־אֵ֣לֶּה תִשְׁכַּ֔חְנָה וְאָנֹכִ֖י לֹ֥א אֶשְׁכָּחֵֽךְ׃ (Will a woman forget

---

40. Dahmen, *TDOT* 13:455.

her pregnancy of son in her womb? Even though she will forget, my Lord will not forget you).

Most of the English translations of this verse have missed the Hebrew idiom עולה מרחם. Here, עולה מרחם means "get into pregnancy." However, it is also a metaphorical expression of God's love compared to a woman who carries a baby in her womb. It is crucial to notice those words of God's attribute. חסד, רב-, אמת, רחום—all of those words contain the meaning of bearing, enduring, and faithful love. There is no price on it. There is no condition on it. This is what "God has declared" (ויקרא יהוה) by himself, not what people have requested of God. Isaiah 49:13 shows that נחם is the Father's expression of heartbroken emotion with suffering compassion (רחם):

רָנּוּ שָׁמַיִם וְגִילִי אָרֶץ יִפְצְחוּ הָרִים רִנָּה כִּי־נִחַם יְהוָה עַמּוֹ וַעֲנִיָּו יְרַחֵם׃

The sky, cry out! The earth, rejoice! Mountains, break out! Because God has deeply sighed for His people with compassion, and His eyes are filled with mercy!

Therefore, according to the author's understanding, נחם is connected directly to רחם emotionally, and it might be the outcome of God's רחם. Because of רחם, which is a priceless love, God has initiated the mission of restoration and reconciliation with humankind at any price. Thus, it is not a wonder to find so many stories of a heartbroken father toward his child or a king toward his people in Jesus' parables. Jesus has demonstrated God's רחמים and נחם as the initial motivation for *missio Dei* throughout the Gospels (i.e., Matt 21:3–46; 22:1–14).

3.3. A Study of חסד

חסד is one of the most profound terms among Hebrew words in the OT, which unlocks the entire mystery of the biblical theology of God's ברית. It is also the word of God's love that has been the most investigated, compared to רחמים, חסד, and אמת. It is like a master key to unlock the mystery of God's attributes, the creation, the election of Israel, covenant, Jesus' messiahship, and more. The author even dares to say that the entire Christian church and missions are the products of חסד. Therefore, it is no wonder to find so many writings on חסד in OT studies. Hence, the study of חסד will be dealt with much more seriously here, compared to other words.

Despite the significance of חסד in the Bible, it has not been long since scholars started paying attention to this Hebrew word. It was only in 1927 when the first work on חסד was published by Nelson Glueck.[41] After Glueck's monumental work, more works followed throughout the twentieth century. Gerald Larue summarized well most of the research of חסד after Glueck, until Hebrew Union College published Glueck's work in an English version in 1967. After Glueck, Gordon Clark lists a few more works after 1967, including his study of *hesed* published in 1993.[42] Among that summary of prior studies, Sakenfeld's is one of the most prominent. All of them have not only suggested their own translation of the Hebrew term חסד but have also agreed that there is no equivalent term in English.[43] Morris explains, "The term occurs 245 times in the Old Testament, and no translation comes close to using a single equivalent."[44]

Most of those works have different methodologies of research. Nevertheless, their research results are not significantly different on the understanding of the meaning of חסד. The issue of the study of חסד will be explained further in this chapter.

It is not the author's intention to criticize those previous studies, nor to develop a new theory of the meaning of חסד in this book. Nevertheless, חסד is one of the most important keys to unlocking the mystery of *missio Dei* and God's love in John 3:16. Therefore, it will be valuable to reference those previous studies to define the true meaning of God's love, in order to lay a foundation for the author's research on God's love and *missio Dei* through the understanding of the meaning of חסד. In this context, a few previous works on חסד will be discussed here in order to lay a background for the research on God's love and *missio Dei*, the main themes of this study.

3.3.1. Review of Previous Studies on חסד

3.3.1.1. Nelson Glueck's Understanding of חסד

Nelson Glueck is the pioneer of research of חסד in the OT. With his research on חסד, the meaning of בריתות and God's attributes became much

---

41. Glueck, Hesed *in the Bible*.

42. Clark, *Word* Hesed.

43. Morris, *Testaments of Love*, 66. See also Sakenfeld, *Meaning of* Hesed, 233; Jacob, *Theology of Old Testament*, 103.

44. Morris, *Testaments of Love*, 66n1.

clearer. The most important finding on חסד by Glueck is the meaning of "requirement" in חסד. Sakenfeld explains,

> For Glueck this passage provided an important key to the understanding of *hesed*, particularly because of the "requirement" form of the first part of Abraham's statement: "This is your Hesed which you must do."... He saw the basis of the narrative in duty-oriented conduct based in reciprocity which obligated all members of a family to assist one another.[45]

Although Glueck's research methodology is not clear, it seems that he used an exegetical study of the narrative for understanding of חסד and determined the meaning of חסד from the context of narrative. The main keyword of Glueck's study is, in fact, "obligation." Glueck tries to understand חסד in the context of "reciprocal conduct" in human-human and in human-God relationships. This mutual practice of חסד is especially crucial in the context of human to human relationships. Then, he concludes the meaning of חסד in secular use for humans' relationships as "piety, kindness, and love of mankind," which is "conduct corresponding to a mutual relationship of rights and duties."[46]

In the religious meaning, Glueck has also put the meaning of חסד in the context of the relationship between humans and God or God and humans, which is "reciprocal conduct."[47] In this context, Glueck shows the connection between ברית and חסד. Based on Ps 50:5, Glueck explains:

> The close connection between *ḥesed* and *bᵉrith* is clearly in evidence in this verse, for חסידי is parallel with כרתי בריתי. However, this does not mean that hesed is a synonym for *bᵉrith*, as Elbogen maintains. Ḥesed is the premise and effect of a *bᵉrith*; it constitutes the very essence of a *bᵉrith* but is not yet a b e rith, even though there can be no *bᵉrith* without *ḥesed*. The Ḥasidim fulfill their covenantal obligations in that they practice *ḥesed* and may, for this reason, be designated as כרתי בריתי.[48]

Therefore, חסד is the foundation of ברית (covenant) in the viewpoint of Glueck. Based on ברית with חסד, Glueck puts the religious meaning of חסד in the relationship between humans and God. In this context, Glueck states,

---

45. Sakenfeld, *Meaning of* Hesed, 26.
46. Glueck, Hesed *in the Bible*, 54.
47. Glueck, Hesed *in the Bible*, 56.
48. Glueck, Hesed *in the Bible*, 68.

"As a reciprocal ethical and religious conduct, חסד fulfills the demands of loyalty, justice, righteousness, and honesty. These concepts are embraced in its meaning."[49] His understanding of חסד as a "reciprocal conduct" was groundbreaking in its time. Yet, the attribute of love in the meaning of חסד is not a main theme for Glueck, although he has a clue about it:

> The *hesed* of God is very closely related to His *rahamim* but distinguished from it by its more positive character. The characteristic of loyalty which belongs to the concept of *hesed* is alien to the concept of *rahamim*.[50]

3.3.1.2. KATHARINE DOOB SAKENFELD

Katharine Sakenfeld effectively points out a strength and weakness in Glueck's work throughout her dissertation, which was published in 1978. Mainly, Sakenfeld argues that Glueck's understanding of חסד as obligation "in terms of customary law" is not a proper interpretation.

> חסד is not a legal right but a moral right and as such can also be a gift. Glueck's need to refute the traditional translation of חסד, *Gnade* in German and loving-kindness in English after Coverdale, led him to a false dichotomy between obligatory action and action freely done.[51]

Sakenfeld defines the meaning of חסד according to the context in each period of its history and according to categories of usage. She summarizes the general meaning of חסד as the "deliverance or protection as a responsible keeping of faith with another with whom one is in a relationship."[52] Her keyword for defining חסד is the same as that of Glueck: "relationship." However, the usage of the word חסד varies greatly in each context and in each period. Therefore, various English terms can be used to translate חסד. First, the secular usage חסד in the First Temple period was mainly among family members or in political relationships. In this context, "the use of חסד for the first action has been described as an extended or dependent usage."[53] However, Sakenfeld argues that the secular use of חסד has never been "a

---

49. Glueck, Hesed *in the Bible*, 69.
50. Glueck, Hesed *in the Bible*, 102.
51. Sakenfeld, *Meaning of* Hesed, 3.
52. Sakenfeld, *Meaning of* Hesed, 80.
53. Sakenfeld, *Meaning of* Hesed, 234.

special favor; rather it is always the provision for an essential need."[54] Her notion on "the acts of חסד" between the superior party and the party in need is quite useful to explain the meaning of God's love. The needy party always depends on the superior party's acts of חסד in the Bible; otherwise, the weaker party faces catastrophe. However, the superior party is not obligated to take an action of חסד to them. This is the crucial point of the act of חסד according to Sakenfeld.

After the exile period, the meaning of חסד in secular usage changes. It is used as "favor" or "beauty," which is similar to חן, as Sakenfeld notices in Esther. But more frequently, the word is used for "pious act," which was probably adopted from religious usage.[55] This is probably the outcome of the Israelites' experience of the destruction of the temple and exile to Babylon. The meaning of "faithfulness" had been fully integrated in the usage of חסד at this point.

The second usage of חסד is as a religious term. Sakenfeld categorizes four areas of this usage.[56] The first area is in the case when an honest person seeks God's justice and protection from persecutors. The second area is the restoring of a relationship that has been broken. The "third and major area of theological usage is that of God's חסד for his covenanted people in the Mosaic tradition."[57] This issue will be discussed in depth later in this book. The final category that Sakenfeld notes is "in the special understanding of God's preservation of the Davidic dynasty."[58] One crucial observation that Sakenfeld makes is the difference between רחמים and וחסד. These two words are often combined together, but they do not hold the same meaning. The exegetical study in this chapter will demonstrate the difference in meaning of the two Hebrew words. Simply put, Sakenfeld's thesis can be summarized as follows: the single word of חסד delivers the greatness of God's faithfulness and everlasting, pious love upon his people, despite the people's unfaithfulness and God's judgment. In *Faithfulness in Action*,

---

54. Sakenfeld, *Meaning of* Hesed, 234. It is interesting to see that Sakenfeld rejects Glueck's view of obligation of חסד, and yet she still stays with the same connotation as Glueck had in the case of "discrete units." However, it seems to the author that Sakenfeld's critics on Glueck are also right, concerning the concept of prior and secondary act in the usage of חסד (*Meaning of* Hesed, 59). As she mentioned, Glueck has failed to notice these acts of חסד in the Bible.

55. Sakenfeld, *Meaning of* Hesed, 236.
56. Sakenfeld, *Meaning of* Hesed, 237.
57. Sakenfeld, *Meaning of* Hesed, 237.
58. Sakenfeld, *Meaning of* Hesed, 238.

which Sakenfeld published in 1985 as "the overture" to her previous book on חסד, she leans towards the direction of "loyalty and faithfulness" as the major meaning of חסד.

3.3.1.3. Other Studies on חסד before Gordon R. Clark

A few studies of חסד are summarized in an introduction of Glueck's study by Gerald Larue and in Sackenfeld's article. One of the critical works is Hans Joachim Stoebe's writing.[59] There are some other crucial unpublished works, like Boone Bowen's dissertation in 1938 or Sidney Hill's paper on חסד in 1957.[60] Edmund Jacob published *Theology of the Old Testament* in 1958. He interpreted חסד with a similar connotation as רחם but with power and fidelity. The uniqueness of Jacob's study of חסד is defining God himself as חסד according to Jer 3:12 and Ps 144:2. Jacob believes that God is not only an actor of חסד but also that חסד is what God is.[61]

Stoebe's study is critical for this research, because Stoebe examines three synonyms of God's love: רחמים, חן, חסד. He noticed that חסד is never combined with חן in the Hebrew Scripture.[62] Through a systematic analysis of a wide selection of texts, he figured out that חסד has its own connotation different from רחמים and חסד. חן in particular might have a sense with the same connotation as טוב. He saw that חסד shares a common connotation with רחמים but does not hold an identical meaning. Stoebe concludes that חסד is goodness and kindness: *Güte, Freundlichkeit*.[63]

3.3.1.4. Gordon Clark

Gordon Clark took his research methodology of the word חסד on a different path than the previous works. He used linguistic analysis of lexical fields for a comparative study of חסד with other conjoined Hebrew words,[64] while other scholars used the method of biblical literature analysis or exegetical study. Nevertheless, all of the studies have strengths and weaknesses. Most

---

59. Stoebe, "Bedeutung des Wortes," 244.
60. Bowen, "Study of Chesed"; Hill, "Servant of the Lord."
61. Jacob, *Theology of Old Testament*, 105.
62. Gerald A. Larue, in Glueck, Hesed *in the Bible*, 14.
63. Stoebe, "Bedeutung des Wortes," 244.
64. See Clark, *Word Hesed*.

scholars did not focus on God's motivation for his חסד, although they did great work defining the meaning of חסד in different contexts of the texts.

Clark's analysis of the lexical structure of חסד helps one to understand the word's conjunction with other words. Through his research, he found that חסד is used more frequently with רחמים and אמת in the biblical Hebrew text. Clark found that "the relationship between חסד and רחמים is very complex—so complex, indeed, that sometimes these elements seem to be interchanged in certain context. Yet there are features that distinguish רחמים from חסד."[65] He also found that אמת is a crucial word connecting humans to God's חסד. In this conjunction of words, he found how חסד, רחמים, and אמת function with each other. In such a case in Dan 9, he found how God's חסד worked among people whom God loves, even though the people were rebellious. Those rebellious Israelites still experienced God's רחמים.

Glueck and Sakenfeld both recognize the difference between these two words but in completely different connotations. Glueck understands these words in the context of obligation. He understands that רחמים does not include obligation.[66] Sakenfeld approached these terms from a different direction. Unlike Glueck, she does not see the obligatory meaning of חסד. In secular usage, חסד worked in patronage and kingship relationships. Furthermore, Sakenfeld pays little notice to the interaction of those two words (רחמים and אמת) in Scripture, which is crucial to understanding the meaning of חסד in context. The meaning of חסד cannot be fully described without the conjuncture of meanings of רחמים and אמת.

This is the point where Clark's research makes a significant distinction. Clark sees that חסד functions differently when God is an agent of the word and when a human is the agent. Clark criticizes Sakenfeld for the weakness of her inductive study methodology. First, "she has not considered whether these features [the characteristic features of חסד] are also characteristic of other words besides חסד."[67] Second, the concept of personal commitment in the word חסד is not clear in Sakenfeld's work, although the difference between חסד and טוב is clearly distinguished in her work. Clark writes,

> This feature has developed as the study proceeded, for חסד refers to an act which one person/party performs for benefit of another person/party, an act based in the mutual commitment between them. It is precisely this basic characteristic of personal

65. Clark, *Word* Hesed, 161.
66. Glueck, Hesed *in the Bible*, 62.
67. Clark, *Word* Hesed, 233.

commitment that has provided a means of distinguishing between חסד and טוב.[68]

However, Clark's mathematical linguistic analysis of lexical fields has a problem. Since language is a tool to convey the expression of human's emotion, it cannot be fully analyzed by mathematical parameters. In particular, his lexical field analysis cannot define the motivation for חסד from the human side or from God's side.

3.3.1.5. Menahem Qadari's Categorization of the Usage of חסד

Categorizing the usage of חסד helps in understanding the diversity of its meanings in the Bible. Glueck divides the usage of חסד into six categories.[69] Sakenfeld categorizes the usage of the term into three themes: secular use, God to humans, and humans to God.[70] She attempts further clarifying the meaning of חסד through exegetical study of the prophetic literature, Psalms, and other books in the OT. Clark uses a completely different methodology of research than the previous scholars, by making a linguistic analysis of the lexical field. However, he also notices the categorization of the usage of חסד in the covenant in the three cases above.[71]

Menahem Qadari, an Israeli Jewish scholar, divides the usage of חסד into two groups: good deeds with love and grace, and the usage of חסד with conjunctive verbs.[72]

1. חסד—Good deeds with love and grace: there are three different types of usages in this case.

A. חסד between Humans as Friends

This case of חסד simply means "good deeds or loyal kindness" (Gen 24:49; 47:29). The origin of the meaning in this context has a connection to the hypothetical proto-Aramaic root חסד, which became Aramaic and later

---

68. Clark, *Word* Hesed, 233.
69. Glueck, Hesed *in the Bible*, 37.
70. Sakenfeld, *Meaning of* Hesed. See chs. 2–4.
71. Clark, *Word* Hesed, 124.
72. Qadari, "חסד," מילון העברית המקראית, 326.

Hebrew, and then Arabic with the language's introduction into Palestine by invading tribes. An analysis of the interpretation of the Arabic word *hassad*, which originally appears to have referred to a gathering in preparation for battle, led Masing to associate the term with potlatch rituals[73]. In such a ritual, a beneficent act might be regarded as a favor or, should one be unable to reciprocate, as an insult. The one who demonstrated favor or חסד stood above the receiver. The stem חסד originally meant a definite action characteristic of a potlatch giver or a similar person.

When Qadari defines the usage of חסד between humans as friends (Isa 16:5; 2 Sam 2:6; Prov 21:21), the חסד to humans is always illustrated as a wish of God's חסד to his friend. It means that חסד never comes from humans but only from God. In this human relationship, there are a few meanings contained in חסד: faithfulness, justice, goodness, judgment, love and mercy, the law of love, and justification.[74]

Isaiah 16:5 conveys the meaning of חסד as "faithfulness": וְהוּכַן בַּחֶסֶד כִּסֵּא וְיָשַׁב עָלָיו בֶּאֱמֶת בְּאֹהֶל דָּוִד שֹׁפֵט וְדֹרֵשׁ מִשְׁפָּט וּמְהִר צֶדֶק. In fact, this verse fully clarifies the meaning of חסד in the human relationship. The faithfulness, justice, and judgment in this verse are based on David's חסד, which God has given to him.

However, BDB brings some other cases of using חסד between humans, which is "kindness of men towards men, in doing favors and benefits."[75] In this case, the word mostly appears as חֲסָדַי, *hassadai* (1 Sam 20:15; 2 Sam 16:17; Prov 19:22; 20:6). This kind of usage can be found only eleven times in the whole Bible, so it can be ignored in the author's research here. In addition, even though חסד is used between humans, it is usually one-sided without expecting any compensation for it. חסד is mostly used to describe relationships between humans and God, or God and humans.

B. Humans' חסד toward God

The word חסד is also used in humans' relationship with God in the OT, and depending on who is the one having a relationship of חסד, the connotation in each context changes. When humans describe their חסד toward God, it is usually translated as "piety." Hosea 6:4 explains this case: וְחַסְדְּכֶם

---

73. Masing, "Begriff *Hesed*."
74. Qadari, "חסד," מילון העברית המקראית, 323.
75. "חסד," BDB 338.

כַּעֲנַן־בֹּקֶר. BDB translates this verse as "Your piety is like a morning cloud."[76] Qadari defines a few connotations of חסד in this case: faithfulness, piety, knowledge of God, and piety to the Almighty God.[77] Hosea 6:6 shows one of these cases: כִּי חֶסֶד חָפַצְתִּי וְלֹא־זָבַח וְדַעַת אֱלֹהִים מֵעֹלוֹת. BDB agrees with Qadari's understanding of חסד in this verse.[78]

An interesting issue here is the usage of חסד with משפט (Zech 7:9; Hos 12:7). Sometimes *hesed* with *mishpat* (grace and judgment) expresses judgment and grace between two people groups through wars (Mic 6:8). However, most of the time חסד is used to ask God to avoid God's judgment to people doing חסד (good deeds) toward God (1 Sam 20:14; Hos 12:7; Neh 13:14; Hos 4:1).

Sakenfeld added an appendix in her book on חסיד. She noticed that the usage of the form חסיד can be found mostly in Psalms. Her understanding of חסיד is "loyalty," based on her interpretation of Deut 33:8. She understands חסיד as a Hebrew term describing the relationship between God and humans. "Those who were the recipients of God's חסד (as the one called is the recipient of a call, the one appointed is the recipient of an appointment) were designated חסידים."[79] However, it seems to this author that Sakenfeld puts herself in a self-contradiction here, because she understands that a Hebrew *qatil* form "designated an office or function" and is "an original passive that could easily acquire a stative or active meaning."[80] This means that חסיד should be based on self-willingness for loyalty, not just on "recipients of God's חסד." In this case, חסיד should be understood as "piety" with "loyalty."

C. God's חסד toward Humans

Qadari defines this category of חסד mainly as grace, love, mercy, and faithfulness. Psalm 21:8 expresses God's חסד to his people: כִּי־הַמֶּלֶךְ בֹּטֵחַ בַּיהוָה וּבְחֶסֶד עֶלְיוֹן בַּל־יִמּוֹט. In this case, חסד can hold any of the meanings above. God's חסד is always unconditional and everlasting (Ps 23:6; 106:1). God's salvation is the consequence of his חסד (Ps 13:6). God's חסד never fails and

---

76. BDB 338.
77. Qadari, "חסד," מילון העברית המקראית, 326.
78. BDB 338n3.
79. Sakenfeld, *Meaning of* Hesed, 242.
80. Sakenfeld, *Meaning of* Hesed, 241.

will never cease (Isa 54:10; Ps 107:43).⁸¹ When Scripture talks about God's חסד toward humans, it often comes with a combination of other words like רחמים, צדקה, אמת, or חסד לעולם (Prov 7:20; Exod 34:6, Ps 25:10; 3:11).

2. The Usage of חסד with Conjunctive Verbs (i.e., עושה חסד עם)

When חסד comes with a conjunctive verb, it expresses an activity of God's חסד, as we can see in 2 Sam 3:8, אֶעֱשֶׂה־חֶסֶד עִם־בֵּית. In this case, it is used as a reminder of God's חסד or his plan of חסד for his people (Josh 2:12). God's חסד is unchangeable and everlasting. In fact, more usage of חסד in the Bible is a part of God's attribute: וַאֲנִי ׀ כְּזַיִת רַעֲנָן בְּבֵית אֱלֹהִים בָּטַחְתִּי בְחֶסֶד־אֱלֹהִים עוֹלָם וָעֶד (But I am like a fresh olive tree in the house of God. I trust in the pious love of God forever and ever [Ps 52:10]).

God's חסד comes down from heaven (Ps 21:8), is devoted (Gen 32:11), and is true love (חסד ואמת [Ps 25:10]). God's חסד has been given to those who believe in him (Ps 88:12). In many cases, God's חסד toward people has been described as the foundation of ברית. Boone Bowen noticed that Exod 15:13 is the revelation of God's covenantal חסד to Moses.⁸² He states that the Deuteronomist never uses חסד as a human quality, and when the term is used in reference to God it is always in close relationship to ברית. The nations are the recipient of the divine חסד, and the conditions under which Israel obtains the benefits of this חסד are stipulated. Both Israel and אלהים have covenantal responsibilities, and unless Israel obeys and loves אלהים, the nation cannot expect to receive the divine חסד.⁸³

In summary, Glueck present the meaning of חסד as a mutual obligation, and it means loyalty, justice, righteousness, and honesty. Bowen is not far away from Glueck, although he is not familiar with much of Glueck's work. Bowen sees that חסד is a mutual obligation between God and Israel. Bowen defines חסד as the agent in God's forgiveness and redemption because of God's love. He translates חסד as "a loyal kindness and loving kindness."⁸⁴ Stoebe states that חסד characterizes God and means goodness, grace, and affability.⁸⁵ Sakenfeld has widely criticized Glueck's concept of חסד "within relationship," although she recognizes it is Glueck's contribution

81. Qadari, מילון העברית המקראית, 326.
82. Bowen, "Study of *Hesed*," 43.
83. Bowen, "Study of *Hesed*," 135.
84. Bowen, "Study of *Hesed*," 135.
85. Stoebe, "Bedeutung des Wortes *Hasad*."

to the study of חסד, because the meaning of חסד in a wide open relationship makes things ambiguous. For Sakenfeld, חסד is a "specific action in special situation" by a superior party.[86] She translates חסד mainly as "loyalty and faithfulness." After a long examination of lexical fields of words combined with חסד in a Hebrew text, Clark agrees with Stoebe that there are no equivalent words in Western languages to translate it properly. However, Clark understands that טוב is "a substitute for חסד," which means *Güte* in German. He finds that חסד is sometimes very similar to רחמים and אמת but is in contrast to אהב.[87] Clark concludes:

> חסד is not merely an attitude or an emotion; it is an emotion that leads to an activity beneficial to the recipient.... Use of the word in the Hebrew Bible indicates that חסד is characteristic of God rather than human beings; it is rooted in the divine nature, and it is expressed because of how He is, not because of what humanity is or needs or desires or deserves. Yahweh's tenacious commitment to Israel even in the face of their blatant and persistent rebellion demonstrates that חסד is an enduring quality of God. This commitment leads him to punish his wayward people and to regulate their punishment in such a way that they desire to return to him. Although it is not at the time apparent to Israel, חסד יהוה is still available and Yahweh awaits the opportunity to manifest it again when his people repent and return to him.[88]

Clark defines the meanings of חסד according to various contexts: grace, mercy, faithfulness, compassion, reliability, and confidence. Nevertheless, חסד is far away from the meaning of אהב, "love."

3.3.1.6. What Is Missing in Previous Studies on חסד

As the survey above shows, these scholars have covered most of the areas and meanings of חסד in the OT and NT. Glueck laid a great foundation for this research, and those after him succeeded in figuring out the profound meanings and usages of the Hebrew word חסד in the Bible. Finally, Clark concluded the study of חסד at the end of the twentieth century. The author believes that there is not much work remaining in the study of חסד anymore.

---

86. Sakenfeld, *Studies in the Usage*, 73.
87. Sakenfeld, *Studies in the Usage*, 264.
88. Sakenfeld, *Studies in the Usage*, 267.

Philological Study of God's Love

Nevertheless, a connection between the two different meanings of חסד (good and bad) in the Bible has never been clarified. A popular theory that those two different meanings of חסד came from different sources has been accepted and confirmed. However, there is a reason that the author believes that both usages of חסד are connected in meaning with each other. Furthermore, their lexical usage and meanings in the Bible kept changing throughout history. The meaning of חסד that we understand today cannot always be the same as yesterday. Nevertheless, the original meaning is usually embedded in the current meaning in a different way. This is the reason why the etymological study of the Hebrew terms is crucial. This research is an attempt to figure out the original meaning of the Hebrew connotations when God's חסד is used for a specific text.

Throughout the entire OT, we can see that God has only one request for the Israelites: "piety to God." כִּי חֶסֶד חָפַצְתִּי וְלֹא־זָבַח וְדַעַת אֱלֹהִים מֵעֹלוֹת (I was eager for piety, not sacrifice; and for the knowledge of God, not burnt offering [Hos 6:6]).

In fact, Hos 6:6 directly opposes Clark's view. Clark says, "When God is the agent of חסד . . . , God expects אהבה—but never חסד—from His covenant partners."[89] Humans' חסד to God will be explained in a later part of this chapter through Qadari's etymological Hebrew lexicon.

God's piety toward his people has often been ignored in Western theology. When theologians talk about the relationship between God and humans, God's piety is usually translated as "love" or "grace." The author thinks this is the reason why the Hebrew word חסד has often been translated as "kindness" or "mercy" in English Bibles. Luther used the word *Gnade*, which means "grace" in English.[90] In the Christian understanding of God, God's piety to people cannot be considered, but people must have piety to him. However, when God made the covenant, it was an interactive covenant. Especially when God declared, "I will be your God," it was an ultimate and unchangeable pious declaration. There was no need for a human's agreement on it, even if it was against the human's will. The word חסד is the foundation of God's declaration in Exod 6:7, and it is God's revelation of his piety to people. Therefore, חסד is the core of God's covenant with Abraham and Israel. The author supposes that among all the translations of חסד, the ESV has translated Hos 6:6 better than any other English versions

---

89. Sakenfeld, *Studies in the Usage*, 136. There is a gap between the lexical analysis and the biblical textual criticism based on etymology.

90. *LW* 1:135.

of the Bible: "For I desire steadfast love." Here, חסד means "love with piety."⁹¹ Wilhelm Gesenius supports this meaning by defining the origin of the meaning of חסד as "in eager zeal or desire, whence develops kindness and envy."⁹² In this context, חסד is well connected with one of God's names, אֵל קַנָּא, in Exod 34:14, because קנא is a consequence of God's חסד. If God did not have חסד toward people, he would not have any reason to have emotion of קנא toward his creation. כִּי יהוה קַנָּא שְׁמוֹ אֵל קַנָּא הוּא (God is jealous, and His name is God of jealousy).

However, there are different meanings of חסד as in Prov 14:34: צְדָקָה תְרוֹמֵם־גּוֹי וְחֶסֶד לְאֻמִּים חַטָּאת (Righteousness praises a nation, but sin is a shame to people). This verse can confuse readers because two opposite meanings of חסד can be found in the OT: pious love and shame. BDB explains that חסד may have an Arabic or Aramaic origin. The Arabic word (ḥasada, ḥasadun) has two different meanings, kindness and envy, and the initial meaning might come from "eager zeal or desire."⁹³ *TWOT* confirms that there is no origin of this word in Akkadian and Ugarit. In the OT, the Hebrew word חסד comes with various meanings, depending on the situation and context. Gerald Larue conducted a short survey of the studies of חסד in the middle of the twentieth century as the introduction to the English translation of Glueck's Hesed *in the Bible*. Larue wrote short summaries, like one of Norman Snaith's study of חסד. "In analyzing the etymology of חסד Snaith noted that in Lev 20:17 and in Prov 14:34 חסד refers to 'shame, reproach or defilement,' and in Prov 25:10 the corresponding verb form has the same significance. Elsewhere the very opposite meaning—love—is reflected."⁹⁴ Snaith assumed that the "bad" meaning of חסד came from Aramaic influence, and the "good" meaning of the word came from Hebrew to Aramaic and Syriac. In fact, the classic study of חסד by Glueck supports the opinion that both meanings were combined in the word חסד. Glueck takes a perspective of חסד from ancient societies, which is "a bonding deity of two different communities [city-states]" by a covenant.⁹⁵ In this case, the word contains two contradictory meanings at the same time: shame (if the covenant is broken) and conditional love (if the covenant is kept).⁹⁶

91. BDB 338n3.
92. Gesenius, *Gesenius' Hebrew Grammar*, 191.
93. BDB 338.
94. Gerald A. Larue, in Glueck, Hesed *in the Bible*, 8–9.
95. Glueck, Hesed *in the Bible*, 37.
96. Cf. R. Laird Harris, "חסד," *TWOT* 305 (Strong's 698).

Philological Study of God's Love

Snaith prefers Gesenius's suggestion that the primary meaning of חסד is "keenness" or "ardent zeal," and that the word developed along two lines—one revealing itself in love and kindness toward a person, and the other in emulation ending in envy or ambition.[97] As Larue summarizes, most other studies of חסד more or less reach similar conclusions: "חסד denotes attitude of loyalty and faithfulness which should be observed by both parties in a covenant."[98] Israeli scholars like Qadari and Even-Shushan describe חסד in similar understanding with these Western scholars, but they also have some different perspectives as native Hebrew speakers.

Even-Shusan posits that the "bad" meaning of חסד comes from the *piel* form of חשד of Aramaic.[99] As the author mentioned previously, there have been many exchanges of letters in the process of immigration of languages. So, the author guesses that Even-Shushan's perspective is right: ש and ס were exchanged between Aramaic and Hebrew during the language immigration (Prov 25:9–10).

In conclusion of the etymological study of חסד, while various meanings of חסד can be seen in the Bible, the foundation of the meanings shows God's pious and everlasting love toward his creations. חסד is often used in people's relationships; however, even in those cases, providers and recipients of the meaning of חסד are evident, and חסד contains the meaning of loyal love or steadfast love with piety. In many cases in the Bible, God is illustrated as the provider of חסד to people. It can also be seen that חסד is often used with אמת and ברית. In this case, חסד is shown as the fundamental foundation of ברית. This proves that חסד with רחמים lays the foundation and motivation for *missio Dei* and serves as the backbone of the whole Scripture, which is the blueprint of *missio Dei*.

3.4. A Study of אמת

God's love can be described in the simplest way as "everlasting, faithful, and unconditional." חסד, the keyword of God's love in the OT, mostly occurs in combination with אמת or רחמים. The word אמת appears 126 times in the OT.[100] Clark found that אמת has been combineD 51 times with חסד in the

---

97. Snaith, *Distinctive Ideas*, 96.
98. Gerald A. Larue, in Glueck, Hesed *in the Bible*, 8.
99. Even-Shushan, "חסד," *Milon Hahadash Le'ivrit*, 2:473.
100. "אמת," *TDOT* 1:309.

OT.¹⁰¹ *TDNT* explains, "It is used absolutely to denote a reality which is to be regarded as אָמֵן 'firm,' and therefore solid, valid, or binding."¹⁰² The origin of this Hebrew word has not been found from other Semitic languages,¹⁰³ and אמת was derived from אמן.¹⁰⁴ Jepsen quotes from H. Bauer-P. Leander that the phonetic development of Hebrew אמת progressed in this way: *amintu>amittu>amatt>āmaht*.¹⁰⁵ According to Einar Brønno, the morphology of Hebrew has various exchanges between the vowels, and ā and ē is one of those cases. This Semitic morphological tradition already existed in the Akkadian texts from El Amarna. In El Amarna texts, *imitt* often came out from *imint*.¹⁰⁶ Here we can already see vowel and consonant exchanges, as we saw in the morphological case of exchanging למנ"ר in the previous chapter.¹⁰⁷ Nevertheless, אמת might originate from Hebrew and have been influenced later by other Semitic languages such as Arabic and Syriac.¹⁰⁸

Jepsen sees that אמת is used both for human beings and for God. When אמת is used in human relationships, it means "really true," because אמת is used of things that have proven to be reliable."¹⁰⁹ Jepsen took an example from Josh 2:12, וּנְתַתֶּם לִי אוֹת אֱמֶת, but several other examples can be found, such as Exod 18:21; Isa 43:9; and Mic 7:20. As most scholars have noticed, אמת is often combined with a few other words, such as דבר, משפט, חסד, and שלום. When אמת is used with דבר, it is always used as a modifier of דבר, not as a coordination conjunction.¹¹⁰ What that means is that אמת with דבר means the "word of truth, or reliable truth." Jepsen explains its use in 1 Kgs 10:6 and Deut 13:15 as meaning "It is true; it is real." However, as Jepsen notices, "It is very difficult to translate accurately the meaning of אמת."¹¹¹

---

101. Clark, *Word Hesed*, 235.

102. Gottfried Quell et al., "Ἀλήθεια," *TDNT* 1:232.

103. Gerhard von Rad, "אמת," *TDOT* 1:292–306; Julius Schniewind, "Ἀγγελία," *TDNT* 1:58.

104. *EB* mentions, "היא נגזרת מן השורשים אמן" (1:435).

105. Rad, *TDOT* 1:309.

106. Brønno, *Studien über hebräische Morphologie*, 157.

107. Qimron, *Biblical Hebrew*, 33–34.

108. Rad, *TDOT* 1:313.

109. Rad, *TDOT* 1:313.

110. See 2 Sam 7:28; 1 Kgs 10:6.

111. Rad, *TDOT* 1:311.

Philological Study of God's Love

The usage of אמת for God describes one aspect of God's divine nature: faithfulness. אמת is used with חסד, as mentioned in the previous study of חסד. In fact, רחמים, חסד, and אמת cannot be separated when we talk about God's divine nature and his love. Just as the Trinity explains God as one in three different persons, God's love is one in three different characters. רחמים, חסד, and אמת explain God's love but three different attributes of it. When St. John declares "God is love," אמת is an identity of God, as Ps 31:6 describes: בְּיָדְךָ אַפְקִיד רוּחִי פָּדִיתָה אוֹתִי יהוה אֵל אֱמֶת. The LXX translates אל אמת as θεὸς τῆς ἀληθείας. Luther follows the LXX translation, *treuer Gott*, and some English translations like KJV and NIV do so too. But the ESV and RSV translate it as "faithful God." However, neither the LXX nor other European languages can convey the full connotation of the Hebrew word אמת, because most of them translate אמת by itself with no connection to חסד. One thing we have to notice is that humans should speak or do only אמת to God, because our God is the God of אמת, as Jepsen mentions.[112] As he describes, אמת is often portrayed in Psalms as God's actions in the OT, and God keeps אמת. In this context, אמת means truth with reliability based on חסד, although there is no mention of חסד in the text, because the connotations of those two words cannot be separated in their meanings. Therefore, אמת without love of חסד cannot be "reliable" anymore.[113] Clark found that אמת is combined with חסד over fifty times in the OT, and is mostly used to describe God's relationship toward human beings. It is never used to express humans' relationship to God. Clark goes further by defining חסד ואמת as a hendiadys.[114] Hendiadys is a Western linguistic concept, not Semitic. After the tenth century, when Hebrew grammar began to develop with the influence of Arab languages, the concept of hendiadys came to Hebrew, but most of the Jewish rabbis rejected the concept and understood it as an idiom. The German Hebrew scholar Gesenius also agreed with this rejection in the nineteenth century.[115]

אמת should be understood as one dimension of God's love but needs to be combined with other attributes of God's love in order to complete its shape, because אמת is not God's duty but his nature. If חסד ואמת are

---

112. Rad, *TDOT* 1:315.

113. According to Merriam-Webster, *hendiadys* is "the expression of an idea by the use of two usually independent words connected by *and* (such as *nice and warm*) instead of the usual combination of independent word and its modifier (such as *nicely warm*)."

114. Clark, *Word Hesed*, 237.

115. Lillas, "Hendiadys in Hebrew Bible," 94.

interpreted as hendiadys, then אמת ומשפט cannot be interpreted properly, because God's חסד ואמת and רחמים are the core of God's משפטים. God's משפט exists to keep God's אמת as Ezek 18:9 mentions: וּמִשְׁפָּטַי שָׁמַר לַעֲשׂוֹת אֱמֶת צַדִּיק. God's משפט is also parallel with חסד and שלום (Mic 6:8; Hos 12:7; Zech 8:16). No such משפט for just judgment without love exists in the Bible, because God's love is to keep his אמת and שלום with חסד (Ps 19:10).

אמת has been translated into various words in English: faithfulness, reliability, trustworthiness, stability, truth, fidelity.[116] BDB describes אמת as an attribute of God.[117] However, these translations in English—especially when these are used in a single word—can cover only a partial meaning of אמת in the Hebrew context of God's love. Therefore, אמת contains all of those meanings, but all of these words cannot be put in one sentence.

3.5. A Study of חנן

3.5.1. Context and Usage

When the OT explains God's love, one of the Hebrew terms for God's love is חנן. However, חנן is a little different than חסד, רחמים, אמת, because חנן expresses an action of חסד and רחמים rather than an attribute of God's love. Even-Shushan's concordance explains the meaning of חנן as an "action of רחם and חסד."[118] The word is never used as an objective noun in Scripture, and it is never connected with חסד by a coordinate conjunction such as ו. As Freedman in *TDOT* has noticed, חנן in the OT appears mostly in the *qal* or *hitpael* form, which is used to express simple actions.[119] Particularly, the most common usage of חנן in the OT is חנני or חנון. In the OT, חנני is used eighteen times, and חנון is used twenty-five times. It is very interesting to notice that חנון comes with חסד only twice (2 Sam 10:2; 1 Chr 19:2) in the OT, and both sentences in 2 Sam 10:2 and 1 Chr 19:2 are identical. So, the text was probably copied from one to the other. In this text, two words (חנון and חסד) are connected to the preposition עם, and the main verb is עשה. It is clear that חנן is not used with חסד, but used more frequently with רחם. Freedman in *TDOT* prefers to translate חנן as "grace or favor." In a

---

116. See "אמת," BDB 54; Jack B. Scott, "אמת," *TWOT* 51 (Strong's 116); "אמת," *DBL* §622.

117. "תמא," BDB 54.1.

118. Even-Shushan, *Milon Hahadash Le Ivrit*, 2:717.

119. D. N. Freedman et al., "חנן," *TDOT* 5:24.

human-relationship context, "favor" will presumably fit. However, in the relationship between God and human, "grace" would be a better meaning. Freedman compares חן in the Hebrew idiom מוצא חן בעיני אלהים with חנן.[120] Although these two words have the same root, the meaning is completely different. חן in this idiom is used as "like, fond." Freedman interprets חן in this idiom as "please." חן and חנן should be distinguished in the OT context, because the context of usage is completely different. חן is more connected to the context of "favor," while חנן is used more in the expression of God's action of love toward humans. Exodus 34:6 and 33:19 are the examples. יְהוָה אֵל רַחוּם וְחַנּוּן אֶרֶךְ אַפַּיִם וְרַב־חֶסֶד וֶאֱמֶת (Exod 34:6). God is gracious. In this sentence, all of the Hebrew expressions for God's love have been used and defined the attributes of God's love. The words here are used in the verbal-noun form: חנן, רחום, which defines God's action of love. Most of the English translations have some problems in delivering an exact meaning of those Hebrew words because they are a noun and a verb at the same time, which can be translated as an adjective that defines אל. By using a verbal-noun form to define אל, these Hebrew terms express "what" God is and "who" God is. God's love is not only a noun but is also an action. His love is much more than a metaphysical phenomenon, as in the Hellenistic concept of love. It is real and in action, always. חנן is a proper term to express the action of God's love. However, the meaning of חנן is a much more complex term than "favor" or "grace" in English.

3.5.2. Etymology

In order to clarify the meaning of חן, etymological study can serve as a great tool. *TWOT* and *TDOT* offer the Akkadian source, *enēnu*.[121] In this case, "asking to grant a favor" would be the right meaning for the word; it usually appears as the *qal* form in Hebrew. However, an Akkadian word *hanānu* could be more identical to חן in the Hebrew context. The Ugaritic and Arabic words also confirm this meaning. In Ugaritic, *ḥnn* is equivalent with the *hitpael* form in Hebrew. And this form immigrates to Arabic later: *ḥanna*. As *TDOT* notes, in the EA 137 text from El Amarna, *enēnu* is used with the meaning of "doing a favor."[122] But *hanānu* in Akkadian, *ḥnn* in Ugaritic, and *ḥanna* in Arabic are used for the expression of "be gracious."

---

120. Gen 33:3; 2 Sam 14:22.
121. Freedman et al., *TDOT* 5:22.
122. Freedman et al., *TDOT* 5:22.

TWOT explains, "The *Hithpael* stem means 'to beseech,' as Gen 42:21 where the brothers recalled how Joseph had pleaded with them."[123] Some scholars, like Bangor Ad-Thomas, mention that חן originally meant "bend, bow, incline," and was developed into the form of חנן or חננו later, which means "condescension of bestowing a favor."[124] Ad-Thomas understands חין or תחנון as "sufficient." He translates Exod 34:6, יְהוָֹה אֵל רַחוּם וְחַנּוּן, and explains the verse:

> There we are told that Yahweh will listen to the cry of the poor man if harshly treated, because he is חנון. It does not matter whether the one who is in distress is righteous or not, i.e. in this case, whether the poor debtor has redeemed his pledge or not, his want and consequent supplication to Yahweh are sufficient, for Yahweh is חנון. And yet, it must not be supposed that Yahweh will condone wickedness in a suppliant, it is simply that he will not allow anyone else to act unjustly towards him.[125]

It is interesting to notice that Psalms uses the חונן form nineteen times. It is a form of the humans' request to God "to be gracious" to them.[126] When one is lonely or in distress (Ps 25:16; 31:9), there is no one of whom that person can ask חן and רחם but the Lord God.

3.5.3. Meaning

As we noticed above, the Hebrew word חן, חנן is used in various forms, but mostly in the *poal* or *hitpael* form. There are some other forms used in the OT, like the *hup'al* or *nip'al* form, but the *nip'al* form must be a grammatical mistake of the text (Jer 22:23). As we saw from the various examples, חנן is basically an expression of an "action" rather than a descriptive or stative noun. Therefore, each form has slightly different connotations depending on each context of the sentence. Nevertheless, those forms contain a common ground of meaning, which is based on God's love (רחם and חסד). Established on God's love, it can be understood as "bestowing God's grace" or "doing favor."

Since חנן does not represent an attribute of God's love, the word will not be discussed further to define God's love and motivation for *missio Dei*

---

123. Edwin Yamauchi, "חָנַן," *TWOT* 302 (Strong's 694).
124. Ad-Thomas, "Aspects of Root *Hnn*," 128.
125. Ad-Thomas, "Aspects of Root *Hnn*," 140.
126. Yamauchi, *TWOT* 302.

in this study. Only רחמים, חסד, and אמת will serve as keywords for this research.

4. Findings from the Studies of Hebrew Words of God's Love

The difficulties of the translation of the Hebrew words for God's love have been mentioned a few times in this chapter. Nevertheless, the study of the Hebrew words has produced some valuable clues in understanding the original meanings of the Hebrew expressions for God's love. Table 1 in the appendix shows the comparison of translations of each Hebrew term in Greek and English.

Through the study of נחם, the following findings were revealed:

1. נחם in Gen 6:6 is an expression of God's broken heart indicating his emotional feeling as the Father of all creation, the feeling of agony because of the humans' betrayal. In this case, Maier's translation of נחם, "grieved, suffered," fits better in the context than any other. Then, God's word איכה in Gen 3:9 can be understood better as the first emotional expression of God, the Father. This word can be understood with the undertone "How dare you do this to me?" These emotional expressions of God as the Father signal significant clues of God's motivation for *missio Dei*. A crucial issue to notice here is that נחם has two different meanings that might come from two different origins of the word: agony and love. Nevertheless, both meanings perfectly present the Father's emotional aftermath following his own creation's betrayal with his still ongoing love for his children.

2. נחם is a consequence of God's love as the Father of all creation, and its etymological meaning of נחם was originally "breathing hard, deep sigh," which usually comes out of a painful heart or agony, or as an expression of a broken heart from a harsh event in a life.

3. נחם is not an attribute of God's love but an expression and action from God's love. By the expression of נחם, God's motivation for the mission toward humanity has been signaled, which is fully an action of his love.

4. נחם is a premise of God's action of love as a "suffering God," and it is the fundamental action of emotion based on God's חסד, רחם, and אמת.

5. נחם characterizes God's אמת, חסד, רחם in a real action in *missio Dei* because God loves us, but suffers at the same time because of his love and the humans' betrayal.

6. Therefore, without understanding נחם, the meaning of God's רחם, חסד, and אמת cannot be clarified. Paradoxically, God's hard labor, endurance, faithfulness, piety, and trustworthiness toward people come because of the human wickedness and betrayal.

Through the study of רחם, the following findings were revealed:

1. There is a variation of forms of רחם in Hebrew, such as רַחִים or רֶחֶם. These have different meanings, but an etymological study gives a clue to analyze the original meaning of the Hebrew words, because those words contain a connotation of God's love despite their derivation from different etymological sources. רַחִים shows God's unceasing, hard labor of love toward his children, and רֶחֶם indicates God's endurance, which is a symbol of a mother's compassion for the child in her womb. רחם in Exod 34:6 explains God's love and compassion full of endurance, and God's unceasing labor toward his people.

2. Therefore, God's רחם presents that his love is unconditional and priceless, even when his children go away from him by betraying him. God's love has never been the "give-and-take" type, because לֹא כַחֲטָאֵינוּ עָשָׂה לָנוּ וְלֹא כַעֲוֹנֹתֵינוּ גָּמַל עָלֵינוּ (Ps 103:10). Instead, God cleans our sin and restores us as his children in his kingdom (Ps 103:3–5). This concept of "unconditional and priceless" love with a hard labor and extreme, enduring character is crucial to understanding the attribute of God's love toward his creation, because this attribute is directly connected to God's election and בריתות, as found in a later chapter.

Through the study of חסד, the following findings were revealed:

1. חסד is the "key" to unlocking the mystery of God's election and בריתות. In fact, with רחם and אמת, it forms the entire backbone of the Holy Scripture of God, because the entire Bible has been built upon it.

2. From Nelson Glueck to Gordon Clark, there have been intensive studies on חסד since the twentieth century, and these have continued until today. Among those studies, scholars have many disagreements and agreements with each other. In spite of that, they all agree on a few core concepts of the Hebrew word חסד:

Philological Study of God's Love

a. None of the translations of חסד in any language can be identical to the original Hebrew meaning.

b. An action of חסד describes only a "relationship" between God and humans or humans and humans. And God is always the "provider" of חסד to his people.

c. חסד contains a meaning of "obligation" and "duty."

d. חסד cannot be separated from רחמים and אמת.

e. God's חסד is everlasting and cannot be changed, because it is about loyalty and piety with the love of God as the Father.

f. חסד can be translated into different connotations depending on the text and depending on the relationship, either between God and humans or humans and humans. Nevertheless, the basic connotation of loyalty does not change.

g. The key meanings of חסד in English are faithfulness, loyalty, and piety with an everlasting love or grace when it is described as the attribute of God's love. These key concepts of חסד are the basic foundation of God's election and בריתות with Israel.

Through the study of אמת, the following findings were revealed:

1. If חסד and רחמים exist without אמת, God's love becomes unreliable. Like other Hebrew words, אמת has no equivalent word to translate into other languages. רחמים, חסד, and אמת describe different dimensions of God's love, but together they form one love of God.

2. God's חסד without אמת cannot be reliable anymore. The key concept of אמת is "reliability and truth." It is translated in the English Bible as faithfulness, reliability, trustworthiness, truth, and fidelity.

3. The Holy Spirit is the Spirit of אמת (John 14:17). God's אמת is revealed through the Holy Spirit.

Through the study of חנן, the following findings were revealed:

1. חנן is one of the most used words to express God's love in the OT, along with רחם, חסד, אמת. But the word has slightly different characteristics than those three key Hebrew words of God's love. While the three keywords present the attribute of God's love, חנן describes more of an "action" of God's love. The conjugation of חנן is not so different either. Therefore, חנן does not define God's love itself but defines the

action of God's love. The etymological study of חנן also confirms the characteristic of the word.

2. חנן is translated in the English Bible as "grace" or "mercy," but it is better to understand it as "bestowing God's love or doing God's favor."

5. Conclusion

The first research question was "How does God's love in John 3:16 justify God's motivation for *missio Dei* as the work of the triune God in the OT?" The premise of the research was based on the assumption that οὕτως in the verse John 3:16 explains God's Radical Love.

Through the study in this chapter, the true meaning of God's love has been crystallized. God's love is radical, unlimited, unconditional, loyal, trustworthy, and undefinable in human understanding. Therefore, it is not proper to say just "love," but it should be "Love," because there is no equivalent love in this universe. God's love is the only one in the whole universe. Therefore, God's love should be marked as "God's Radical Love."

The research shows that most foreign languages, including Greek, do not deliver the full dimensions of God's Radical Love in the "translated" Bibles. The English word *love* is too general of a word to express the full picture of God's Radical Love.

Through the study of Hebrew words and their etymological study from the ancient Semitic languages, the full dimension of God's Radical Love has been defined. רחם presents God's enduring and hard-labored love toward his people. It will continue no matter what his children do to him. It is much more of a mother-like love toward her children. It is an unconditional love of the Creator. חסד represents God's piety, fidelity, loyalty, and faithfulness in his love toward humanity. חסד is everlasting and continuous until the kingdom comes. God's judgment and righteousness are based on his חסד. חסד portrays a fatherlike love toward people. אמת describes the reliability of God's חסד and רחמים. Based on אמת, God's love is always faithful and trustworthy. These three dimensions figure into the one love of God, our Father, who has designed *missio Dei*. Simply put, God's love is radical, uncompromisable, and unchangeable even by God himself.

Luther has explained John 3:16 by using John 3:14, saying that v. 14 is what οὕτως means: "God does not confine Himself to giving us His Son in His incarnation, but He also delivers Him into death for us. He has Him lifted up as Moses lifted up the serpent."[127] In fact, John 3:14 explains God's self-giving love, which is an outcome of God's Radical Love. Therefore, οὕτως indicates God's Radical Love.

Thus, οὕτως in John 3:16 does justify God's motivation for *missio Dei* as the work of the triune God in the OT. The word οὕτως cannot be explained without God's Radical Love from the OT.

---

127. *LW* 22:354.

Chapter Four

The Radical Love of God and B'rith (ברית)

1. Etymology of B'rith

Much of Christian theology has been strongly influenced by the Reformers, such as Martin Luther and John Calvin, and their thought has impacted the theology of the covenant as well. The Hebrew term *b'rith* (ברית) has been translated in various terms depending on each denominational doctrine, such as covenant or promise. However, those words don't convey the original meaning of the *b'rith*, because there is no term among foreign languages exactly equivalent, as most OT scholars have agreed. For example, William J. Dumbrell writes,

> For the development of our argument it may be most helpful if some discussion is advanced at this point on the highly significant Hebrew term *B'rith*. As has been indicated the customary translation of this word has been "covenant." In recent years however in a number of technical studies the adequacy of that rendering has been called into question.[1]

Weinfeld also explains in his writing of *b'rith* in *TDOT*, "The etymology of Bergtheim is not altogether clear." He demonstrates the variety of the etymology of *b'rith* from various Semitic languages. For an example, he takes ברה as a possible root of *b'rith*, which means "to eat or dine" in a festival meal and is *biritu* from Akkadian. But, as he has also noticed, *birit* in Akkadian means "between, among," which later became *bein* (בין)

---

1. Dumbrell 2013, 15.

The Radical Love of God and B'rith (ברית)

in Hebrew. He also takes note of E. Kutsch's suggestion that *baru* (to look) in Akkadian is related to *b'rith* in Hebrew.[2]

The *Encyclopedia Bible* explains that there are two different possible sources of the origin of *b'rith*. First, it might be from ברא (or ברה) as Weinfeld defines it in *TDOT*. *EM* explains that a meal sharing was a part of the *b'rith* ceremony when they "ברה-cut" the sacrifice of the *b'rith*, because it was grilled as a meal later.

Second, *EM* suggests that the most probable origin of the Hebrew word may be from *ba'tar*, which may have originated from Arabic with letter repositioning.[3] In the Semitic language, letter repositioning often happened in the transition into foreign languages during ancient times.[4] The Hebrew word *ba'tar* (בתר) means "cut, dissect, divide," according to the Evan-Shushan Hebrew-Hebrew dictionary. Therefore, the Hebrew word *b'rith* was widely used in the ancient Middle Eastern world as an act of a two-part agreement on an issue with a sacrifice and a meal.

However, the author believes that there is a missing part in the etymology of the *b'rith* from Weinfeld or *EM*. The most important issue is that *b'rith* was not created by God but rather through human culture and had already been well embedded in the people's cognition during the Old Testament period. God used the human culture to deliver his messages of *b'rith*. When God spoke about *b'rith* to Noah, Abraham, or Moses, they did not question what it was. This is a very crucial part of understanding the word *b'rith*. All of those people in the Old Testament were already accustomed to the culture of *b'rith*, thus accepting God's offer for *b'rith* with them without any doubt or questions. Jakob Jocz agrees with this understanding:

> The idea that the covenant tradition was a later invention is now dismissed by most scholars. It is assumed, however, that the concept of a covenant with God derives from the sociological structure of ancient society which was amphictyonically constituted. Tribal life depended upon the co-operation within the related groups and tribal leagues came about under political pressure.[5]

---

2. "ברית," *TDOT* 2:254.
3. "ברית," *EB* 2:348.
4. See the case of למנר"נ in Kim, "Radical Love," 87.
5. Jocz, *Covenant*, 21.

Picture 1. Calchas, the Greek seer at Troy, inspecting the liver. The lungs lie ready on the table in front of him. This decoration appears on an Etruscan mirror and was reproduced by Aeree Yoo as the above image in 2024. Used with permission.

One of the crucial parts of the ancient Near Eastern cultural context of *b'rith* is the omen of the liver, which was called *bārûtu* in Akkadian. The *bārûtu* is

> a monumental ancient Mesopotamian compendium of the science of extispicy or sacrificial omens stretching over around a hundred cuneiform tablets which was assembled in the Neo-Assyrian/Babylonian period based upon earlier recensions.[6]

---

6. Starr, "*Bārûtu*," 46.

The Radical Love of God and B'rith (ברית)

Some archaeologists also have found ceramics in the shape of a sheep liver (haruspex), which had been used by a *bārû*, a Babylonian priest practicing extispicy with sacrificed animals. This omen had been popular in most of the Mediterranean and Middle Eastern area throughout the Hellenistic period. Cicero writes of this liver omen,

> Let us laugh at the soothsayers (*haruspex*), brand them as frauds and impostors and scorn their calling, even though a very wise man, Tiberius Gracchus, and the results and circumstances of his death have given proof of its trustworthiness.[7]

The *barutu* practice is also mentioned in the book of Ezekiel: "For the king of Babylon will stop at the fork in the road, at the junction of the two roads, to seek an omen: He will cast lots with arrows, he will consult his idols, he will examine the liver" (Ezek 21:21). Although this activity of divination is not directly connected to the *b'rith*, it draws a picture of the cultural background in the ancient Middle East, one that uses lamb livers as a source of omen because livers were considered as seats of feeling, passion, and life. This is also well expressed in the Bible (Lam 2:11; Prov 7:22–23; Job 20:25). In Hebrew, liver is כבד, which means "heavy" because it is the heaviest organ in the body. Many historical resources from the ancient Middle East confirm that the liver is considered the source of life, as Prov 7:23 explains.

עַד יְפַלַּח חֵץ כְּבֵדוֹ כְּמַהֵר צִפּוֹר אֶל־פָּח וְלֹא־יָדַע כִּי־בְנַפְשׁוֹ הוּא

Till an arrow pierces its liver; a bird rushes into a snare; he does not know that it will cost him his life. (Prov 7:23 ESV)

In Judaism, the liver is also considered a crucial piece of sacrifice, because it is considered a source of life.[8] Therefore, the ancient culture that is related to *b'rith* is highly connected to the liver, because the liver is thought to be the source of life and the center of emotion. Based on this cultural background of the ancient Middle East, a few facts of *b'rith* can be conjectured:

a. The etymology shows that the term *karath b'rith* (כרת ברית) might be derived from "cutting a liver," which could hold the symbolism of "sharing life." When two groups of people (בין) or two people made a

---

7. Cicero, "On Divination," 2.1.
8. See Rambam on Lev 3:4: *Ar.* 20a, *Sanh.* 49.

b'rith, they cut an animal in two pieces as Abraham did (Gen 15:10). Then, they may have cut the liver in two pieces too.

b. Since the liver was considered the seat of life and emotion and a divine tool to see signs of the future, the *b'rith* was meant to be a "blood covenant," as James Lindemann describes in his book *Covenant: The Blood Is the Life*. Thus, when two sides cut a liver, it could symbolize sharing lives, emotion, and even the mind and soul.

c. Therefore, breaking a *b'rith* meant breaking a life commitment. The side that has broken the commitment must pay with his life. Concerning the *b'rith* between God and humanity, the side that breaks *b'rith* is humanity. It should be the humans who pay the price of death, but God has taken the penalty and paid by his life on the cross.

2. Meaning of *B'rith*

In *TDNT*, Weinfeld hints at the meaning of *b'rith* but does not paint its full picture in the OT, as mentioned in the previous section. This lexiconic discrepancy of the translation of *b'rith* into different languages has been shared with many biblical scholars, such as Dumbrell and Jocz.[9] Additionally, Weinfeld describes the incongruity between the Hebrew word *b'rith* and its Greek translation *diathêkē*. The etymology of *b'rith* is not altogether clear. He also notes,

> The common term for covenant in Greek is *synthêkē*. The LXX, however, for theological reasons, renders *B'rith* with *diathêkē*, which rather means "will" or "testament," which in a sense renders the original meaning of *B'rith*.[10]

Still, none of these Greek words translates the exact meaning of *b'rith*, as Weinfeld mentions.[11] Nonetheless, the foreign terms *covenant* or *promise*[12] will remain in use since the denominational doctrine would not be easily changed, regardless of what anyone says about *b'rith*. The traditional meaning of the covenant hence is still understood as "agreement or settlement between two parties," "imposition, liability," or "obligation," based on

---

9. Weinfeld, *TDOT* 2: 254. See also Dumbrell 2013, 17; Jocz, *Covenant*, 15–19.
10. Weinfeld, *TDOT* 2:256.
11. Weinfeld, *TDOT* 2:256.
12. *LW* 2:71–72.

The Radical Love of God and B'rith (ברית)

each denominational doctrine. Nevertheless, the true meaning of *b'rith* and the election of Israel must be clarified here in the context of God's Radical Love: *racham, hesed,* and *emeth*. God's Radical Love is the fundamental motivation and foundation of *b'rith* and God's election of Israel.

The theme of *b'rith* has been a burning issue for many biblical and theological scholars, and many of those scholars have tried to clarify its true meaning from various perspectives: biblical, linguistic, theological, and even anthropological. After a few centuries of studies on *b'rith*, several conclusions have emerged. Despite such a diverse understanding of *b'rith*, all conclusions share common facts:

a. *B'rith* is a covenant, treaty, compact, and a mutual agreement with an obligation of two covenantal parts. Nevertheless, it is unconditional between God and humans, mainly from God's side.

b. *B'rith* is what God has asked humans to do in the relationship with him.

c. *B'rith* is not God's favoritism of Israel. "There is no favoritism with God, God only elects those who deserve it."[13] The election of Israel is just a "role" for *missio Dei*.

d. *B'rith* is fully based on God's חסד.

Nevertheless, the author believes that the most crucial meaning of *b'rith* is the blood covenant with life commitment and with God's *hesed* (Gen 15:9–21). As mentioned above, *b'rith* is truly a mutual agreement, one that also has a commitment of life or death. When one side breaks the *b'rith*, they should pay back with their life because they had committed to *b'rith* in blood, which means life. A blood covenant contains a self-cursed oath in the case of covenant breaking, as Jeremiah says in Jer 34:18–19:

> And the men who transgressed my covenant and did not keep the terms of the covenant that they made before me, I will make them like the calf that they cut in two and passed between its parts the officials of Judah, the officials of Jerusalem, the eunuchs, the priests, and all the people of the land who passed between the parts of the calf. (ESV)

The most classic and crucial blood covenant in the Bible is the Abrahamic *b'rith* (Gen 15:9–21). The main elements of the Abrahamic covenant are five sacrificial animals and God's oath. Before the *b'rith*, God tells Abraham

---

13. Jocz, *Covenant*, 23–24.

to "cut animals in half" and then passes with fire between those sacrifices. The blood of the sacrifices on the floor is burned, and the sacrifices themselves are accepted. God then makes a *b'rith* with Abraham. In this passage, God is the only one who speaks. It means that God is the one who makes the *b'rith*, not Abraham. Abraham is just a participant and the object of the *b'rith*, not the subject. The blood involved in this covenant indicates the life from which the blood comes. God states in Lev 17:11,

> For the life of the flesh is in the blood, and I have given it for you on the altar to make atonement for your souls, for it is the blood that makes atonement by the life. (ESV)

Therefore, wasting blood, which happens through the breaking of the *b'rith*, can be paid only by blood. Humans have broken the *b'rith*, and they need to pay by blood. But because of God's Radical Love, God took the cross and gave himself as the blood sacrifice for all the sins of humanity, because there is no forgiveness of sins without blood (Heb 9:22).

Therefore, Jesus on the cross is the ultimate outcome of God's bloody *b'rith*. The *b'rith* is God's prophetic epic for *missio Dei* through the blood on the cross by himself, as described in Heb 9:24–28. All of humanity becomes the spiritual heirs of the *b'rith* in Christ (Gal 3:29).

Simply said, *b'rith* means God's promise and oath to bring the ultimate salvation through his blood on the cross, by paying with his life for the humans' sin. Moreover, all *b'rith* in the Bible contain promises of the new land. *B'rith* is thus the promise to restore God's creation and his kingdom (Isa 11:6–9; Heb 11:13–16). The fundamental motivation is God's Radical Love.

3. God's Radical Love and *B'rith*

Among theologians, the term *covenantal love* has been widely used for centuries. The author believes that covenantal love is another expression of God's Radical Love. This is because the Hebrew term *b'rith* has been combined with other Hebrew terms, *hesed* (חסד) and *emeth* (אמת), several times in the OT, confirming God's Radical Love as the fundamental motivation for *b'rith*.[14] *TWOT* explains,

> The phrase *Hesed* and *Emeth* mentioned above is thought by some to argue for the concept of loyalty or fidelity in *Hesed*. It

---

14. Deut 7:9, 12; 1 Kgs 8:23; 2 Chr 6:14; 1 Sam 20:8; Neh 1:5, 9:32; Dan 9:4. Ps 25:6–10.

The Radical Love of God and *B'rith* (ברית)

occurs some twenty-five times with about seven more in less close connection.[15]

TWOT also quotes Stoebe, mentioning that Deut 7:9, 12 is just "a paraphrase of Ex. 34:6."[16] וְיָדַעְתָּ כִּי־יְהוָה אֱלֹהֶיךָ הוּא הָאֱלֹהִים הָאֵל הַנֶּאֱמָן שֹׁמֵר הַבְּרִית וְהַחֶסֶד לְאֹהֲבָיו וּלְשֹׁמְרֵי מִצְוֺתָו לְאֶלֶף דּוֹר: (Deut 7:9). Psalm 25:6–10 shows the *b'rith* is created because of God's Radical Love (חסד, רחם, אמת) in order to deal with humans' sin.

זְכֹר־רַחֲמֶיךָ יְהוָה וַחֲסָדֶיךָ כִּי מֵעוֹלָם הֵמָּה:
חַטֹּאות נְעוּרַי ׀ וּפְשָׁעַי אַל־תִּזְכֹּר כְּחַסְדְּךָ זְכָר־לִי־אַתָּה לְמַעַן טוּבְךָ יְהוָה:
טוֹב־וְיָשָׁר יְהוָה עַל־כֵּן יוֹרֶה חַטָּאִים בַּדָּרֶךְ:
יַדְרֵךְ עֲנָוִים בַּמִּשְׁפָּט וִילַמֵּד עֲנָוִים דַּרְכּוֹ:
כָּל־אָרְחוֹת יְהוָה חֶסֶד וֶאֱמֶת לְנֹצְרֵי בְרִיתוֹ וְעֵדֹתָיו:

Without God's ואמת, חסד, רחם, it is impossible to understand God's ברית, because God's *racham*, *hesed*, and *emeth* are the flesh and bones of *b'rith*, which is God's blueprint for *missio Dei*. As God promised Abraham the salvation of his descendants from Egypt, God presented his *missio Dei* through *b'rith* to bring the salvation of the entire humanity from the slavery of sin and restore his kingdom again. The Israelites' slavery in Egypt four hundred years hints at the entire human history in the darkness of sin after the fall from Eden. The journey of the Israelites in the desert for forty years indicates God's work of salvation for the entire humanity through *missio Dei* based on his Radical Love. No matter how hardened the hearts of the Israelites are, God will continue his salvation work until his kingdom comes.

As stated before, *b'rith* is not just a legal contract between God and humans but the blueprint of *missio Dei* with God's Radical Love. The story of Hosea confirms God's covenantal love toward Israel in Hos 3:1–5: "And the LORD said to me, go again, love a woman who is loved by another man and is an adulteress, even as the LORD loves the children of Israel, though they turn to other gods and love cakes of raisins." Although humans have always betrayed God's love and the *b'rith*, God will never give up loving his children until "the children of Israel . . . return to God" (Hos 3:5). This represents God's Radical Love in *b'rith*. This covenantal love lays the foundation of his kenotic love on the cross for the salvation of humanity through Jesus.

---

15. R. Laird Harris, "חסד," *TWOT* 307 (Strong's 698).

16. Harris, *TWOT* 307.

4. B'rith, Election, and *Missio Dei*

Jocz clarifies the covenant's connection with God's election. Election "is inseparable from the biblical doctrine of God." Jocz reviews a few arguments by several scholars, such as G. Ernest Wright and H. H. Rowley. He disputes their arguments on God's election of Israel due to a couple of errors that they made. Jocz can't accept Wright's theory of "separating election from the covenant." He argues that Rowley is "wrong when he declares that 'when the service is withheld the election loses its meaning, and therefore fails,'" although he agrees with Rowley's understanding of election for service. Then, he disputes Rowley's idea of the "election without covenant," describing it as a "theological impossibility," because "covenant means election, and election is for covenant."[17] Here, Jocz's understanding of the connection between covenant and election is clear: they are one inseparable body.

Since the covenant and election are rooted in God's Radical Love, they are not "depending upon men's loyalty." If they are, Jocz states, "then, God has chosen a wrong partner."[18] Psalm 103:10 endorses his argument: "He does not deal with us according to our sins, nor repay us according to our iniquities." This passage shows that God's covenant is unconditional and a one-sided commitment from God, and so is election. Jocz defines God as שומר הברית וחסד, according to Deut 7:9, 12. He also outlines God's attribute of his love, faithfulness, and enduring love: *hesed*.[19] Then, Jocz concludes on the study of the election:

> Election then is the inseparable concomitant of the covenant as the conditionless and the irrevocable will of God to be present to His people. The heart of the Torah is the declaration that the Creator of the universe condescends to take man under His protection and to become Israel's God. This is the Great Manifesto of man's franchise: "I am Yhvh their God."[20]

The author has found that Jocz's statement is the most agreeable explanation of covenant and election, despite some missing parts in the context of *missio Dei*, because God's *b'rith* is everlasting, as 1 Chr 16:17 mentions:

---

17. Jocz, *Covenant*, 40.
18. Jocz, *Covenant*, 40.
19. Jocz, *Covenant*, 42.
20. Jocz, *Covenant*, 43.

The Radical Love of God and *B'rith* (ברית)

ויעמידה ליעקב לחק לישראל ברית עולם. Here, the Hebrew term עולם means "eternity, everlasting."[21] God's *b'rith* cannot ever be terminated.

Since the covenant and election present God's attributes and characteristics of his Radical Love, it is crucial to understand the two terms in the light of *missio Dei*, since they are not just one-time historical events. The entire human history has been shaped in the context of *missio Dei*, which has been presented by the covenant and election. Therefore, it is crucial to understand God's purpose of the covenant and election through the Israelites.

What is the main reason God has chosen Israel to make the covenant? Why Israel? Why the covenant? These questions can be answered only by understanding God's Radical Love. The creation has been corrupted by humans' sin. The perfection (טוב) of the creation has been destroyed by humans' disobedience. As the author mentioned in chapter 3, God felt great frustration and agony in his heart at seeing the human sin (Gen 3:9; 6:6).[22] Nevertheless, God's Radical Love is unceasing and everlasting regardless of humans' sinful actions, as are his covenant and election of Israel.

Deuteronomy explains clearly why God chose Israel. God chose Israel as a sample of the entire "stiff-necked" humanity. God is omniscient and knew that Israel would betray him and break the covenant. Nevertheless, he kept punishing their sins and kept restoring them with his Radical Love, as Ps 78 explains. Israel was chosen as the עם סגולה and בבת עיניו. His anger and fury were aroused when the Israelites caused נחם in God's heart with their sins against him. Despite their unfaithfulness, God could not forsake Israel, because God's *b'rith* and election are everlasting (ברית עולם) and irrevocable (Rom 11:28–29). For this reason, Jocz rejects the idea of Wright's theory of separation between covenant and election and Rowley's theory of the revocable covenant.[23]

Then, why Israel? Why the covenant? God did not pick any other people (Amos 3:1) but Israel, so that God could show his Radical Love and how to deal with humans' sin through Israel's rebellion against God (3:2). "Only you have I chosen of all the families of the earth; therefore, I will punish you for all your sins" (Amos 3:1–2). God's election does not show his favoritism of Israel above all nations. Instead, Israel was chosen because they were the עם המעט מכל העמים (Deut 7:7). Israel had the smallest number of people

---

21. Allen A. Macrae, "עלם," *TWOT* 672 (Strong's 1613).
22. See the meaning of איכה and נחם in ch. 3 of this book.
23. Jocz, *Covenant*, 40.

in the area at that time (it could be connoted that they were "worthless people"). They did not have anything but God—no kingdom, no land. God said that this was the reason that he had chosen Israel—to make them "holy people" for God and "treasure people" out of nothing: כִּי עַם קָדוֹשׁ אַתָּה לַיהוה אֱלֹהֶיךָ בְּךָ בָּחַר יהוה אֱלֹהֶיךָ לִהְיוֹת לוֹ לְעַם סְגֻלָּה מִכֹּל הָעַמִּים אֲשֶׁר עַל־פְּנֵי הָאֲדָמָה: (Deut 7:6). God had a full plan for Israel, and his commitment to the plan was the covenant. As the author mentioned in chapter 2.5, God revealed his plan of *missio Dei* through the election of Abraham: וְנִבְרְכוּ בְךָ כֹּל מִשְׁפְּחֹת הָאֲדָמָה: (Gen 12:3). Blessing (ברכה) in the OT means submission (kneeling down) to God. He created a master plan of *missio Dei* to bring salvation to all humanity through Abraham's children (Israel).

In the Bible, God chose the most miserable (מעט) group of people to designate as his messenger and to reveal himself as God of all nations. He chose Moses and sent him to Pharaoh to let the Israelites and Egyptians know that יהוה is God (Exod 10:2), using the ten plagues to reveal himself. God chose Abraham to make him the father of the nations (אב להם). He made it clear, when he chose Ezekiel and gave him a mission among the Babylonians and Israelites, that "they shall know that I am the Lord" (Ezek 6:10).

In fact, Israelites were held to higher expectations in God's eyes as the "people of the high priest," "holy people," and "treasure people," but they failed to uphold them (Ps 78). God had already expected that Israel would fail their mission on earth. The secret of Israel's calling was, in fact, that their failure to be the light of the world was actually half of the mission that God had given. God revealed himself and his Radical Love through Israelite rebellion and unfaithfulness, and through the success of missions, such as conquering Canaan and other nations. All the enemies of Israelites saw that Israel became invincible when God was with them.

Michael. A. Grisanti accurately points out what Israel's mission was through election. Based on his study of Isa 40–55, he clarifies Israel's mission among all nations through the covenant and election. Through his study, Grisanti has tried to figure out Israel's relationship to the nations.

> In describing Israel's relationship to the nations, Isaiah 40–55 represents three loci of tension: either divine blessings for Israel alone or for the entire world also, Israel as either an active witness or a passive one, and either the nations as subject to Israel or as coequal with Israel in their standing before God. Israel's mission

The Radical Love of God and B'rith (ברית)

to the world is either centripetal (inward moving) or centrifugal (outward moving).[24]

Grisanti defines two different roles of Israel by election: nationalism (salvation is only for Israel) and universalism (salvation is for the entire humanity through Israel). He points out that many scholars have misunderstood the context of Isa 40–55 by separating these two functions of Israel. However, they are one for Israel. God made *b'rith* with only Israel to promise her restoration, but at the same time Israel was called to be "a kingdom of priests" and "a holy nation." Grisanti determines, based on his study of Isa 40–55, that "Yahweh intended that Israel function in a mediatorial or representative role before the nations."[25] Then, he argues that Israel was called to be a missional nation to the world in two different ways: active (centrifugal) and passive (centripetal). Whether through nationalistic or universalistic mission, God has used Israel to take his name to the world. The prophecy of Isaiah sounds mainly like a nationalistic mission, but it is actually nationalistic and passive universalism. Grisanti explains,

> Several posit that Isaiah 40–55 contains a commission for Israel to be a passive witness. In other words, Israel is not commanded to do missionary work, but to serve as a sign of God's glory among the nations. Israel has no other mission to the heathen than to be the chosen people. Martin-Achard argues that "it is by means of the life of His people that the God of Israel produces the light of the world" (i.e., gentiles—Isa 49:6). By its very existence in the world, Israel will assume its mediatorial function of representing Yahweh to the world.[26]

Then, he quotes from Oswalt:

> Israel's function is that of witness as opposed to proselytizer. . . . Israel, by its life and words, is to demonstrate what God is like and what he is doing. Beyond this, it is God who will do the drawing and the bringing of the nations to himself. . . . If Israel will simply be the Israel of God, the nations will be drawn to him.[27]

Indeed, most of the time in the OT, Israel were passive missionaries by being punished for their unfaithfulness to God and being restored by God's

---

24. Grisanti, "Israel's Mission," 39.
25. Grisanti, "Israel's Mission," 59.
26. Grisanti, "Israel's Mission," 54.
27. John N. Oswalt; quoted in Grisanti, "Israel's Mission," 54.

חסד and רחם. Since Israel was God's firstborn child, they were used as a pedagogical tool for the nations, as mentioned in Isa 40:2: "Speak tenderly to Jerusalem, and proclaim to her that her hard service has been completed, that her sin has been paid for, that she has received from the Lord's hand double for all her sins." St. Paul also describes in Rom 11:11–12, "Again I ask: Did they stumble so as to fall beyond recovery? Not at all! Rather, because of their transgression, salvation has come to the gentiles to make Israel envious. But if their transgression means riches for the world, and their loss means riches for the gentiles, how much greater riches will their fullness bring!"

The *b'rith* and God's election of Israel represent the full blueprint of *missio Dei*. They also orchestrate God's Radical Love (חסד, רחם, אמת), which is the fundamental foundation and motivation for *missio Dei*. Furthermore, God has called Israel to be mediator and missionary to the nations. God's mission through Israel has not been completed yet, but will remain ongoing until his kingdom comes.

5. Conclusion

The Hebrew term ברית has been the core of many theological arguments for centuries. First of all, the meaning of the Hebrew word is not clear and is almost impossible to translate precisely. Various scholars have tried to figure out its etymology but have mostly drawn ambiguous conclusions. The author's interpretation of ברית may not be so different, or it may be even more vague. Nevertheless, the understanding and interpretation of ברית in the cultural context of the ancient Middle East might provide an inkling for a new perspective of the Hebrew term ברית. This is because the Hebrew word כרת means cutting the sacrifice, and the liver was a crucial part of sacrifice at that time.

Therefore, the Hebrew term can be translated either way, as covenant or promise, but the author insists on using the Hebrew term by itself, as *hosanna* or *amen* are used. This is due to the fact that foreign translated words could totally change the concept of the original Hebrew word.

The true meaning of *b'rith* is God's promise and oath to bring the ultimate salvation of humanity from sin through his blood on the cross. It is a fully planned map for *missio Dei*. God has revealed this salvific plan in *missio Dei* through the *b'rith* and election of Israel. Israel was called to be the centripetal and centrifugal missionary nation to the world.

CHAPTER FIVE

Understanding *Missio Dei* through Christology and Pneumatology in Light of John 3:16

1. Introduction

IN THIS CHAPTER, THE second research question will be explored. This question is about the "what" of *missio Dei*: "What is God doing through *missio Dei* in his creation?" The question should be answered according to the findings of the first research question above.

The key verse of this research, John 3:16, lays a firm foundation of Christology. In chapter 3, the author attempted to define the meaning of God's love through the philological study of Semitic languages and the Hebrew Scripture, which covers the first phrase of John 3:16, "God has so loved the world." Through the philological study, the meaning of God's Radical Love has been uncovered, and the research has concluded that God's Radical Love through חסד, רחם, ואמת is God's fundamental motivation for *missio Dei*. John 3:16 describes that God's Radical Love (חסד,רחם, ואמת) is also the initial motivation for God to give his begotten Son to sinful humanity, so that they can have salvation through the Son and not perish. Therefore, Christology must be discussed as the means of *missio Dei*, because it is the first and most fundamental consequence of God's motivation for *missio Dei*: his Radical Love (חסד, רחמים ואמת).

This chapter is not about defining the meaning of Christology, nor about the controversy of Christology discussed for two millennia, since the very beginning of Christianity. It would not only be an irrelevant discussion in this research context, but also an igniting point of wasteful debates, since each denominational doctrine has a different understanding of Christology. Furthermore, this research is not about Christology but about *missio Dei* based on John 3:16. In this research, Christology is considered the means of *missio Dei*, not the goal of it.

2. God's Radical Love as the Foundation of Christology

According to John 3:16, God's initial motivation for giving us his only Son is his Radical Love, which is ואמת, חסד, רחמים as we have seen in previous chapters. It is radical because ואמת, חסד, רחמים are beyond humans' comprehension of love. After Adam's sin, the entire creation was contaminated and cursed. The Father's heart was torn in seeing the betrayal of his own creation that broke the harmony of the perfect creation (Gen 3:9). Then, God brought judgment to the first humans and the serpent. Interestingly, the completion of the serpent's judgment was promised not in Eden but by "a son of woman" in the future. Why didn't God judge the serpent on the spot for an everlasting time but postpone the punishment to the future? Was God not able to do it? Or didn't God want to do it? These questions can be answered only by understanding the full picture of God's Radical Love, as mentioned above, because the concept of judgment cannot be understood without full comprehension of רחמים, חסד, ואמת.

In Gen 3:15, God promised the salvation of his creation, which is the complete restoration of the perfection that the initial creation was in the beginning. God promised Christ, who is the only "woman's son" in human history, to all human beings. Then, the second research question should be asked here again. "What does God want to do for *missio Dei* through Christ?" Or, "What is the role of Christ in *missio Dei*?" Understanding of the work and role of Christ among evangelical denominations shares similar Christology and soteriology in the majority of areas, but simultaneously huge differences in opinion exist among them. The author is not going to march into the turmoil of debating the controversy now, since it does not help this research at all. Instead, the author will take Luther's Christology as the basic foundation of this thesis and will compare it to the author's view of Christology based on his theory of God's Radical Love.

The key actions of God's salvation through Christ have been described in John 3:16. The phrase "Whoever believes in him" can be an action justified by faith, and "should not perish" is about reconciliation and salvation.

And then, "but have eternal life" may be a description about ἔσχατον. Therefore, there are four missions of Christ that God has given to the Son: 1) justification (or purification), 2) reconciliation, 3) salvation, and 4) restoration of God's kingdom and kingship of the Lord (which can also be considered the restoration of the creation).

However, prior to these missions of the Son, God did one incredible action from his Radical Love (חסד, רחמים, אמת) for the world: "he gave his only Son." The phrase τὸν μονογενῆ ἔδωκεν can probably find a parallel context in ἑαυτὸν ἐκένωσεν μορφὴν δούλου λαβών in Phil 2:7. Saint Paul explains that this "self-giving action" is a result of God's Radical Love in Gal 2:20.[1] Due to his Radical Love, God (λόγος) has incarnated in a δοῦλος form and had a great humiliation (*Erniedrigung*). This is the self-giving action of God through Jesus, which is the meaning of κένωσις. Therefore, it would not be an exaggeration to say that κένωσις is the very beginning point of *missio Dei* through Jesus Christ in this world. Thus, all four categories of the Son's mission must be understood based on God's initial action for Christ of "emptying himself" through humiliation.

3. κένωσις

3.1. Theological Study of κένωσις

The theology of κένωσις is the core of incarnation in Christology, because God's salvific mission for humanity is conducted by the kenotic (self-giving) love of God through Jesus, the second person in the Trinity. The following chapter will demonstrate the details of this issue. As D. M. Baillie noticed, the theology of kenosis has been developed only in the modern era as a part of the theology of incarnation, although the term has been used far before, as with Zinzendorf.[2] From around Justin Martyr's time to contemporary Christology, the theology of incarnation has been a mysterious stumbling stone, as has the theology of κένωσις. Since the Chalcedonian Creed, the theology of incarnation has focused mainly on the ontological and soteriological work of the Lord Jesus Christ. It seems that Baillie had the same issue. He insisted on leaving the theology of incarnation as "God's paradox of Christology," which no human being would ever understand.

---

1. Gal 2:20: ζῶ δὲ οὐκέτι ἐγώ, ζῇ δὲ ἐν ἐμοὶ Χριστός· ὃ δὲ νῦν ζῶ ἐν σαρκί, ἐν πίστει ζῶ τῇ τοῦ υἱοῦ τοῦ θεοῦ τοῦ ἀγαπήσαντός με καὶ παραδόντος ἑαυτὸν ὑπὲρ ἐμοῦ.

2. Baillie, *God Was in Christ*, 94.

Despite the controversy of the incarnation in Christian theology, a short survey of the previous understanding of God's incarnation in the concept of κένωσις and theology of God's suffering may be a necessary process to clarify the direction of this research. This is because liberal theologians viewed κένωσις with a negative connotation.[3] Therefore, there is a strong objection to κένωσις theology among evangelical scholars, as Baillie mentions in his book.[4] Such objection is a result of misunderstanding the concept of God's Radical Love, and also of misinterpretation of the OT. In fact, Luther illuminated this issue very clearly.

Although Luther quoted Phil 2:5–7 over fifty-five times in his sermons and writings,[5] he never conceptualized the term of κένωσις in his life. Nevertheless, he clarified the servanthood concept of κένωσις as a part of the incarnation.

> St. Paul speaks of it this way in Philippians 2:6, 7: Jesus Christ, "though He was in the form of God, did not count equality with God a thing to be grasped, but emptied Himself, taking the form of a servant." He says that Christ emptied Himself of the divine form; that is, He did not use His divine might nor let His almighty power be seen but withdrew it when He suffered. In this emptying and humiliation, the devil tried all his hellish might.[6]

Luther focused on God's divine incarnation, God who became a man by "emptying" his divine form, or on his "servanthood" after emptying his glory.[7] He took a form even lower than that of a man.[8] This means that God became humiliated (*Erniedrigung*) by taking a servant form. Most of the interpretation in commentaries of Phil 2:7 by Luther describe Jesus' symbiotic identity as God and man, as Dennis Ngien explains.[9] In Luther's perspective, κένωσις is about being incarnated without emptying himself of God's glory. But the divine form was "resumed . . . before he had fulfilled

---

3. As Baillie summarizes in his book, many liberal theologians interpret κένωσις as "emptying God's divinity." Therefore, Jesus died as a true human being on the cross. Those liberals missed Luther's understanding of the Greek words μορφὴν δούλου. There is no mention of "emptying God's divine attribute" in the Bible.

4. Baillie, *God Was in Christ*, 94–96.

5. Based on the St. Louis edition in English.

6. *LW* 12:127.

7. *LW* 10:88: "[He made himself lower] than the angels, namely, by the incarnation. 'He emptied Himself, etc.'" See also *LW* 15:307.

8. *LW* 25:140.

9. Ngien, *Suffering of God*, 59–62.

this office of a servant."¹⁰ Jesus takes back the form of God and his glory when he is with the Father. In Luther's understanding, humiliation is the core of κένωσις, which served to exchange our sin for his divine glory, to save humanity.¹¹ In other words, God emptied his divinity to carry away the sinful nature of humanity through humiliation, suffering, and death on the cross.¹² Although the divinity itself did not suffer, this humiliation and suffering on the cross may connect directly to the emotion of נחם.

While this research is not about clarifying Jesus' deity, it is very crucial to approach the issue at least once here in order to avoid confusion with the theory of anti-kenoticism. The most crucial understanding of κένωσις in Luther's Christology is the connection between κένωσις and Jesus' deity as incarnated man. Most advocates of the historical Jesus have believed that Jesus "emptied" his deity and became a pure human.¹³ However, Luther clarified this issue long before Bultmann, Moltmann, or Harnack. Luther noted in his commentary on Philippians that God's divine μορφῆ, not "divine being," was "emptied."

> Diese Worte "göttliche Gestalt" werden nicht in einerlei Weise erklärt. Etliche meinen, Paulus wolle dadurch das göttliche Wesen und die Natur in Christo verstehen, also daß Christus sei wahrer Gott gewesen, und habe sich doch heruntergelassen. Wiewohl nun das wahr ist, daß Christus wahrer Gott ist, so redet doch Paulus hier nicht von seinem göttlichen heimlichen Wesen. Denn eben dasselbe Wörtlein "morphe" oder "forma" braucht er hernach, da er spricht, Christus habe Knechtsgestalt angenommen. Daselbst kann er "Knechtsgestalt" nicht ein Wesen eines natürlichen Knechts heißen, der von Art eine knechtische Natur an sich hat, weil Christus nicht von Art, sondern aus gutem Willen und aus Gnaden unser Knecht worden ist. Darum kann auch "göttliche Gestalt" hier nicht eben heißen sein göttlich Wesen. Denn das göttliehe Wesen kann niemand sehen, aber die göttliche Gestalt sah man. Wohlan wir wollen deutlich davon reden und St. Paulus hell an den Tag bringen.¹⁴

Therefore, Luther believed that God was in Christ because Christ is God. God had just emptied his "forma" to come down to the human

10. *LW* 24:190.
11. *LW* 29:142.
12. See FC 8:16; SD 8:50, 65, 87.
13. Baillie, *God Was in Christ*, 39–48.
14. WA 34:195–96.

world, and taken *Knechtsgestalt*. Nevertheless, he never emptied his divine attributes from Christ. God's motivation for "emptying his μορφῇ" is his love and his obedience to the Father. Therefore, κένωσις lays a missiological foundation of Jesus' obedience and Radical Love to the Father.

> Aber das alles tat er wahrlich nicht, weil wir's würdig wären oder verdient hätten. Denn wer wollte eines solchen Verdienstes einer solchen Person würdig sein! Sondern (er tat's), daß er dem Vater gehorsam würde.[15]

Consequently, God's suffering and humiliation by κένωσις in Luther's theology is the outcome of the Father's love, and ultimately of God's plan of salvation for humanity by taking the humans' position to take their sin away.[16] This κένωσις is parallel to Jesus' crucifixion in letting people avoid God's judgment and wrath. Therefore, Luther's understanding of κένωσις corresponds with John 3:16.

John Calvin had a similar view to Luther's on God's incarnation in Jesus, with a little discrepancy. Calvin believed that Jesus was fully the son of man, because "he took not on him the nature of angels, but he took on him the seed of Abraham" who had flesh and blood.[17] He agreed with Luther on God's willingness of "voluntarily debas[ing] himself" but took a path that was a bit different by saying God "suffered his Divinity to be hidden behind of the veil of humanity."[18] In Luther's perspective, God's divinity didn't suffer. Furthermore, Calvin believed that God would have a new glory after his humiliation.[19] Nevertheless, Calvin confirmed the deity of Jesus.[20]

John Wesley took a slightly different position on κένωσις from that of the two Reformers. He believed that Jesus temporarily emptied himself of everything, including his "divine fullness," until "he received them again at his exaltation," in order to take the punishment of the "fallen creatures."

> He was content to forego the glories of the Creator, and to appear in the form of a creature; nay, to be made in the likeness of the fallen creatures; and not only to share the disgrace, but to suffer the punishment, due to the meanest and vilest among them all. He

---

15. WA 34:201.
16. *LW* 35:390.
17. *ICR* 8:1.
18. *ICR* 8:2.
19. *ICR* 8:2.
20. *t*8:1.

emptied himself—Of that divine fullness, which he received again at his exaltation. Though he remained full, yet he appeared as if he had been empty; for he veiled his fullness from the sight of men and angels. Yea, he not only veiled, but, in some sense, renounced, the glory which he had before the world began. Taking—And by that very act emptying himself. The form of a servant—The form, the likeness, the fashion, though not exactly the same, are yet nearly related to each other. The form expresses something absolute; the likeness refers to other things of the same kind; the fashion respects what appears to sight and sense. Being made in the likeness of men—A real man, like other men. Hereby he took the form of a servant.[21]

However, this position does not fully correspond with Jesus' ministry in the Synoptics. The first Synoptic and John's Gospel orchestrated Jesus' divinity throughout his ministry on the earth, from birth to resurrection. He was the λόγος who became flesh. Wesley's understanding of κένωσις contradicts Isa 9:5. The baby was פֶּלֶא יוֹעֵץ אֵל גִּבּוֹר אֲבִיעַד שַׂר־שָׁלוֹם. Accordingly, God didn't "empty himself" but emptied his divine form only. Therefore, this research will take Luther's theology of κένωσις as its foundation of theology, because Jesus was born as אל גיבור—Almighty God.

Yet, there are a few objections to the kenotic theory, as Baillie mentions in his book. He points out two main objections:

1. What happened to the rest of the world while God was absent in his position of the Creator and Maintainer when he came to the world as baby Jesus?

2. Was the κένωσις (kenosis) merely temporary? He was God, then man, and then God again?[22]

These claims of anti-kenotic theologians reveal a lack of the full picture of κένωσις. God is God, and God has sent "his begotten Son," but the Son is God's incarnation, or the second person in the Trinity. Therefore, what Vicedom mentions is right: "God sent Himself in His Son."[23] This is a great paradox to explain, and this is the point that most anti-kenotic theologians do not comprehend. God is still the Creator and the Sovereign of the universe, although he has sent his begotten Son—*Knechtsgestalt* in

---

21. Wesley, *Wesley's Notes on Bible*, 499.
22. Baillie, *God Was in Christ*, 95–97.
23. Vicedom, *Mission of God*, 83.

Luther's terms. He is omnipresent. Therefore, the liberal theologians' questions of God's absence while he is in the human Jesus cannot reflect who God really is. Terence Fretheim noticed this concern. God's "general presence" has been revealed in several places in the OT. Fretheim quotes from 1 Kgs 8:27: "The highest heavens cannot contain you." And then, Job confesses to the Lord, "I know that you can do all things, and that no purpose of yours can be thwarted" (Job 42:1). Fretheim explains, "God is believed to be continuously present, yet God will also be especially at certain times; God is believed to be everywhere present, yet God will also be especially present in certain places."[24]

Therefore, κένωσις does not limit God's presence and divinity in Christ, since God is omnipotent and omnipresent. Furthermore, John 3:16 reminds one that "God has sent his begotten Son." God is God, and he became man and God, and he is the Son of God. This paradox can be explained only in Trinitarian theology. Furthermore, if God really emptied his divinity from Christ, then God could not have been the principle agent of *missio Dei* anymore, since he had ceased to be God. Then, the meaning and function of Christ in *missio Dei* may be diminished. This issue will be clarified further in the section of exegetical study.

3.2. Exegetical Study of κένωσις

The initial biblical foundation of κένωσις is Phil 2:5–6 in the NT. As Luther declared above, the Son is God and man.[25] Therefore, when St. John

---

24. Fretheim, *Suffering of God*, 61–62.

25. There are many different theological theories of Christology concerning the divinity of Christ. However, as Luther pointed out, based on Gen 4:1, Messiah should be God-Man, not a man with divinity (*LW* 15:321). Luther noticed the function of the Hebrew word את. Havah, Adam's wife, gave birth to Cain, and she thought of him as the seed of woman because he was the first human who was born from a woman. This is the reason that she said, וַתֹּאמֶר קָנִיתִי אִישׁ אֶת־יְהוָה, although Havah did not understand what she was describing. This verse has been mysterious because it is almost impossible to translate into any other language. Arnold G. Fruchtenbaum, a Messianic Jewish theologian, discusses this problem in his book *Messianic Christology*. Fruchtenbaum compares the grammatical structure of Gen 4:1 to 4:2, וַתֹּסֶף לָלֶדֶת אֶת־אָחִיו אֶת־הָבֶל. This sentence shows how the sentence of 4:1 is supposed to be. As אָחִיו is הָבֶל in the second verse, the first verse might be איש את יהוה, קניתי את איש. Therefore, God became a man, and Havah understood it clearly. She just did not know that the seed of woman was not Cain but Jesus, who came after long generations. This concept of God-Man Messiah is not new, and Luther had a similar conclusion by understanding the function of the Hebrew word את in Gen 4:1. "All other Hebraists would also be obliged to admit this if they scrutinized

states, "He gave his only Son," it might be an initial description of κένωσις in the NT. Saint Paul clarifies it in Phil 2:6: "Christ Jesus: who, being in very nature God, did not consider equality with God." Theologians have described this verse as "Christ's self-emptying." This is the beginning point of the theology of κένωσις. John 3:16 reveals that God's initial motivation for the mission is God's Radical Love: חסד,רחמים, ואמת. Since the entire OT is about God's Radical Love, the initial meaning of κένωσις may be possible to trace from the OT. Understanding κένωσις from the OT context in fact will clarify the meaning and purpose of κένωσις in Phil 2:6. Unfortunately, Western theologians have narrowed their understanding of κένωσις only to the case of Jesus Christ, not paying much attention to κένωσις in the OT. This is because Phil 2:7 is the only case talking about God's self-emptying. However, as Luther mentioned, all of the OT is about Jesus.[26] Then, Jesus' κένωσις should also be found in the OT, because κένωσις is the beginning of Christology and the fundamental foundation of the Christian mission principle.

According to Phil 2:5–8, Jesus experienced three consequences of κένωσις:

1. Humiliation

2. Suffering

3. Death on a cross

As Luther pointed out in "Last Word of David," these consequences were driven by God's love.[27] Hence, God's kenotic love can be traced from the OT, where God's Radical Love (חסד,אמת, רחמים) is fully revealed.

3.3. κένωσις in the OT

Genesis 3:15: וְאֵיבָה ׀ אָשִׁית בֵּינְךָ וּבֵין הָאִשָּׁה וּבֵין זַרְעֲךָ וּבֵין זַרְעָהּ הוּא יְשׁוּפְךָ רֹאשׁ וְאַתָּה תְּשׁוּפֶנּוּ עָקֵב׃

---

the text closely and if they believed that this Seed of the woman is Jehovah, that is, God and man" ("Last Words of David," *LW* 15:321). Some rabbis have understood this verse in a similar way, as Fruchtenbaum notices. "The Jerusalem Targum, an Aramaic translation, read, 'I have gotten a man: the angel of Jehovah'" (Fruchtenbaum, *Messianic Christology*, 15). Therefore, it is very clear that God became a man who is Christ.

26. *LW* 15:312–14.

27. *LW* 15:332.

The OT Christology begins with the humiliation of the "Seed" (in Luther's terminology) as a consequence of κένωσις. According to *TDNT*, the literal meanings of κένωσις are "empty," "without content," and figurative meanings are "hollow," "vain," "of a person." Oepke explains in *TDNT* that the word was initially used for the genitive form of objects since the time of Homer. He also mentions that ריק or פחז could usually be equivalent to κένωσις in Hebrew. The LXX has sometimes translated אמללה as κένωσις when the word is used as a verb.[28] אמלל means to become empty handed. However, those Hebrew words have a slightly different connotation than what St. Paul meant in Phil 2:6–7, and the following sections will explain why. In fact, there is no exact sentence in the OT that has used κένωσις in same context as Phil 2:6–7. Rather, some passages contain the meaning of κένωσις but not the word.

The first example of κένωσις in the OT may be Gen 3:15. "The seed of woman" means Jesus Christ, according to St. Paul: "Now the promises were made to Abraham and to his offspring. It does not say, 'And to offspring,' referring to many, but referring to one, 'And to your offspring,' who is Christ" (Gal 3:16 ESV).

Although most commentaries and Christian theologians agree that this is the first gospel in the OT, they mostly ignore the crucial theological point that this verse is the first declaration of κένωσις in the entire Bible. According to ancient Jewish traditions or Middle Eastern culture, being called the seed of a woman is an extreme humiliation. All children and all sons in ancient Middle Eastern families were the seed of man. Being one who has no father was a great shame for a man. Women were not counted as part of the family. The Pentateuch shows various examples of this case. Chapter 4 in Genesis begins with the family tree of Adam. There are only men's names listed, and all the descendants are described as the men's seed. This tradition keeps going throughout the Pentateuch. Even in the book of Exodus, only the number of men is counted (Exod 12:37). Furthermore, Judg 11:1–2 confirms the shameful fact of being the son of a woman. Jephthah the Gileadite is described as the son of a woman who is a prostitute: וַתֵּלֶד אֵשֶׁת־גִּלְעָד לוֹ בָּנִים וַיִּגְדְּלוּ בְנֵי־הָאִשָּׁה וַיְגָרְשׁוּ אֶת־יִפְתָּח וַיֹּאמְרוּ לוֹ לֹא־תִנְחַל בְּבֵית־אָבִינוּ כִּי בֶן־אִשָּׁה אַחֶרֶת אָתָּה׃ (Judg 11:2). In v. 2, he is just described as one of בְנֵי־הָאִשָּׁה. It is a shameful name for a person to be the son of a woman, especially one who is a prostitute. Phyllis Bird describes in her book *Missing Persons and Mistaken Identities* that a married wife "was regarded as

---

28. Albrecht Oepke, "Κενός," *TDNT* 3:659–60. See also Jer 14:2; 15:9.

the exclusive property of her husband," and the violation of the marriage norm "was ranked the same as murder and major religious offenses as a transgression demanding the death penalty" (Lev 20:10; Exod 20:14) by Moses' law.[29] She points out the issue of the patriarchal family structure of ancient Israel. A married wife's adultery was considered a "robbery" of the husband's honor. This is the ethical conceptualization of the patriarchal society of ancient Israel. For this reason, a son of a woman was already cursed from his birth, and being a son of a woman was an extreme humiliation in that society.

It is clear that the Virgin Mary is not the case of a prostitute nor of adultery. Nevertheless, the act of Joseph, the Virgin Mary's fiancé, can be comprehended in the cultural context. Joseph expressed emotions of shame toward his bride, who would be the mother of a child with no father. It meant to him that Mary had had an inappropriate relationship with a man. Phyllis Bird writes that a woman who had committed adultery was regarded as a person who had "dishonored a member of society."[30] Nevertheless, Joseph was a kind and humble person and did not want to cause any risk to Mary's life by publicizing his fiancée's pregnancy. "And her husband Joseph, being a just man and unwilling to put her to shame, resolved to divorce her quietly" (Matt 1:19). According to the Jewish Torah, if a woman became pregnant with no father, it meant that she might have had an inappropriate relationship with a man, and such a woman should be stoned to death (Lev 20:13). The Christ was born as "a son of woman," as Gal 4:4 describes. This is an incredible paradox of the history of salvation and is also a very crucial fact in understanding the concept of *missio Dei*, because the full theology of *missio Dei* is embedded in the term. Although there is no word of κένωσις in Gen 3:15, the passage clearly demonstrates that Messiah will come to the human world in human form, and the first consequence of κένωσις is the worst humiliation as a "seed of a woman." Luther sees that the first step of Christ's humiliation is his birth to Mary.[31] Therefore, "emptying" God's form (incarnation) and taking all of the humans' humiliations by being in the worst humiliation God can receive among human beings is the first step of *missio Dei* through Christ Jesus in the human world. Furthermore, this humiliation through κένωσις is an action of God's Radical Love (Ps 103:13).

---

29. Bird, *Missing Persons*, 23.
30. Bird, *Missing Persons*, 199.
31. LC 2.25.

Isaiah 7:1-17

Isaiah 7 is well known as a messianic prophetic chapter. In this chapter, the prophet states that the Son will be born of a virgin. This verse has ignited controversial arguments among theologians for millennia, and these have not finished yet. Verse 14, "a sign: the virgin will be with child and will give birth to a son," has especially been a hermeneutical enigma. There are two hermeneutical problems: 1) sign; 2) the meaning of העלמה (*almah*) in Hebrew. Many discussions of this theological problem have been written and published until today, with no clear stamp on the answer. Nevertheless, most theologians agree that this is a prophecy of the birth of Jesus, and that he will be born of a virgin or unmarried woman. In fact, this confirms the discussion of Gen 3:15 here, because it is in the same context, taking the same issue. The theological controversy of this passage will not be discussed here, because that is a different issue than this research. Nevertheless, the passage is another confirmation of God's κένωσις since God will be born in the human form of a sinner, a virgin. Mary cannot be excluded from this category. The debate of whether העלמה means a virgin or an unmarried woman is not a critical issue for this thesis. The most crucial issue in this research is that Christ came in human form. It means that God emptied his כבוד (holiness; δόξα) to come as Christ to human beings. Even so, it does not mean that God emptied his divinity in Christ. Isaiah 9:5 confirms that the child is God: כִּי־יֶ֣לֶד יֻלַּד־לָ֗נוּ בֵּ֚ן נִתַּן־לָ֔נוּ וַתְּהִ֥י הַמִּשְׂרָ֖ה עַל־שִׁכְמ֑וֹ וַיִּקְרָ֨א שְׁמ֜וֹ פֶּ֠לֶא יוֹעֵץ֙ אֵ֣ל גִּבּ֔וֹר אֲבִיעַ֖ד שַׂר־שָׁלֽוֹם: This verse drags Christology into an unending maze, because the child is clearly אל יועץ and אביעד, who is God and the Father himself. This verse seems to be contradicted directly in St. Paul's description: "For all have sinned and fall short of the glory of God" (Rom 3:23). King David confesses that he was born in sin in Ps 51:5: "Behold, I was brought forth in iniquity, and in sin did my mother conceive me." Therefore, the divine child who is born as Christ, and who is Almighty God and Everlasting Father, was born in a sinful human form so that Christ could take all humans' sins on himself, although God is not a sinner at all (Rom 4:25; John 1:29). God gave his Son in a sinner's form to humans, to take all of their sin (Gal 2:20). Therefore, Isa 7 and 9 represent another case of κένωσις. God emptied his divine form and took a sinner's shape by being born as a helpless baby. Nevertheless, Christ is still God. This point of view is confirmed by Luther's view of κένωσις as mentioned above and rejects the theology of divine vacancy in human Jesus after emptying ἐν μορφῇ θεοῦ.

God came to the world as God in Jesus, was in Jesus, and died on the cross as God carrying out our sins and our judgment.

Psalm 113:6

The translation of Ps 113:6, הַמַּשְׁפִּילִי לִרְאוֹת בַּשָּׁמַיִם וּבָאָרֶץ, has been controversial. There are many different interpretations of the Hebrew word הַמַּשְׁפִּילִי among different versions of the Bible—not only in the English Bible but also in different languages. Luther translated the verse as "Der oben thront in der Höhe, der herniederschaut in die Tiefe" (Lutherbibel), which is similar to how the NIV translates it: "He bends down to look at the heavens and the earth." The new Lutherbibel (2017) has modernized the word *herniederschaut* to *niederschaut*. In the context of Hebrew, *herniederschaut* could be a closer meaning to הַמַּשְׁפִּילִי, although *niederschaut* would not make a big difference in the meaning of the sentence. The ESV and most of the other modern English translations focus on God's attitude and his physical action: "Who looks far down on the heavens and the earth?" Contrastingly, the Authorized Version (KJV) translates this verse as "Who humbleth himself to behold the things that are in heaven, and in the earth!" The revised version of the Korean Bible has followed the KJV translation for this verse. The trickiest phrase of the translation of this verse in Hebrew is הַמַּשְׁפִּילִי לִרְאוֹת בַּ-.

First of all, according to Engelken, the word שָׁפֵל is a very popular word among all Semitic languages.[32] Engelken says that the literal meaning of the word among those languages basically expresses "to make low physically."[33] But its meaning in the Hebrew Bible is mainly "humiliation by God" as a result of rebellious acts toward him. In fact, when a man made himself "crouch" or "sink low," it meant subordination or humiliation in the ancient Middle Eastern culture. H. J. Austel explains that the most important use of שָׁפֵל, though the idea of "being low" in the physical sense underlies the verb and its derivatives, is in the figurative sense of "abasement," "humbling," "humility."[34]

In Ps 113:6, the word שָׁפֵל appears in *hiphil* form. It means to "cause someone to become low" or "make someone be humiliated." הַמַּשְׁפִּילִי has the suffix י which means "myself" or "God" in Hebrew grammar. The

---

32. Hermann Engelken, "שפל," *TDOT* 15:442.
33. Engelken, *TDOT* 15:442.
34. Hermann J. Austel, "שָׁפֵל," *TWOT* 950 (Strong's 2445).

psalmist of 113:6 is not God. Therefore the suffix, י cannot be the psalmist himself but God. Therefore, the suffix י, who is God, is the subject of the verb השפיל. From vv. 6 to 9, the format of the sentences is the same: each verb includes the subject as a suffix form. The KJV translates the verse in this way too. Therefore, the Hebrew word הַמַּשְׁפִּילִי in Ps 113:6 can be translated as "God has humiliated/humbled himself."

Now, the Hebrew word לִרְאוֹת בַּ- is translated in most English Bibles as "to look far down" (RSV, ESV) or "to look at" (NIV). However, grammatically, the verb ראה usually takes the preposition את when it is used with the meaning of "look at." The preposition ב basically means "spatial." Bruce Waltke explains the preposition: "The preposition ב marks the location in or at a point on a surface, within an area, and amid a domain. It marks, with verbs of movement, both goals ('in, into') and areas moved through."[35] Therefore, לִרְאוֹת בַּ- may be translated as "look through" or "look from a place." Even-Shushan explains, "ראה ב-; ראה בדבר מה: היה נוכח בשעת" in something" means that "something exists in that spatial/periodical."[36] Psalm 118:7 shows an example: יְהוָה לִי בְּעֹזְרָי וַאֲנִי אֶרְאֶה בְשֹׂנְאָי. Ecclesiastes 3:22 shows a similar case: כִּי-הוּא חֶלְקוֹ כִּי מִי יְבִיאֶנּוּ לִרְאוֹת בְּמֶה שֶׁיִּהְיֶה אַחֲרָיו: God or a person is looking from a certain situation. Furthermore, the infinitive form ל can be considered as just an infinitive form, but it can also be translated as "in order to." Therefore, Ps 113:6 can be translated to "God has humbled/humiliated himself so that he can see into the heaven, and also into the earth."

The verse Ps 113:6 thus presents God's κένωσις. God has humbled himself, or put himself in a "humiliated" situation, so that he can see the human world at the same level of human beings. However, God can also see the cosmos in the divine position as God simultaneously.

Isaiah 53

Isaiah 53 is one of the key chapters for Christology in the OT, and so it is for the concept of κένωσις. Isaiah 53 presents the full picture of κένωσις of the Christ and self-giving God. As John 3:16 describes, "God has given his begotten Son" for the salvation of humanity out of his radical and ultimate love of his children. But the Christ came to the world with the worst humiliation, and so died on the cross. In fact, Isa 53 foreshadowed the entire

---

35. Waltke, *Biblical Hebrew Syntax*, 196.
36. Even-Shushan, "שפל," *Milon Hahadash Le Ivrit*, 5:2436.

picture of Christ Jesus' suffering, humiliation, and self-giving for humanity. Furthermore, it pictures the complete blueprint of *missio Dei* through Jesus' humiliation, self-giving, and the Radical Love of God (Isa 53:5).

Luther often used this chapter to portray the self-giving Christology of the OT in his teaching of the Pentateuch or Psalms.[37] He clarifies the goal of Isa 53 in his interpretation by quoting Gal 3:13: "Here Paul solves the whole difficulty with one word, saying . . . He became a curse FOR US. For us, I say, not for Himself."[38] This explains the entire chapter of Isa 53. Humiliation of Christ was cardinal, because it was what God planned as the core of *missio Dei* to bring salvation to humanity (Isa 53:10–11). Through his humiliation, all of humankind would be delivered from their sins (Isa 53:12). By humiliation, Christ fulfilled (יִשְׂבָּע) his mission. In fact, most English translations translate יִשְׂבָּע as "satisfied," but this verse must share a similar connotation with 1 Chr 23:1 and 2 Chr 24:15, וְדָוִיד זָקֵן וְשָׂבַע יָמִים. David was not "satisfied" with his days but fulfilled (שָׂבַע) his life and died (1 Chr 23:1; 2 Chr 24:15). This means David lived his life the way God allowed him to. In Isa 53:11, Christ took the punishment and fulfilled his mission on the cross. The key issue here is that the humiliation of Christ is the core of the crucifixion and of humanity's salvation. Luther pictures the humiliation of Jesus as the humiliation of all of humanity.[39]

In his commentary on Isa 53, Luther divides the chapter into three sections: 1–6, 7–9, and 10–12. The keywords of Luther's interpretation for the first part of Isa 53 are "suffering" and "*missio Dei*," although Luther never uses the term *missio Dei*.

> So far the prophet has completed one paragraph concerning Christ as the Servant hanging on the cross, and concerning His completely absurd appearance and concerning His exalted kingdom, so that the kings will shut their mouths. Therefore I conclude that after His death Christ will have an eternal kingdom.[40]

Luther sees that Jesus' suffering on the cross was directly connected to the kingdom of God. Jesus took our griefs, our sorrow, and suffered for us (v. 4) so that we could follow him to his kingdom through justification by faith in Jesus' suffering and crucifixion "for us."

---

37. See *LW* 11:35.
38. *LW* 9:216.
39. *LW* 11:36–37.
40. *LW* 17:219.

We have heard that in these paragraphs there was a description of Christ's person with respect to His suffering and His glorification. This passage forms the basis for the church's faith that Christ's kingdom is not of this world. Now follows what He would accomplish by His suffering, whether He suffered for His own sake or for the sake of others. And this is the second part of our understanding and justification, to know that Christ suffered and was cursed and killed, but FOR US.[41]

Therefore, Luther confirms the purpose of Jesus' humiliation and suffering based on v. 4: "Surely He has borne our griefs and carried our sorrows; yet we esteemed Him stricken, smitten by God, and afflicted." This describes the purpose of Christ's suffering. It was not for himself and his own sins but for our sins and griefs. He bore what we should have suffered. The humiliation and suffering of Jesus were not for someone else but for the entire humanity. Jesus carried all of the humiliation and suffering of humanity on himself and died on the cross, which was the worst humiliation in his society, because his suffering and humiliation on the cross would bring "the peace of God" and "healing of wounds" (v. 5) to all humans. This is the grand plan of *missio Dei* that God made for the salvation of humanity. "All we like sheep have gone astray; we have turned—everyone—to his own way; and the LORD has laid on him the iniquity of us all" (v. 6).

The Creator of the universe, God, had to come down in a human form, born to a woman, who was the beginning point of sin. Jesus was born in such humiliation in order to carry every human sin on himself. As Ngien writes, Luther connects this humiliation and God's suffering directly to Jesus' cross.[42] Jesus' cross is truly the final conclusion of God's κένωσις. Fretheim explains that God's humiliation and suffering are directly connected to the human's.[43] This suffering was prophesied throughout the OT.

For the second part of Isa 53 (vv. 7–9), Luther uses the key phrase of "Jesus' duty for suffering with love."[44] Luther explains v. 7:

> That paragraph expresses the will and the patience of Christ as He suffers, that He does not even think of vengeance. This is the way for Christians to suffer, that they endure very patiently without threats and curses, yea, that they pray for and bless their

---

41. *LW* 17:220–21.
42. Ngien, *Suffering of God*, 175–76.
43. Fretheim, *Suffering of God*, 108.
44. *LW* 17:226.

tormentors. Therefore he depicts Christ's patience by comparing Him in a most felicitous way with a sheep. This is the force of that crucifixion, that such a Christ will suffer who is described as overflowing in suffering like that of sheep, with His whole heart filled with love.[45]

Jesus was slaughtered like a lamb in silence. Saint Paul describes him as the Lamb of Passover (1 Cor 5:7) who cleaned out sin. Luther understands from v. 8 that Jesus "was not dead but has taken away" God's oppression and judgment on humanity.[46]

In the last part of Isa 53 (vv. 10–12), Luther concludes the mission of Jesus.

> Now he describes the fruit of His passion, and this is His fruit, that He will have His future kingdom according to the statement: "He sits at the right hand of the Father, from thence He shall come."[47]

Jesus sacrificed his soul to see "his seed" and to please the Lord God, because Jesus had done the greatest part of *missio Dei*: being the sacrifice for the entire humanity through his humiliation and death on the cross. This is the reason why Jesus would succeed (יצלח) with his hand to fulfill God's desire (חפץ). Various English translations of Isa 53:10 gave a bit of a different connotation to the Hebrew text וְחֵפֶץ יְהוָה בְּיָדוֹ יִצְלָח. The KJV translates the Hebrew word חפץ as "pleasure," and the ESV as "will." Luther translates it as *Vorhaben*, which means "plan or intention." *TWOT* explains that "the basic meaning is to feel great favor towards something."[48] Therefore, in this context, "desire" or "will" would be better terms to translate the Hebrew word חפץ in Isa 53:10. It was God's will to crucify his begotten Son for the salvation of humankind. In fact, the entire Bible covers Jesus' humiliation and crucifixion for humanity, because those are the core of *missio Dei*.

3.4. Conclusion of the Exegetical Study of κένωσις in the OT

κένωσις in the NT has been widely discussed among NT scholars in the last century. However, many of those arguments have led to the wrong theological conclusion, because κένωσις is not about the question of God's

---

45. *LW* 17:227.
46. *LW* 17:227.
47. *LW* 17:228.
48. Leon J. Wood, "חָפֵץ," *TWOT* 310 (Strong's 712).

divine existence in Jesus but is about who God is. First of all, God is self-existent with his free will. No human being (creature) can define who he is and what he is supposed to be. As Peter Berger describes, the "absolute reality (God)" cannot be modified nor influenced by a humanistic process to create a "nomos."[49] According to Berger, God exists as the absolute reality, and he does not receive any influence from humans' "externalization, objectification, and internalization" process to generate a social nomos in their society,[50] even though God emptied his "form" of divinity in the baby Jesus. He is still "the absolute reality," whether he is in a human form or not. This means that the humiliation of God, after God became incarnated in Jesus, is derived from his Radical Love, and it is completely his free will to do it. Furthermore, the question of the divinity of Jesus is useless, since Jesus is God no matter what form he is in. His humiliation is absolutely an integral component for the justification of the entire humanity, because God put himself even in the lowest level of humanity to communicate with them.[51] Furthermore, the humiliation was done by Jesus' ultimate obedience through his free will.

Johannes von Hofmann's Christology and theology of κένωσις can also fit well in this perspective. For Hofmann, "God is the self-determination of God,"[52] which is "an absolute realty" in Berger's terms. Matthew Becker describes this in his book:

> Hofmann's Trinitarian view of God is grounded in the divine love, which is the cause of God's free decision to self-differentiate God's self in history and give God's self (divine kenosis or "divine self-emptying") in history in order to realize in the human Jesus a new humanity.[53]

All of the actions of the incarnated Christ are fully done by his free will, based on his Radical Love. According to Becker, Hofmann presents God's self-giving as the freedom of God. God cannot be limited in any time, situation, or thing. This free will of God has been revealed through human history.

Second, God is love. In his love, he can limit himself as a human, so that he can communicate with humanity. Hofmann writes that God's will

---

49. Berger, *Sacred Canopy*, 19.
50. Berger, *Sacred Canopy*, 4.
51. WSC 8:1–2; Phil 2:5–11.
52. Becker, *Self-Giving God*, 179.
53. Becker, *Self-Giving God*, xix.

for humiliation in a human form and self-giving love is a way of God's communication with humanity. Becker says,

> The doctrine of the *communicato idiomatum* stresses the real communication of the specifically divine attributes or properties to the human nature in Christ's person and activity. This communication between the two natures in Christ means that there is a genuine condescension of God into the depth of human existence and a genuine communication of the full majesty of God into the man Jesus. So Lutheran theologians generally affirm that "the finite is capable of the infinite" (*finitum capax infiniti*). By God's condescension into the finite, which God creates, preserves, and redeems, God makes the finite capable of receiving God, so that God is revealed in the form of a humble servant.[54]

This statement clearly concludes the exegetical study of κένωσις in the OT. From Genesis throughout the OT, God presents his free will to show his Radical Love. All of the humiliation that God took in a human form—being the son of woman, making himself lower than his creation, being a lamb of Passover—is because of his חסד, רחמים, אמת. His humiliation and self-giving reveal who God is and what God's love is. God had already set the plan of *missio Dei* based on his love from the beginning of creation. The final goal of *missio Dei* is to reconcile with all of humanity and to give them eternal life in God's "new" Jerusalem through Jesus. Therefore, κένωσις is not just a work of Christ, but it is what Christ is, because κένωσις does not only reveal God's Radical Love for the salvation of the entire humanity but also shows an example of ultimate obedience until crucifixion on the cross. Throughout the exegetical study of κένωσις in the OT, a few major actions of *missio Dei* could be observed:

1. God had already planned and processed κένωσις at the very moment of humans' fall by sin in Genesis because of his Radical Love toward humanity. Humiliation and self-giving were fully God's will and plan for humanity.

2. κένωσις is an ultimate example of obedience to God, and the incarnated God (the Son) demonstrated it on the cross with the worst humiliation.

3. The fundamental goal of κένωσις is to bring salvation to the entire humanity by placing all of humans' sorrow and suffering by sin on the Passover Lamb (Jesus).

---

54. Becker, *Self-Giving God*, 175.

4. Therefore, the key phrases of the kenotic love of Jesus are ultimate submission and Radical Love (אמת, חסד, רחם) by κένωσις (self-giving even to the worst humiliation and death on the cross).

In other words, there would be no *missio Dei* without κένωσις, and this is a crucial issue to understand the next research question: "How can we carry out *missio Dei*?"

4. The Holy Spirit and God's Radical Love

The works of the Holy Spirit in *missio Dei* are too enormous to describe in full in this small book, and it is not necessary to go through the entire pneumatology for this research subject either. Therefore, this section will describe briefly how God's Radical Love is related to the work of the Holy Spirit in *missio Dei*. The work of the Holy Spirit is a crucial issue in defining *missio Dei* as a work of the triune God, and God's Radical Love has mainly been revealed through the work of the Holy Spirit in the OT and in history. The works of the Holy Spirit in the context of *missio Dei* based on NT systematic theology have been well documented by Schulz in his article "Tension in the Pneumatology of the *Missio Dei* Concept" and later in his book *Mission from the Cross: The Lutheran Theology of Mission*. Schulz has mainly focused on the work of salvation, sanctification, and forgiveness of sin through the Holy Spirit with the holy sacraments. According to Schulz, the Holy Spirit brings people to the church to have blessings of "forgiveness of sins and [to have] comforting words of the entire gospel" through the holy sacraments.[55] Through the Holy Spirit's work of sanctification and salvation in the church, believers receive their relationship with God. Therefore, according to Schulz, the church becomes the core of the Holy Spirit's activity for *missio Dei*.[56] But people outside of the church, "natural man" in his book,[57] cannot have such blessings by the gifts of the Holy Spirit.[58] It is interesting to notice that the work of the Holy Spirit was the main theme of Luther's work. Schulz quotes from Regin Prenter:

> The Danish theologian Regin Prenter points out that in the theology of Martin Luther, the Holy Spirit receives central place even

---

55. Schulz, "Tension in Pneumatology," 101.
56. Schulz, *Mission from the Cross*, 95–97.
57. Schulz, *Mission from the Cross*, 117.
58. Schulz, "Tension in Pneumatology," 102.

in such doctrines as justification, Scripture, the Sacraments, the Church, and ethics.[59]

Strikingly, Luther used the term *the Spirit* over thirteen thousand times in the fifty-five volumes of Luther's works in the English version alone, and must have used it much more in his entire works. It is used far more frequently than other key theological terms such as *justification* or *sacraments*, which are used over seven hundred times each. Schulz defines the Holy Spirit as the main dynamic of the mission: "Without the Holy Spirit, the mission of God and of the Church would not continue."[60] God's economy is revealed only through the Holy Spirit.[61]

Most theological writings of the Holy Spirit's ministry relating to *missio Dei* have been based mainly on the NT. There are few writings on the work of the Holy Spirit in the context of *missio Dei* according to the OT so far. Additionally, there are not many works on God's Radical Love through the Holy Spirit based on the OT context as of yet. Therefore, this chapter will be dedicated to defining what the Holy Spirit does for *missio Dei* with God's Radical Love, based on an exegetical study of the OT. Afterward, this study will check the discrepancy of the Holy Spirit's works between the OT and the NT. Finally, this study will be able to conclusively confirm the phrase οὕτως γὰρ ἠγάπησεν ὁ θεὸς τὸν κόσμον in John 3:16 in the context of the OT.

4.1. Exegetical Study of the OT on the Work of the Holy Spirit with God's Radical Love

Wonsuk Ma has defined four traditions in his study of the Holy Spirit in the book of Isaiah.

1. רוח (*ruach*: Spirit) is used to refer to the incomparable quality of God, according to Isa 31:3.

2. רוח (*ruach*: Spirit) is a superhuman element granted to God's chosen vessels, and this is the dominant tradition in preexilic Isaianic thinking (Isa 11:1–3; 23:5–6)

---

59. Schulz, *Mission from the Cross*, 103.
60. Schulz, *Mission from the Cross*, 134.
61. Schulz, *Mission from the Cross*, 139.

3. The most obvious impression is that the Spirit of God seems to function as one of the various divine agents.

4. רוח (*ruach*: Spirit) is the prophetic Spirit.[62]

The study on the Holy Spirit in the book of Isaiah is valuable for this research, because Ma defines how the Holy Spirit has worked in the OT in context of the mission. Based on Ma's clues about the Holy Spirit's mission, with some help from other sources, the work of the Holy Spirit based on God's Radical Love in the OT context may be classified in the following categories:

1. Creation, preservation (restoring and giving life)
2. Giving knowledge of God and the Scriptures (חוכמת, חוכמת ליראת ה', תורה)
3. Sanctification, transformation (healing), and salvation (Isa 61)
4. Κήρυγμα, prophecy, and eschaton

Ma includes some other categories, such as representing God or anointing leadership. However, this chapter does not need to include those categories, since some of them are already incorporated in other categories or do not clearly present God's Radical Love through the ministry of the Holy Spirit. Consequently, those categories are omitted in this research.

There is often ambiguity between God's work and the Holy Spirit's ministry in the OT. Many researchers or commentaries have engaged with this case. However, the Father, Son, and Holy Spirit are one in the Trinity; consequently, it can be understood that their works are one in mission too. As Vicedom mentions, God and the Son sent the Son and the Holy Spirit.[63] Therefore, God became the Sender and the One sent at the same time, because of his Radical Love. In this context, as God is love (1 John 4:6), so is the Holy Spirit. Nevertheless, there are different roles for each person of in the Trinity in terms of *missio Dei*. Hence, this research will try to make those differences clear as much as possible.

---

62. Ma, *Until the Spirit Comes*, 67–69.
63. Vicedom, *Mission of God*, 48.

4.1.1. Creation and Preservation

The Holy Spirit is the agent of creation. As Ps 33:5 and John 1:1 describe, the Word of God has created the universe. The acting agent of creation is the Holy Spirit. God sent the Holy Spirit for creation. Therefore, the creation work of the Holy Spirit is too enormous to list in this tiny thesis. Thus, in this book, the work of the Holy Spirit will be focused on only in the context of God's Radical Love. The work of the Holy Spirit with God's Radical Love has been since the beginning of the creation, according to what Gen 1:2 describes, וְרוּחַ אֱלֹהִים מְרַחֶפֶת עַל־פְּנֵי הַמָּיִם. And Ps 89:3 mentions, כִּי־אָמַרְתִּי עוֹלָם חֶסֶד יִבָּנֶה שָׁמַיִם. Therefore, God created the universe with his Radical Love (חסד) through the work of the Holy Spirit from the beginning. As Luther understood, וְרוּחַ אֱלֹהִים in this verse cannot be "wind," since the universe had not been created yet.[64] Without God's חסד, there could not be God's creation of the universe. Psalm 33:5–6 also explains God's creation in his love by the Holy Spirit: אֹהֵב צְדָקָה וּמִשְׁפָּט חֶסֶד יְהוָה מָלְאָה הָאָרֶץ בִּדְבַר יְהוָה שָׁמַיִם נַעֲשׂוּ וּבְרוּחַ פִּיו כָּל־צְבָאָם. God's Word reveals the work of the Holy Spirit and God's action with חסד on the earth.

God's will for creation has always been good. Schulz explains,

> God's intentions for the world are entirely good because He loves it and is willing to preserve it. In fact, a straight line can be drawn between God's love for creation and the cross.[65]

God was with the Word, and it was טוב in God's eyes.[66] טוב can be the only outcome of God's love. In Judaism, טוב is another side of אהבה, as W. Grundmann notices: "The Rabbis have the constant formula: הַטּוֹב וְהַמֵּטִיב."[67] This confession expresses the perfectly good being of God, which consists of his goodness. Therefore, the work of the Holy Spirit may be uncovered through God's attribute of טוב.

Isaiah 40:12–13 also describes the universe's creation. The Spirit of God is described as an acting agent of the creation in Isa 40:13. Ma mentions that the Holy Spirit plays "a definite role" in every stage of the creation and re-creation, and Isa 34:16 "has a strong allusion to the creation theme."[68]

---

64. *LW* 1:9.
65. Schulz, *Mission from the Cross*, 111.
66. See ch. 3 on the Hebrew word טוב.
67. Walter Grundmann, "Ἀγαθός," *TDNT* 2:14.
68. Ma, *Until the Spirit Comes*, 109.

The Holy Spirit is not only an agent of creation but also a Preserver of creation. The Holy Spirit sustains the running of the universe, as Isa 40:12–13 describes, "Who has measured the Spirit of the Lord, or what man shows him his counsel?" God's knowledge and power are as unlimited as his love. Psalm 136:6–9 mentions that God created the world, preserves creation, and keeps it running with rules he created, because of his everlasting חסד.

As the Preserver of creation, the Holy Spirit gives life and restores wounded and broken hearts. Various Hebrew words are used for this context. In Gen 2:7, God blows נשמת חיים into Adam's nostril, and then Adam gets נפש חייה. Two Hebrew words must be clarified here: נפש, נשמה. First, נפש חיה means "soul of his life" in Hebrew. The Hebrew words נפש חיה were translated in various ways, because it is very difficult to find a word equivalent to נפש in English. The Hebrew word נפש has many different meanings, depending on the context of each sentence containing the word. However, two of the most crucial meanings must be mentioned here. Although this word isn't directly related to the work of the Holy Spirit as the Preserver of creation, נפש shows the foundation of God's work among humanity as the Creator and Preserver, because it indicates how *missio Dei* works for the creation. According to *TWOT*, "The original, concrete meaning of the word was probably 'to breathe.'"[69] However, the word is used in various contexts with various connotations. Two issues can be pointed out here: first, God has blown his life (חייה) into human beings, unlike any other creatures on earth. Second, most usages of נפש in the Bible are used for the meaning of "soul, life, and love."[70] The soul that God gave to Adam was the soul of God's life. And נפש is often used with אהבה in the OT.[71] These two issues can lead us to guess, therefore, that God created humans to connect with God and to seek God's love always. Consequently, God's love is hidden in every human gene. That is why all humans seek something supernatural with which to be connected, without knowing what the reason is exactly.

Related to this Hebrew word נפש, God blows נשמת חיים into Adam. In the Bible, נשמה and נפש are often used together or mixed with each other. Job describes how God's Spirit has created him and gives him "soul of life": רוּחַ־אֵל עָשָׂתְנִי וְנִשְׁמַת שַׁדַּי תְּחַיֵּנִי (Job 33:4). *TWOT* explains about the Hebrew word נשמה: "This noun, when used in reference to man, generally signifies

---

69. Bruce K. Waltke, "נֶפֶשׁ," *TWOT* 588 (Strong's 1395).
70. Waltke, *TWOT* 588.
71. Waltke, *TWOT* 588.

the breath of life. It is frequently found in combination with *rûaḥ* 'spirit' and seems synonymous with *nepeš* (soul, spirit)."[72]

However, נשמה is often translated as "spirit" in English Bibles, such as the KJV. God has given life to humans and preserves their נשמה or נפש. Thus, the Hebrew idiom נִשְׁמַת־רוּחַ חַיִּים בְּאַפָּיו means "as breathed in by God, it is God's breath in man."[73] Furthermore, "God is love" (1 John 4:8), and his breath of love is always in human beings. Hence, all humankind has an instinct to seek God's love and to spiritually link with him, whether he believes in God or not. This is the main reason why so many different religions have been created, because human beings were created with God's breath in them, and it is impossible to undo that without dying. Then, in Gen 2:17, God tells Adam and Eve the truth: כִּי בְּיוֹם אֲכָלְךָ מִמֶּנּוּ מוֹת תָּמוּת. The snake has whispered in the woman's ear that she will not die after eating the fruit from the tree of life, but that is a complete lie, "for the wages of sin is death" (Rom 6:23). God does not talk about a physical death here but a spiritual death, which is a disconnection between God and creation, and which is the contamination of the entire creation by sin.

As the Preserver of creation, this is the point where the Holy Spirit comes in, to work for salvation and restoration through sanctification. Since humans lost a spiritual connection to their Creator by sin, they have been trying to find someone else as their god. But the Holy Spirit sanctifies them to have salvation and restoration through the blood of Jesus. As the third article of the Apostles' Creed declares, sanctification is part of the process for salvation and restoration: "I believe in the Holy Spirit, the holy Christian church, the communion of saints, the forgiveness of sins, the resurrection of the body, and the life everlasting. Amen."[74] It means that sanctification is also part of the preservation ministry of the Holy Spirit for God's creation. A further discussion on sanctification is coming in the following section.

The OT shows many cases of the salvation and restoration of Israel through the Holy Spirit's work. The most prominent passage for salvation and restoration by the Holy Spirit may be Ezek 36:26—37:10. God promises to pour a new spirit and new heart on Israel, וְנָתַתִּי לָכֶם לֵב חָדָשׁ וְרוּחַ חֲדָשָׁה (36:26), and he also promises to give them his Spirit, וְאֶת־רוּחִי אֶתֵּן בְּקִרְבְּכֶם (36:27). Furthermore, the entire chapter of Ezek 36 is covered by

---

72. Milton C. Fisher, "נָשַׁם," *TWOT* 605 (Strong's 1433).

73. "נְשָׁמָה," BDB 675.

74. Commission on Worship, *Lutheran Service Book*, 159.

the connotation of God's Radical Love promising salvation and sanctification to Israel through the restoration. Ma has also noticed this point in his study of the Holy Spirit's work in the book Isaiah.

> In an implicit reference, the same רוח is expected to consummate the restoration of the national fate.... With the ideal figure endowed with God's רוח, the entire journey of restoration will be completed by the work of רוח.[75]

The ministry of the Holy Spirit for restoration and salvation has been revealed throughout the history of Israel. Ma writes,

> God's restoration of Israel is the ultimate goal of Isaianic eschatology. "In that day (ביום ההוא)" the members of the restored community will experience God's cleansing through the Spirit of משפט and fire (Is. 4:4).[76]

Ezekiel 37 demonstrates God's restoration. Indeed, the dried bones symbolize Israel in this chapter. Israel will be resurrected by the Word of God, and God gives them רוח וחיים to resurrect as a whole. This chapter reveals the restoration of the creation and reveals the preservation ministry of the Holy Spirit.

In fact, God's judgment is based on his Radical Love, אמת. This will be discussed in the chapter on God's righteousness and judgment with God's Radical Love. The ministry of the Holy Spirit for the creation and its preservation is its major work, as demonstrated so far. There is also crossover work among various ministries of the Holy Spirit, such as restoration through sanctification, salvation through judgment, etc. The ministry of the Holy Spirit often appears in multiple ministries simultaneously. Such cases will be described throughout the coming chapters.

4.1.2. Giving Knowledge of God and Scripture

Luther was always heavily focused on God's word, *sola Scriptura*. Luther's understanding of the acts of the Holy Spirit is only through his word. Luther writes, "Knowledge indeed gives form to the soul, but the Holy Spirit

---

75. Ma, *Until the Spirit Comes*, 212.
76. Ma, *Until the Spirit Comes*, 212.

alone gives grace and ointment, that is, growth."⁷⁷ He also explains how the Holy Spirit works to make people understand the word:

> For we have a God who is able to give more than we understand or ask for. Even though we do not know what we should ask for and how, nevertheless the Spirit of God, who dwells in the hearts of the godly, sighs and groans for us within us with inexpressible groaning and also procures inexpressible and incomprehensible things.⁷⁸

In fact, there are several verses in the OT telling that the Holy Spirit gives חכמה דעת to understand God's word and his love. וְנָחָה עָלָיו רוּחַ יְהוָה רוּחַ חָכְמָה וּבִינָה רוּחַ עֵצָה וּגְבוּרָה רוּחַ דַּעַת וְיִרְאַת יְהוָה (Isa 11:2). Through having the Spirit of God, people will gain the understanding and knowledge of God. The OT often uses the term חכמה with רוח, because Jewish people understood that the primary knowledge that one should have is יראת ה׳ as Prov 9:10 describes: תְּחִלַּת חָכְמָה יִרְאַת יְהוָה וְדַעַת קְדֹשִׁים בִּינָה. In Judaism, חכמה בינה ודעת is the outcome of the Holy Spirit's ministry. One of the famous Jewish rabbis in the Middle Ages, Ibn Ezra, commented on Isa 11:2: "*The Spirit of the Lord*, that is, *the spirit of wisdom and understanding*, such as, *e.g.*, was assigned to Joshua (Deut 34:9)."⁷⁹ Therefore, the wisdom to know God and his love comes from the Holy Spirit.

Without the Holy Spirit, people cannot have בינה on God's love either. Luther said that people cannot understand God's love and word without the Holy Spirit, because humanity was disconnected from God by a corrupted nature.

> Our nature is so corrupt that it no longer knows God unless it is enlightened by the Word and the Spirit of God. How, then, can it love God without the Holy Spirit? It is true that there is no desire for anything that is unknown. Hence our nature cannot love God, whom it does not know; but it loves an idol and the dream of its heart. Furthermore, it is so completely bound up in its love for the creatures that even after it has learned to know God from the Word, it still disregards Him and despises His Word, as the examples of our own people show.⁸⁰

---

77. *LW* 10:219.
78. *LW* 3:159.
79. Ibn Ezra, "Ibn Ezra on Isaiah 11:2"; emphasis original. מהשניים הנראים: והנה פרש וכן כתוב על יהושע בתורה, כי רוח יי היא רוח חכמה ובינה (Deut 34:19).
80. *LW* 2:124.

As Zech 4:6 mentions, "Not by might, nor by power, but by my Spirit." The Holy Spirit is the only one who can make humanity to understand God's word and God's love. What St. Paul describes about the Holy Spirit in Eph 6:14–17 is remarkable: "And take the helmet of salvation, and the sword of the Spirit, which is the word of God" (v. 17). The Holy Spirit has a sword, and it is the word of God. The Holy Spirit uses God's word as the sword. God's word through the Holy Spirit has power to destroy any barrier to *missio Dei*. Consequently, as Jesus has described the Holy Spirit as the Helper (παράκλητον [John 14:16]), all believers must have the Holy Spirit so that they can understand their Lord and his Radical Love.

4.1.3. Sanctification, Transformation (Healing), and Salvation

The Holy Spirit as the Sanctifier is a well-known concept among theologians. Luther has defined the Holy Spirit as the Sanctifier, as Schulz mentions in his book.[81] As Schulz sees, from Luther's perspective, sanctification is the main work of the Holy Spirit. In fact, most definitions of the Holy Spirit as Sanctifier are mainly based on the NT.

God loves his children. He does not just love them but does so radically. He loves all sinners. He loves Saddam Hussein, Kim Jong Un, even ISIS members, but he hates the sin in their hearts. This is the reason why God wants to sanctify them through the blood of Jesus on the cross. God's mission is to destroy sin completely from his creation (Ezek 36:33). God wants to cleanse all of his children because of his Radical Love. Sanctification is an action of God's Radical Love.

The Formula of Concord explains that the wage of "original sin is death and eternal damnation." There is no way for humans to escape from the "domination of devil" by themselves. Therefore, their nature is corrupted and evil.[82] However, the mission of Christ on the cross "covers" them in Jesus' blood to receive eternal forgiveness for their sins, and the Holy Spirit cleanses them (Heb 9:14). The sanctification is fully by God's grace, and humans do not deserve to have it. Titus 3:5 explains, "He saved us, not on the basis of deeds which we have done in righteousness, but according to His mercy, by the washing of regeneration and renewing by the Holy Spirit."

Saint Paul argues in 1 Cor 6:9–20 that we became sanctified by the Holy Spirit and became "the temple of the Holy Spirit."

---

81. Schulz, *Mission from the Cross*, 135.
82. FC 1:13.

> But you were washed, you were sanctified, you were justified in the name of the Lord Jesus Christ and by the Spirit of our God.... Or do you not know that your body is a temple of the Holy Spirit within you, whom you have from God? (1 Cor 6:9, 19)

As the result of the sanctification by the Holy Spirit, St. Paul teaches in Gal 5:22–23, Christians will receive the "fruits of the Holy Spirit" such as "love, joy, peace, endurance, kindness, goodness, faithfulness, and self-control." Therefore, the NT clearly describes the sanctification ministry of the Holy Spirit. Nevertheless, the sanctification ministry of the Holy Spirit in the OT context has not been clarified much among theologians so far.

In the context of the OT, as described in the previous section, sanctification may be a part of the Holy Spirit's preservation ministry, because sanctification cannot be separated from the process of salvation and restoration of God's creation. As the previous section has presented, salvation and restoration are part of the process of preserving God's creation. Therefore, it is impossible to separate the sanctification from the preservation ministry. Nevertheless, this research will allocate one whole section for sanctification, including transformation and healing as the result of salvation, since it is one of the most crucial works of the Holy Spirit. The section will be narrowed to focus on how God's Radical Love becomes the foundation of the Holy Spirit's sanctification ministry.

The most prominent chapter of sanctification by the Holy Spirit in the OT may be Ps 51:12–21. This chapter is the confession of King David about his sinful heart after committing a sinful episode with Uria and Bathsheva. He is crying out of his sin and praying for the sanctification of his sinful heart. Truly, God creates a pure heart among Christians and gives the Spirit to renew it. God's Holy Spirit will dwell in Christians and will give the joy of salvation. David knew that God is the only source of salvation from his sinful life. One interesting term in this verse is רוח נדיבה. Leonard J. Coppes explains, "The root נדב connotes an uncompelled and free movement of the will unto divine service or sacrifice." Coppes also clarifies that the word has the connotation of "no cost."[83]

> This noun denotes that which is offered voluntarily. It is used three times adverbially to describe acts. Other words translated "free" are ⁂innām, costing no money; nāqâ, having no guilt; and ⁂āpaš, not being enslaved.[84]

83. Leonard J. Coppes, "נדב," *TWOT* 554 (Strong's 1299).
84. Coppes, *TWOT* 554.

Therefore, the Hebrew word נדב shares a similar connotation with one of the attributes of God's Radical Love, רחם, because רחם has an attribute of enduring and self-giving love, and this matches the meaning of נדב, which is "free-will offering."[85] Therefore, רוח נדיבה presents here God's Radical Love through the Holy Spirit who sanctifies people. Through the רוח נדיבה, Christians learn how to love others and how to serve others with God's kenotic love.

As Ps 51:12 presents, God is trying to preserve the creation by renewal and restoration. In this context, Isa 61:1–3 presents the Holy Spirit's ministry of sanctification through healing and restoration. Through the restoration by the Holy Spirit, God's righteousness is revealed to the world. In this verse, sanctification offers freedom from bondage and brings salvation. The Holy Spirit turns mourning to joy, changes the spirit of darkness into praises of the Lord. The Holy Spirit heals the broken hearts, and then finally brings his people to glorify God. This is the promise of the restoration of God's kingdom. And all these things happen when רוּחַ אֲדֹנָי יְהוִה עָלָי יַעַן מָשַׁח יְהוָה אֹתִי. This is truly a spiritual anointing and true sanctification by the Holy Spirit. The verse reveals that sanctification enacts total transformation. And all of this process has been fully based on God's Radical Love, because the entire chapter of Isa 61 is covered with God's love vocabularies, promising salvation and restoration through sanctification.

4.1.4. Κήρυγμα and Prophecy

The Bible begins with God's Word and the Holy Spirit. *Missio Dei* through God's Radical Love has been performed through God's Word and the Holy Spirit, which were given by the Father and the Son. In the creation dynamic, the Word and the Holy Spirit are the acting agents of creation and preservation. When the Word and the Holy Spirit are in action, the Greek word κήρυγμα is used in the NT. κήρυγμα is usually translated in English as "news," "declaration," "enquiry," etc.[86] κήρυγμα is a known and typical term from the NT,[87] but not from the OT. This is because κήρυγμα is known as preaching the gospel of Jesus in the context of the NT. However, it is rare to find any research on the κήρυγμα of the Holy Spirit in the context of the OT.

---

85. Coppes, *TWOT* 554.
86. Victor P. Hamilton, "פָּגַע," *TWOT* 715 (Strong's 1731).
87. See Gerhard Friedrich, "Κῆρυξ," *TDNT* 3:698.

In fact, the entire Bible is the κήρυγμα of God's kingdom, and God has sent the Holy Spirit as the agent of κήρυγμα. However, the term κήρυγμα was not frequently used in the OT. Instead, the Word was used to give the message of κήρυγμα to all prophets. In fact, most of the books of prophecy usually start with דבר יהוה היי אל. All of the prophecies in the Bible come from God, and those are דבר יהוה. Most introductions to the prophecies in the Bible do not clarify that דבר יהוה came through the Holy Spirit. However, there are several cases demonstrating that דבר יהוה came through from the Holy Spirit. Psalm 33:6 explains how the Word and the Holy Spirit become the dynamics of creation: בִּדְבַר יְהוָה שָׁמַיִם נַעֲשׂוּ וּבְרוּחַ פִּיו כָּל־צְבָאָם. God's Word was the source of creation and is the action of his Radical Love. John 1:1 explains that θεὸς ἦν ὁ λόγος. 1 John 4:16 says: Ὁ θεὸς ἀγάπη ἐστίν. Therefore, דבר יהוה is God's Radical Love.

Consequently, the Word of God has created the world with God's Radical Love, and the Spirit from his mouth had the action of creation. In the OT time, the prophecies were God's κήρυγμα, and the κήρυγμα were given to prophets through the Holy Spirit in a form of דבר יהוה. King David confirms this issue: "The Spirit of the LORD speaks by me; his word is on my tongue" (1 Sam 23:2 ESV). Ezekiel also confesses, "And as he spoke to me, the Spirit entered into me and set me on my feet, and I heard him speaking to me" (Ezek 2:2 ESV). Therefore, God's words were given to prophets by the Holy Spirit, and prophets declared (κήρυγμα) God's word to people. In this case, κήρυγμα was usually a declaration of God's judgment (משפט) on Israel.

The prophecies in the OT are often related to משפט and God's salvation. To bring God's משפטים and salvation, prophets preached (κήρυγμα) the message of repentance of the people from their sin. Therefore, משפטים and salvation in the OT are directly linked to God's חסד and אמת, with which God wants Israelites to return from their evil life to the Lord. Again, it is critical to understand that God's judgment on Israel has never been לעולם (everlasting). God has always given them κήρυγμα of restoration after משפטים. The initial and emotional motivation for משפטים is נחם as chapter 3 has presented, and נחם is the outcome of God's Radical Love toward his children.

Here, one Hebrew term must be clarified briefly to avoid confusion. The Hebrew term משפט is often translated as "judgment" in English, which is a total mistranslation in many cases in the OT. Robert Culver clarifies this issue in *TWOT*:

The primary sense of *šāpaṭ* is to exercise the processes of government. Since, however, the ancients did not always divide the functions of government, as most modern governments do, between legislative, executive, and judicial functions (and departments) the common translation, "to judge," misleads us. For, the word, judge, as *šāpaṭ* is usually translated, in modern English, means to exercise only the judicial function of government. Unless one wishes in a context of government—civil, religious, or otherwise—consistently to translate as "to govern or rule," the interpreter must seek more specialized words to translate a word of such broad meaning in the modern world scene.[88]

Therefore, the Hebrew word משפט is not a terrifying vocabulary term; rather, it is an expression of God's Radical Love. First Kings 10:9 demonstrates this love language of God.

יְהִי יהוה אֱלֹהֶיךָ בָּרוּךְ אֲשֶׁר חָפֵץ בְּךָ לְתִתְּךָ עַל־כִּסֵּא יִשְׂרָאֵל בְּאַהֲבַת יהוה אֶת־יִשְׂרָאֵל לְעֹלָם וַיְשִׂימְךָ לְמֶלֶךְ לַעֲשׂוֹת מִשְׁפָּט וּצְדָקָה׃

God's משפט and צדקה come from באהבת יהוה. Because God loved King David forever, he crowned him to make God's משפט וצדקה to Israel. Isaiah 16:5 confirms this point again: וְהוּכַן בַּחֶסֶד כִּסֵּא וְיָשַׁב עָלָיו בֶּאֱמֶת בְּאֹהֶל דָּוִד שֹׁפֵט וְדֹרֵשׁ מִשְׁפָּט וּמְהִר צֶדֶק. Therefore, God's משפט and צדקה are a means of exposing God's Radical Love to humanity. Accordingly, the author determines that the Hebrew term משפט in the OT shares a similar connotation with το κήρυγμα in the NT.

The entire chapter of Isa 61 is for τος κήρυγμα of the restoration of Israel. It is God's promise, which has been delivered by the prophet Isaiah to the Israelites after לעשות משפט וצדקה in the promised land of Israel. The LXX translated the Hebrew of Isa 61:1, לִקְרֹא לִשְׁבוּיִם דְּרוֹר וְלַאֲסוּרִים פְּקַח־קוֹחַ, to κηρύξαι αἰχμαλώτοις ἄφεσιν καὶ τυφλοῖς ἀνάβλεψιν. In this sentence, the Hebrew word לקרא is translated as κηρύξαι. Johannes Louw and Eugene Nida explain κηρύσσω as "an announcement of religious truths and principles while urging acceptance and compliance—to preach."[89] κήρυγμα is a variant form of κηρύσσω. Therefore, in the context of the OT, κήρυγμα functions to bring the following messages through the Holy Spirit, which are derived from God's Radical Love:

a. God's righteousness and justice (לעשות משפט וצדקה)

---

88. Robert D. Culver, "שָׁפַט," *TWOT* 947 (Strong's 2443).
89. Louw and Nida, *Greek-English Lexicon*, 416.

b. Salvation and restoration

c. Restoration of God's kingship

d. Sanctification with new Spirit, and destruction of sin and the power of Satan

e. Promise of משיח as the Savior of Israel and of all nations

f. On the day (היום ההוא) Messiah will bring משפט וצדקה to all powers of darkness, and defeat them forever.

g. Promise of eschaton: God has prepared the עולם הבא for his children to have a holy convocation with Jesus in the new kingdom of God.

These messages confirm that God's Radical Love is the foundation of all messages of κήρυγμα in the OT. The Holy Spirit kept delivering God's love message with the hope of eschaton. These messages were delivered by the Holy Spirit to the Israelites and to all nations. God's messages in the Bible are not limited to only the Israelites, because God is God of all the universe that he has created.

4.2. The Holy Spirit's Ministry in the OT and NT: The Discrepancy

Schulz defines the work of the Holy Spirit in three facets:

1. He mediates the gifts.
2. He builds and gathers the church on earth.
3. He equips the church for the continual proclamation of the word.[90]

These clues that the Holy Spirit is the foundation of the church were already considered by Irenaeus in the second century AD,[91] although the concept of the Holy Spirit's ministry in the OT is slightly different than its concept in the NT. The major concept of the Holy Spirit in the OT is as the Creator and Preserver of creation. This concept was discussed from very early on in the Christian era by the church fathers. According to Anthony Briggman, Irenaeus was the first one who conceptualized the Holy Spirit as the Creator.[92] Irenaeus understood the frequent Hebrew expression רוח יהוה in two different ways: the Holy Spirit or "the Spirit of God, which means

---

90. Schulz, "Tension in Pneumatology," 102.
91. Briggman, *Irenaeus of Lyons*, 65.
92. Briggman, *Irenaeus of Lyons*, 43.

that God is the Spirit."[93] However, the greatest work Irenaeus ever did was the clarification of the substance of the Holy Spirit. Briggman explains,

> Irenaeus's understanding of the descent of the Spirit on Jesus at his baptism in the Jordan has garnered a great deal of attention. At issue is the way in which the Holy Spirit, if indeed the descending Spirit should be regarded as the Holy Spirit rather than an impersonal Spirit of power of God, relates to the humanity and divinity of Jesus.[94]

In fact, it is hard to say that there is a difference in the Holy Spirit's ministry in the OT and in the NT, since God, the Holy Spirit, and the Son are one, and they are everlasting beyond time and space. However, it is totally clear according to the study above that there is a difference of pattern in the Holy Spirit's ministry between the OT and the NT. The creation, or anointing leaders, by the Holy Spirit does not happen anymore in the NT history. Furthermore, the ministry of the Holy Spirit in the church frame, or κήρυγμα ministry of Jesus, was not in the OT era either. The author believes that this is a discrepancy created by Jesus Christ, because Jesus accomplished the ultimate preservation of the creation through his blood, as the OT had prophesied.[95] Just as human history has been divided into before Christ and after Christ, the pattern of the Holy Spirit's ministry among humanity has been transformed because all of the prophecies of the Savior have been fulfilled by Jesus Christ.

Nevertheless, there is one thing in the Holy Spirit's ministry that is concrete and continues everlastingly. It is God's ministry through the Holy Spirit to carry out *missio Dei* in his Radical Love. Therefore, the ministry of the Holy Spirit transcends culture, time, and space; it is universal.

4.3. Conclusion

The concept of the Holy Spirit's ministry has been discussed for almost two millennia from Irenaeus until today, and it remains controversial. Nevertheless, the work of the Holy Spirit in *missio Dei* is crystal clear. Louis

---

93. Briggman, *Irenaeus of Lyons*, 44.
94. Briggman, *Irenaeus of Lyons*, 59.
95. Luke 24:27: "And beginning with Moses and all the Prophets, he interpreted to them in all the Scriptures the things concerning himself" (ESV).

Berkhof's summary, which Arthur Glasser quotes in his book *Announcing the Kingdom*, can also serve as a great summary for this section:

> [The Holy Spirit] creates a world of his own, a world of conversion, experience, sanctification; of tongues, prophecy, and miracles; of upbuilding and guiding the church, etc. He appoints ministers; he organizes; he illumines, inspires, and sustains; he intercedes for the saints and helps them in their weaknesses; he searches everything, even the depths of God; he guides into all truth; he grants a variety of gifts; he convinces the world; he declares the things that are to come.[96]

Arthur Glasser explains:

> [The Holy Spirit] is the actual center of the great variety of "kingdom actions." True, Jesus Christ remains the sole center and object of faith, and the Spirit always remains intimately connected with him as the Spirit of Christ.[97]

Therefore, the Holy Spirit is the core of *missio Dei* action, and his action is completely based on God's Radical Love. Through the study of the Holy Spirit in *missio Dei* and God's Radical Love in the context of the OT, the following conclusions can be pointed out.

a. God's creation and preservation are a major part of the Holy Spirit's ministry in carrying out *missio Dei*.

b. The preservation is done through the mediation of the Holy Spirit.

c. Then, through preservation of the word, κήρυγμα by the Holy Spirit of God gives justification/righteousness (לעשות משפט וצדקה) in creation.

d. The Holy Spirit sanctifies humanity through the blood of Jesus.

e. The Holy Spirit renews the creation and humanity by pouring out the new Spirit.

f. The Holy Spirit delivers hope in the eschaton.

Therefore, the work of the Holy Spirit justifies the description of John 3:16 and presents the full picture of *missio Dei* in the OT and NT, because every action of the Holy Spirit reveals Jesus Christ in the NT.

---

96. Louis Berkhof; quoted in Glasser with Van Engen et al., *Announcing the Kingdom*, 261.

97. Glasser with Van Engen et al., *Announcing the Kingdom*, 261.

Chapter Six

Missiological Interpretation of God's Radical Love and a New Definition of *Missio Dei*

1. Introduction

THIS BOOK BEGAN WITH the premise that John 3:16 is the summary of *missio Dei* and that it fully presents God's Radical Love. Therefore, a missiological conclusion of the thesis is necessary here. This conclusion will lead then to conceptualizing a new definition of *missio Dei* based on the interpretation of John 3:16 in the context of the OT.

From the precedent studies in the previous chapters, this study has demonstrated that God's Radical Love, which is אמת, רחם, חסד, is the initial motivation for God's missional action among creation. All of his creation, the work of preservation through the Holy Spirit, and the reconciliation through the Son by covering human sins in his blood are derived from God's Radical Love: אמת, רחם, חסד. To avoid confusion with the general meaning of a worldly love, this thesis has been using capital letters: God's Radical Love. And God's Radical Love includes the three attributes of God's serious love toward humankind.

The etymological study of the three attributes of God's Radical Love in Hebrew terms in chapter 3 reveals that God's Radical Love is at the bottom of God's heart as the Father of all creation, which the Hebrew word נחם presents. Furthermore, the study shows that נחם is God's emotional sequel from God's Radical Love after having been betrayed by his own creation. The Hebrew term נחם is expressed later in the NT again through his

Missiological Interpretation of God's Radical Love

incarnation, in a different term. It was expressed as a kenotic love (self-giving love) on the cross. The cry of Jesus on the cross (אלי אלי למה שבקתני [**Matt** 27:46] is not a cry for himself. It is an expression of God's נחם with a kenotic love derived from God's Radical Love. Therefore, the definition of God's Radical Love is linked to the Father's heart with נחם. This is a crucial point for the missiological interpretation of God's Radical Love and *missio Dei*. The etymological definition of each attribute of God's Radical Love (אמת, רחם, חסד) reveals the Father's heart.

Each attribute presents different aspects of God's Radical Love. Simply summarized, חסד is God's fatherly heart and love. It reveals God's everlasting loyalty and faithfulness to his creation, and it is from God, not from humanity to God. It cannot be changed, even by God himself. As long as the creation continues to exist, God's חסד will not perish, and cannot. God's covenant with Israel is based on God's חסד. Therefore, God's covenant is everlasting and still active now, since God's creation still exists. God's חסד is universal and transcultural, because no human fact can influence or change it. This is the meaning of God's חסד being everlasting (חסד לעולם). In fact, all of the aspects of God's Radical Love are universal, transcultural, and even countercultural. Whenever God's Radical Love has been injected into any human culture, it brings transformation and changes the local culture. No human effort can prevent the transformation.

רחם is God's motherly love with patience and endurance. *Missio Dei*, as the work of the Holy Spirit's preserving ministry, is based on God's חסד and רחם. As Ps 78 confesses, God continues to forgive humanity and brings salvation despite humans' sinful lives and betrayal. God's kenotic love on the cross is deeply rooted in God's רחם and חסד.

In fact, חסד and רחם lay a fundamental foundation for all Christian missions. God's love is universal, transcultural, and countercultural. Without God's Radical Love, no Christian mission is possible. Without God's Radical Love, whatever ministries will be, they will be only humans' work, not a part of *missio Dei*. *Missio Dei* cannot be carried out by any Christian without God's Radical Love (חסד and רחם). To lack God's Radical Love in *missio Dei* is like having no engine in a car.

God's משפט and צדקה are based on God's אמת, because אמת is what God is. He is faithful and is the truth. Since he has created the universe with his אמת, God's משפט is also righteous. God is the only One who can judge the creation on whether it is right or wrong. God declares his "judgment" with his word and also brings salvation after משפט. This is the reason he עושה משפט וצדקה. All of the OT prophecies are based on God's אמת, whether it is really declared (kerygma) as judgment or as hope for restoration. This is the reason why the OT usually uses the Hebrew word אמת with other words, such as דבר, חסד, משפט.

The Hebrew word אמת defines what Christian missions should be. God's word is always straightforward. God does not give people many different ways. He offers only two: life or death. Kerygma must be straightforward. Therefore, a missiological interpretation of contextualization cannot be supported by the concept of God's Radical Love, because humans cannot reform the kerygma of God's אמת, but God's אמת is supposed to do so with human cultures. As God is omnipotent, so is his Radical Love above all humanity and human cultures.

Consequently, the missiological interpretation of God's Radical Love is this:

1. God's Radical Love is everlasting, self-giving, and unconditional to all humanity.
2. God's Radical Love is universal, transcultural, countercultural, and cross-cultural. No human element can alter that fact.
3. Christian mission is an act of carrying out *missio Dei*. Then, it should be based on God's Radical Love. All of the actions of Christian mission are about God's Radical Love and should act according to it. No Radical Love of God means no Christian mission.
4. Contextualization is not biblical according to God's Radical Love, because God's omnipotent power does not need contextualization. God's Radical Love can penetrate any human cultural barrier. *Heilsgeschichte* proves this. However, Christian mission will need a proper injector of kerygma in each human culture without changing the content of gospel. Then, God's Radical Love will transform the object culture.

2. Defining *Missio Dei* in the Light of God's Radical Love

Missio Dei has been defined by many missiologists in the twentieth century, beginning with Hartenstein. Since the definition of *missio Dei* is about defining what God is doing, it must include various understandings and concepts. Humankind can never fully comprehend what God is doing, because humankind is only a creature of God. Whatever humanity tries to understand about God, it falls short of understanding, like a blind man touching an elephant, because they can see only partial features of the Creator. This is the same with the definition of *missio Dei*. How can human beings have a full picture of what God is doing for his creation, as God describes in Job 40–41? Therefore, the new definition of *missio Dei* from this research cannot be more than a partial look, as others are. Nevertheless, the author hopes to bring new insight on *missio Dei* through this research, which has been exposed before, because the Bible informs us on *missio Dei*.

The keywords of most definitions of *missio Dei* by various scholars are "triune God," "mission," "salvation," "reconciliation," and "God's love." Indeed, those are the most significant contents of *missio Dei*. Therefore, the new definition of *missio Dei* in this research cannot reject any previous ones, since those definitions have already been helpful in highlighting various aspects of *missio Dei*. Nevertheless, by paraphrasing John 3:16, *missio Dei* can be described: God has loved the entire creation with his Radical Love, and has given his begotten Son as the result of his kenotic love so that the world and humanity will not perish by God's judgment, but the broken relationship with the creation will be restored through the work of the Holy Spirit, and they will receive eternal life in his kingdom with him. Then, this interpretation of John 3:16 based on the OT context confirms the new perspective on *missio Dei*:

> The *missio Dei* is the preserving and re-creating work of the Creation by the Creator, the triune God, through the work of the Holy Spirit and the Son, motivated by God's Radical Love (רחם, חסד, אמת), until God completely destroys the original sin from creation and restores his kingdom, and until all mankind saved by the blood of Jesus are gathered in holy convocation in God's kingdom.

Meanwhile, God's Radical Love is exposed as the Father's broken heart (נחם) toward humanity and was performed through Jesus' kenotic love on the cross. God's Radical Love is the fundamental motivation and foundation to restore the creation cursed by human sin. Hence, *missio Dei* commands churches and Christians to carry out the work of kerygma in God's Radical Love.

CHAPTER SEVEN

Missiological Application of God's Radical Love and *Missio Dei* in the Messianic Jewish Context in Israel

THROUGHOUT THIS RESEARCH, THE author has tried to determine how John 3:16 defines the motivation for God's *missio Dei* in the context of the OT. The most important finding in the theological/biblical studies from previous chapters was that God's Radical Love is the fundamental and initial motivation for *missio Dei*, which is the work of the triune God. Additionally, these studies also found that God's Radical Love is concurrently universal, supra-cultural, countercultural, and cross-cultural. God's Radical Love is the fundamental motivation and foundation of *missio Dei*, and so should be in Christian mission. Since God is the beginning and termination of mission, the Christian mission should follow his model, derived from God's Radical Mission. This means that the primary foundation of Christian mission should be supra-cultural, countercultural, and cross-cultural, depending on the mission object and situation.

Having said this, this chapter will focus on the last research question, which is about the missiological application of John 3:16 in the context of the God's Radical Love. The final research question is: "How should the Messianic Jewish congregations (Jewish Christian churches) in Israel respond to and participate in *missio Dei*?"

While the author continued with the research for this chapter, he became aware that all of the issues approached are too enormous to describe in one chapter. This chapter should be written, at minimum, in a couple of volumes of books, because this chapter covers all the issues of the modern Israeli society: sociology, anthropology, psychology, politics, ethnography, history, Judaism, and so on and so forth. Therefore, the author has decided not to go in depth on each issue, because it is impossible. Furthermore, the focus of this research is not sociological, anthropological, or ethnographical. The focus is mission theology, to conceptualize *missio Dei* in the context of God's Radical Love of John 3:16 in light of the OT. This is a missiological book, in which the author has conducted research on how to apply the mission theology principle found through this research. Accordingly, the author will focus solely on framing the missiological concept of God's Radical Love in the context of Israeli Jews in this chapter.

In order to answer the research question in this chapter, there will be a few preceding tasks to go through. First of all, it is crucial to frame Jewish history and society to lay a foundation for building a Messianic Jewish missiology based on God's Radical Love. This will help to analyze the current target for *missio Dei* in Israel related to ethnicity, culture, identity, mentality, and religiosity. Second, this study needs to verify what tools are available to carry out *missio Dei* in Israel in the twenty-first century. Third, a methodology to take action for *missio Dei* in Israel should be examined. However, prior to everything, how Messianic Jews in Israel understand *missio Dei* should be explored.

1. *Missio Dei* in the Jewish Context

1.1. A Mini Survey among Israeli Messianic Jewish Leaders

To carry out *missio Dei*, people should first know what *missio Dei* is. How do local Messianic Jewish congregational leaders really view *missio Dei*? To understand how many Messianic Jewish leaders in Israel recognize the terminology, the author carried out a mini survey among eighty-four leaders through email and SNS, who are approximately 30 percent of all Messianic Jewish leaders in Israel, and asked one question: if they had heard of or knew of *missio Dei*.[1] Their answers were clear and short. Only three people

---

1. See Kai and Bodil, *Facts and Myths*. No concrete survey for the number of Messianic Jewish congregations and number of leaders has been done since the Caspari Center did one in 1999. This is because of sensitivity of security due to the persecution by the anti-missionary group Yad L'Achim backed by the Orthodox Jews. Messianic Jews in Israel do not want to be exposed in public because it is dangerous. Therefore, based on that survey, which counted ninety-eight Messianic Jewish congregations in Israel and

answered that they knew the term and defined it in their own words. One described it as "the great sending." The second person described *missio Dei* as

> the plan that God has for the congregations. It can also be determined as the mission of the congregations (churches). What I know about the term is about the missional plans of the churches in Israel and in the world, which must help each other to carry it out in their society, and also to take care of the environment of believers. I think this dialogue is a very important issue in Israel.

His original text in Hebrew is:

> הוא התוכנית שיש לאלוהים עבור הקהילה או אפשר גם *Missio Dei* להגיד המשימה של הקהילה. מה שידוע לי בנושא כאשר מדברים עליו בין קהילות בחו"ל הוא שאלות בנושא תוכן המשימה של הקהילה. האם מדובר רק בלימוד או בישור לאחרים או האם קהילה גם אמורה לעזור ולהיות נוכחת בנושאים חברתיים כמו לדאוג לסביבה וכו. אני חושב שהשיחה הזאת מאוד חשובה בארץ.

The third person responded in English: "*Missio Dei* means God's mission for human beings through His Begotten Son, Jesus, and the Holy Spirit in this world. Moreover, God has chosen Israel to reveal *Missio Dei*."

These three people were the only ones out of eighty-four leaders who had even a clue about the concept of *missio Dei*, although their understanding was not complete. The third person was the only one who mentioned *missio Dei* by the triune God. It is encouraging to see that the second person thinks that the issue of *missio Dei* is a crucial issue to be discussed in Israel. Interestingly, the first two responders had received theological education in the USA. The third person is a native Israeli missionary of the Brethren Church.

The conclusion from the mini survey among Israeli leaders is this: Only fewer than 3 percent of the Messianic Jewish leaders in Israel may have some understanding of *missio Dei*, since it is a Christian term and most Christian terms are not familiar to Jewish people. Stewart Dauermann

---

two other sectors (Jehovah's Witnesses and Mormon), there were around 250 leaders. In Israel, furthermore, there is no such position called a pastor. They call the congregational leaders as elders according to the NT tradition (1 Pet 5:1–6). The head of the elders carries out the role of a senior pastor of each congregation. Therefore, the number of eighty-four leaders means mainly elders and includes some female leaders who serve as deaconesses. Therefore, 30 percent is just a guess through the author's twenty-eight years of ministry experience in Israel, and there isn't any concrete number for it.

mentions, "The term 'mission' is, for most Jewish people, hardly a warm word, but this need not be the case."[2] Until today, the terms *missiology* or *intercultural study* have not been known among most Messianic Jews in Israel. Therefore, it is no wonder that the term *missio Dei* is not known among Messianic Jewish leaders. This result probably would not be so different even among pastors or missionaries from Korea or the USA. Only a few church leaders or pastors comprehend that they are working in *missio Dei* through their ministries, since the term *missio Dei* is pretty much foreign to most Christians.

1.2. A Short History of the Research on Jewish Mission in Israel

The first person in the history of Europe to initiate the Jewish mission may have been Martin Luther, the Reformer. After he began the Reformation movement in Germany, Luther opened his arms to embrace Jews in his movement, hoping to convert them to the new Protestantism. He wrote a famous article about Jews, "Jesus Was Born as a Jew," in 1523. In the article, Luther mentions Jews, saying, "Therefore, I will cite from Scripture the reasons that move me to believe that Christ was a Jew born of a virgin, that I might perhaps also win some Jews to the Christian faith."[3] Luther understood how Catholics had dealt with Jewish people. He describes in the article that the Catholic way of Jewish proselytization cannot work because they had to try to convert them to Christianity with swords and spears under a cross. Luther criticized those Catholic attitudes.

> If the apostles, who also were Jews, had dealt with us gentiles as we gentiles deal with the Jews, there would never have been a Christian among the gentiles. Since they dealt with us gentiles in such brotherly fashion, we in our turn ought to treat the Jews in a brotherly manner in order that we might convert some of them. For even we ourselves are not yet all very far along, not to speak of having arrived.[4]

However, Luther's mission to Jewish people was not so fruitful in the end. After Luther, the first Jewish mission in Germany was conducted by Franz Delitzsch and his student Hermann Strack. At the time, aggressive

---

2. Dauermann, *Rabbi as Surrogate Priest*, 12.
3. *LW* 45:200.
4. *LW* 45:200–201.

anti-Semitism was heating up around Germany and Europe. In such turmoil, Delitzsch and Strack stood up against anti-Semitism and worked hard to bring Jews to Christianity, bearing quite successful fruit. In 1724, Professor Callenberg founded Institutum Judaicum in Halle. Then, Delitzsch founded the Institutum Judaicum Delitzschianum in Leipzig in 1886.[5] Through the influence of Delitzsch, Strack later created another institute in the University of Berlin. Both institutions became the centers for Jewish mission in Leipzig and Berlin. Since both Delitzsch and Strack were great scholars of Judaism and Hebrew literature, their scholarly work was quite influential to both Jewish Christians and Christians in Germany at that time.[6] However, this was far before the term *Jewish mission* had been conceptualized.

The group who possibly first articulated the term *Jewish mission* is Church's Mission among Jewish People (CMJ), which was founded by Joseph Levi (renamed Joseph Frey), a German Jew who was converted to Christianity by a German Pietist Christian in the late seventeenth century.[7] CMJ created an intensive modern mission strategy to spread the gospel in London and Europe, and also worked among Israeli Jews in Tel Aviv and Jerusalem. With this historical background, the Anglican Church sent the first Jewish bishop, Michael Solomon Alexander, in 1841.[8]

Since the beginning of the twentieth century, many Western Christian organizations have sent their missionaries to Israel.[9] Christian Mission Alliance came in 1890, and Southern Baptists in 1921. German Lutheran churches carried an important role in the Jewish mission from the beginning. Several German colonies in Israel, which were established from the eighteenth century through the beginning of the twentieth century, established churches and orphanages around the nation.[10]

Nevertheless, throughout the history of Israel, the term *Jewish mission* has been foreign or hostile to most Jewish people, as is *missio Dei*. This

---

5. D., "Institutum Judaicum," *JE* 6:609–10.
6. Levenson, "Missionary Protestants as Defenders," 383, 385–86.
7. CMJ USA, "Joseph Frey in America."
8. Crombie, *Jewish Bishop in Jerusalem*, 16.
9. Nerel, "Messianic Jews in *Eretz*-Israel."
10. Goldman, "Architecture of the Templers," 72–75.

might be a great irony because the actual *missio Dei* began in Israel,[11] and now most Jews are hostile to Christians' mission to Jews.[12]

In 1982, a Norwegian Lutheran Church set up a research center, Caspari, in Jerusalem, and started publishing their magazine *Mishkan* from 1984. *Mishkan* is the first theological/missiological research journal on Messianic Jews in Israel, although it has yet to mention the terms *missiology* or *missio Dei*.

In 2012, a small section of the Lausanne Movement had a gathering in New York for a conference, which was focused on Jewish evangelism in the world. They named the conference Lausanne Consultation for Jewish Evangelism (LCJE). LCJE has focused on Jewish evangelism around the world, including Israel. They have published the presentations from their annual conferences from each continent and also from their international general conference. LCJE has developed good insights on the theological issue of Messianic Jews in the world. Nevertheless, not even a single conference has focused on the issue of Jewish mission for the last seven years, nor on the issue of *missio Dei*. In sum, talking about *missio Dei* with Messianic Jewish groups in Israel is a completely untouched task, like discovering a new continent.

---

11. As mentioned at the beginning of this book, *missio Dei* begins with creation and continues through Israel with the election and ברית. In fact, the thesis from which this book is derived was initially designed to build on the issue of God's ברית and God's selection of Israel as part of the demonstration of God's Radical Love, because God's ברית with Israel is the most crucial part of *missio Dei* in the OT. It is, in fact, impossible to get the whole picture of God's Radical Love without comprehension of ברית and his selection. Nevertheless, this section was omitted in the dissertation in order to focus on the mission of God's Radical Love in the modern missiological context. Furthermore, the theme can also be a controversial part to discuss in a thesis, because the theology of ברית has great complications among various denominational doctrines. For instance, the author does not accept Western theologians' translation of ברית as "promise" or "covenant," because those English terms cannot convey the meaning of God's Radical Love in the context. ברית should be just *Brit* with no translation, as Christians use אמן and הללויה as transliterated terms without translation. The terms *promise* and *covenant* have created different theologies because they brought out different connotations than the original Hebrew terms. Consequently, the issue of ברית did not fit in the dissertation, but it might be looked into in the future.

12. The hostility of Jews toward the Christian gospel was created mainly by Christians in Europe during the Middle Ages, because Christians killed Jews and persecuted them as "Jesus killers" under the cross. Luther was well aware of this Jewish history (*LW* 45:200).

2. Framing a Target for *Missio Dei*

2.1. Ethnicity of Jewish People in Israel

2.1.1. A Long History Short

Israel is a unique place in the world. It has a land smaller than New Jersey, but with a rich history, which is well documented throughout the Bible and academic writings. Many different ethnic groups have been through the land, as the Bible already mentioned and as is also written in the world history of the Middle East. The land has had so many wars throughout history. Throughout her life, "Jerusalem has been attacked 52 times, captured and recaptured 44 times, besieged 23 times, and destroyed twice."[13] The list of invading ethnic groups is long: Egyptians, sea people from Mycenae (Philistine, not Palestine), Assyrians, Babylonians, Persians, Greeks, Romans, Aramaic, Arabs, Mongolians, Ottoman Turks, Napoleon French, and British. Nevertheless, the Jewish population in Israel has never ceased to exist throughout history, despite the rumors that are currently spreading in the world, saying that the Jews left Israel after the invasion of Rome and came back at the end of the nineteenth century to Palestine to claim their ancestors' land, and now Jews "occupy" Palestinian lands. Jewish people have always existed in Jerusalem, Yavneh, Tiberias, and the Zefat area from the Roman period throughout the nineteenth century, although the Jewish population was not so big.[14] "The Encyclopedia Britannica of 1910 gives the population figure [of Jerusalem] as 60,000, of whom 40,000 were Jews."[15]

Even under Islamic conquest by the Umayyad Empire (661–750), the Jewish population was spread out in the entire land of Israel.[16] They were protected by the Umayyad Empire as "the people of the Book" or *dhimmitude*.[17] Karaite Jewish rabbis returned the favor by helping the Umayyad Caliphate to develop Islamic theology.[18] Then, when the Crusade captured Jerusalem and the entire land of Israel, the crusaders cleansed Jewish people

---

13. Akhtar, *Faith and Philosophy of Islam*, 276.

14. Sources on the demographic history of Israel prior to the twentieth century are rare. Roberto Bachi's is the only source for the demographic history of Israel so far. See Bachi, *Population of Israel*, 4–8.

15. Aumann and Academic Committee, *Israel*, 120.

16. Aumann and Academic Committee, *Israel*, 120.

17. Chazan, "Jewish in Europe," 4:629–32.

18. Poluack, *Karaite Judaism*; Lewis, *Jews of Islam*, 67–106.

from the land of Israel because they were considered "Jesus killers" and worse than "Islamic mobs."[19] All Jews were locked up in their synagogues and burned alive with the synagogue by the crusaders. The population of Jewish people barely existed in Israel after being wiped out by the Crusade, but they still did not cease to exist in Israel.[20] When the Ottoman Turks came and conquered "Palestine," the Jewish population increased again. Historically, Jews had a good relationship with Turks, since they had cooperated against the Crusade advance.[21] A French Jewish banker, Rothschild, had bought a huge plot of land in Israel from the Ottoman Turks to move the Jewish people from Russia, where a severe persecution of Jews had been going on at the time.[22] The second Aliyah (Jewish émigrés) founded kibbutzim to turn the desert into the land where "milk and honey flows" (Exod 3:8). Then, the Jewish population grew significantly. Now, Jewish people from mainly Eastern Europe have shaped their cultures there. The Jewish Agency began encouraging Jewish people in the world to move to their ancient homeland, Israel.[23]

When Britain came to Palestine after defeating the Ottoman Turks during the First World War, the Jewish population in Israel had a short hope because of the Balfour Declaration, but it fell again with the White Declaration. Then, Britain tried to control the Jewish population by banning Jewish immigrants. However, this was the time when Jewish Zionism was flourishing in Europe, so many Jewish "floaters" crossed the Mediterranean Sea secretly with the help of a local Jewish armored group, Hagana. The Jewish population kept growing. After the Holocaust in Europe, the world let Jewish people have their own nation in their ancestors' land. By the time Israel had their independence on May 14, 1948, there were around 650,000 Jewish people who had come before the British Mandate or who were émigrés from over seventy countries around the world who had come during the British Mandate.[24] There was a serious diversity of ethnicity and cultures. Nevertheless, they were bound by one spirit and blood, Jewish, no

---

19. Murray, *Crusades*, 2:679–82.
20. Nemoy, "Karaite," 210.
21. Levy, *Jews, Turks, Ottomans*, 6–7.
22. Aumann and Academic Committee, *Israel*, 245–53.
23. See the census of 1922 at https://upload.wikimedia.org/wikipedia/commons/1/12/Survey_of_Palestine_Page_142.jpg (accessed Feb. 5, 2018).
24. Bachi, *Population of Israel*, 4.

matter where they came from or what languages they spoke. Despite the different ethnicities, they were just one people: "Jewish."

In sum, Jews have been spread out in the world and in Israel for two millennia, and have been under persecution and pressure constantly. These rough historical experiences have shaped their foundation of Jewish character and culture. Nevertheless, the souls of all the Israeli Jews are also united in Judaism, no matter what kind of Judaism each Jew has.

2.2. Ethnicity, Identity, and Community

The previous short summary of the history of modern Israel laid a foundation to discuss the goals of *missio Dei* in Israel. To set a clear target, this research will limit the research boundaries to the following: 1) exclusively to the Jewish population in Israel, not Arabs or Jews in diaspora, because the contemporary Jewish population in Israel is the only ministry target of the author; and 2) exclusively to the data on the twenty-first century, although some older data will be used for comparison.

2.2.1. *Ethnicity*

Ethnicity is the core of the cultural matrix in a society, and culture is purely a human product. No people means no culture, because culture is generated from human interactions. Thomas Eriksen summarizes well the concept of ethnicity from various scholars:

- Although ethnicity is widely believed to express cultural differences, there is a variable and complex relationship between ethnicity and culture; and there is certainly no one-to-one relationship between ethnic differences and cultural ones.
- Ethnicity is a property of a relationship between two or several groups, not a property of a group; it exists *between* and not *within* groups.
- Ethnicity is the enduring and systematic communication of cultural differences between groups considering themselves to be distinct. It appears whenever cultural differences are made relevant in social interaction, and it should thus be studied at the level of social life, not at the level of symbolic culture.

- Ethnicity is thus relational and also situational: the ethnic character of a social encounter is contingent on the situation. It is not, in other words, inherent.[25]

As Eriksen describes, ethnicity comes from more than two different ethnic groups, because it is "relational and situational." Ethnicity is mainly a phenomenon of immigration. Therefore, complexity and matrix are embedded in it without any intention. The ethnicity in Israel probably fits very well in Eriksen's ethnicity summary, because the ethnicity in Israel is like walking in a maze—so many different ethnic groups are living in such a small land, but they are of the opinion that they have two different kind of ethnic groups: Jews and non-Jews. It is truly incredible that they think all Jews from all around the world are one ethnic group. But from an outsider's perspective, one does not see that they are one. Israel is a cocktail of all the ethnicities in the world.

After Israel had their independence, the Israeli government and Jewish Agency in different parts of the world encouraged all Jews to move home to Israel. Then, three massive operations for immigration were carried out. In 1948–51, there was a massive Jewish immigration, mainly from Europe and the Middle East.[26] In 1981, Ethiopian Jews were endangered by a civil war, and Israel's government brought over two hundred thousand Ethiopian Jews by 1991.

When Mikhail Gorbachev allowed all Russian Jews to move to Israel in the late 1980s, around one million Russian Jews moved from 1989 to 2006.[27] Since the majority of the population in Israel are Russian immigrants or their descendants, they have shaped a different form of Jewish identity and culture in Israel.

Since the nation of Israel was born, immigration has never ceased. Currently more French Jews and Latin Jews from South America are waiting in the line for immigration, because of the rising anti-Semitism in those areas. Therefore, the diversity of ethnicity is inevitable in Israel. This diversity has become a double-edged sword. On one hand, ethnic diversity brought the richness of culture and languages that became a strong point for their economy and culture. On the other hand, it brought endless sociocultural war among different cultural groups. For instance, the

---

25. Eriksen, ""Ethnic Identity, National Identity."
26. See details in Facts about Israel, "Aliyah."
27. Tolts, "Post-Soviet Jewish Diaspora," 3.

mass immigration from Russia in such a short period greatly shook the entire society of Israel. All of the local Israelis felt a demographic crisis for over ten years, until the Russian Jews became assimilated and absorbed into the Israeli society while creating a new pattern of culture: speeding up secularization. Until the middle of the 1990s, no Jewish shops were open in Israel on Sabbath day, and there was no traffic movement on the roads. On Sabbath, everything was completely shut down. But from the middle of the 1990s, Russian markets started opening on Sabbath because they didn't care about the kosher law, since they were selling pork. It ignited a cultural war between Orthodox Jews and secular Russian Jews. Now, it is not so hard to find a Russian supermarket open on Sabbath in every city in Israel. In fact, strong secularism had already been planted by the founders of the nation, Chaim Weizmann and David Ben-Gurion. The first prime minister, David Ben-Gurion, and most of the Zionist leaders were especially faithful believers in Baruch Spinoza, the creator of secularism.[28] Moreover, Spinoza shaped the entire newborn nation of Israel by his Zionist followers based on his *Tractatus Theologico-Politicus* and *Ethica*, which later created the foundation for the ongoing cultural war between secular and religious Jews.

Eliezer Ben-Rafael and Lior Ben-Chaim made an intensive study of Israeli identity and culture in 2006, and they published it as a project of the Open University of Israel with the title *Jewish Identity in an Era of Multiple Modernities*. They explain that the crisis rises from the transformation of "politics, societies, religions, upheaval of translocation and fashion, achievements . . . etc."[29] Everything in Israel has continued changing so fast, and the population has also changed so quickly. They determine the modern Jewish identity in Israel as follows:

> כניסת יהודים לעידן המודרני, 'רב-מודרני', -או כפי שנבנה אותו, העמידה
> את הזדהותם הקולקטיבית בפני משבר וערערה את אותה זהות שהייתה
> ברורה ומובנת מאליה משך עשרות דורות.[30]

> The entry of Jews into the modern era, or as it was built, "modernized," placed their collective identification before a crisis and undermined the identity that was clear and obvious for decades.

Ben-Rafael and Ben-Chaim categorize Jewish people groups based on their ethnicities, different kinds of Judaism, and various personal social

---

28. Adler, "Zionists and Spinoza."
29. Ben-Rafael and Ben-Chaim, *Jewish Identities*, 11.
30. Ben-Rafael and Ben-Chaim, *Jewish Identities*, 11.

identities. Their goal for the research was to identify Jewish identities among different Jewish groups.

Throughout Israel's history, Jewish people have been dispersed across the world, and they returned to their ancestral homeland relatively recently. As a result, only a small number of Israeli Jews can trace back their family history in Israel for more than four generations, with most having no more than two generations in the country. Therefore, their diverse ethnicities are still alive and active in their blood.

In this context, Ben-Rafael suggests that modern Jews face a crisis of identity, caught between their collective history and the diverse modern cultures they encounter. This identity confusion and conflict have been present since before the founding of the state of Israel, continue to persist today, and are likely to last indefinitely.

This section will bring some cases of ethnic studies that have been done by Israeli social scientists in the twenty-first century. The research of Ben-Rafael and Ben-Chaim is crucial, because they analyze every detail of the Jewish mentality and sociopolitical-religious identity in their book. There are two terms to understand in order to discuss their research. The two key phrases in are "collective identity" and "multiple modernity."

Defining the term *collective identity* is not an easy task. Ben-Rafael and Ben-Chaim present various definitions by many different scholars. Among those definitions, they take the one from Levi-Strauss.

> אנו מקבלים את הגישה הסטרוקטורליסטית הרואה בזהות הקולקטיבית
> שחדרה, ארוכה יותר או ארוכה פחות, תוצר של היסטוריה תרבותית
> המבנים את סדר היום של הקולקטיב. בשל השתרשותה, לערכת הסמלים
> בדימויים העצמיים של חברי הקולקטיב עשויה זהות זו הזאת גם עשויה
> להתחזק או להיחלש- במקרים מסוימים אף להיעלם- בהשפעת נסיבות
> שונות ומשתנות.[31]

> We accept the structuralistic concept that views the collective identity as the product of a longer or shorter cultural history that has penetrated the value of symbols that make the agenda of the collective. Due to its rooting in the self-images of collective societies, this identity may also be strengthened or weakened—in certain cases even disappear—by various and changing circumstances.

Then, they define the term *multiple modernity*, which is different from *multiculturalism*. Multiple modernity is a social phenomenon, and multiculturalism is an ideology of certain groups pursuing the diversity

---

31. Ben-Rafael and Ben-Chaim, *Jewish Identities*, 17.

of cultures in society.³² They describe it as a process of "modern civilization," which is globalization, based on S. N. Eisenstadt and Björn Wittrock's theories:³³

> המושג "רב-מודרניות" מסייע אפוא להבהרת יחסיותן של חוויות מודרניות הערבוב וההפריה, שונות ומדגיש את הדינמיקה שלהן על ההשאלה ההדדית שבין היבטים תרבותיים פרטיקולריים ואוניברסליים.³⁴

> The concept of "modernity" thus helps to clarify the relativity of various modern experiences and emphasizes their dynamics in the borrowing, mixing, and mutual enrichment between particular and universal cultural aspects.

Ben-Rafael and Ben-Chaim see that multiple modernity is related to many different aspects in various areas. One crucial element of those is religion, because religion is always the core of a tradition, regardless of which community or culture it is from.³⁵ Therefore, an old, mysterious Jewish question with no clear answer, which Israel had before being established, "Who is a Jew?," cannot avoid the link with the Jewish religion, Judaism. The first prime minister of Israel, David Ben-Gurion, also faced the controversial question "Who is a Jew?" to define Jewish ethnicity for the Law of Return, which passed in 1950. It created a serious problem, because there is no way that anyone can define Jewish ethnicity by blood. The "Jewish" population has spread out over almost the entire world, mixed, and assimilated with local ethnic groups. The best answer for the question so far is according to Jewish halakah:

> A halakhic definition is: a Jew is one who is born of a Jewish mother or who converts according to the halakha. The traditional criteria thus consist of biology (descent) and religion. In a sense, biology dominates religion, because, according to halakha, someone remains a Jew if born of a Jewish mother, even if he or she converts to another religion, although such a person is referred to as "one who has destroyed himself."³⁶

Ben-Rafael and Ben-Chaim categorize Jewish people groups based on their mother cultures, different denominations of Judaism, and

32. Ben-Rafael and Ben-Chaim, *Jewish Identities*, 12.
33. Ben-Rafael and Ben-Chaim, *Jewish Identities*, 12.
34. Ben-Rafael and Ben-Chaim, *Jewish Identities*, 12.
35. Ben-Rafael and Ben-Chaim, *Jewish Identities*, 13.
36. Metz, "Who Is a Jew?," para. 6.

sociopolitical-religious status. In their categories, it is clear that religion is the core of Jewish people's identity and culture, regardless of the diversity of their birth country. The table 2 that Ben-Rafael and Ben-Chaim created shows that native ethnicity doesn't play a big role in Jewish identity in Israel. This phenomenon is not so different in tables 3 and 4 either.[37] How Israeli Jews shape their identity is basically based on their perception of religion and sociopolitical position. However, that does not mean that there is no ethnic influence on Jewish identity in Israel. Since Jewish immigration has never ceased in Israel, the cultural and social impact is unavoidable. When new Jewish immigrants arrive in Israel, most of them need a minimum of five years to adjust to a new nation as a complete Israeli citizen by learning the language, social system, and culture. During this time, the process of collective identity forms through multiple modernity. After ten years, their identities and mentalities are mostly transformed into "Israeli" in society, although they still have the language and culture from their mother countries. However, their children cease to speak their mother tongue and start speaking Hebrew at home and outside of the home. This is a different situation from immigrants in other Western countries.

Due to globalization, the world has become one huge community by mixing many different ethnicities and cultures. However, most of them create their own communities in the hosting countries, such as Chinatown, Koreatown, little Tokyo, little Istanbul, etc. No matter what country the immigrants came from, people prefer to live together as a homogeneous group, because they have less cultural and life conflict in their diaspora community while in a foreign country.

However, Jewish immigrants in Israel don't do such a thing. They try hard to assimilate into the "home" country. If they fail to do so, then they go back to their mother countries or move to Western countries, like America, Canada, or Germany, with their new Israeli passports. Only some Ethiopian Jews have created their own diaspora, but that is due to economic reasons. Most of them cannot afford to rent apartments by themselves. So, they rent a cheap apartment outside of town and share it with other families. But when they make enough money, they quickly move out from the place to live "normally" like other Israelis.

In summary, ethnicity in Israel is more unique than in any other country in the world. They have an enormous diversity in Israel, but they are only one people who are connected by Jewish history and religious

37. See tables 2–4 in appendix.

traditions. This diversity of ethnicity has created their collective identity of Jewishness in Israel and unique "multiple modernities" in their culture based on Judaism and sociopolitical ideology. Nevertheless, they claim that they are one Jewish ethnic group, regardless of where they originated. Israel has been working hard to form unity among their citizens but has not been successful so far. It is clear that they have conflict between groups that is not ethnic but more likely due to sociopolitical-religious divisions. It reveals that Israel has a serious problem with Jewish identity, even among Israeli Jews.

2.3. Social and Cultural Identity among Israeli Jews

Eriksen writes about culture with ethnicity:

> One may choose not to speak of such features of social reality and everyday life in terms of "culture," but they are no more "invented" than any other social fact. People do not choose their relatives, they cannot choose to do away with their childhood and everything they learned at a tender age. These are aspects of identity that are not chosen, that are incorporated and implicit. People relate to them as reflexive agents, but they do so within limitations that are not chosen. Such limitations form the objective foundations of social identification.[38]

Eriksen is probably right when he says ethnicity is a place where people were born, live, and die. Most Israelis become native Jewish after a few generations have lived in Israel after immigration. In this point of view, Israel has a unique ethnicity, because the cultural and national identity and ethnicity were formed in seventy years. It is the only country with that kind of case. Furthermore, identity and ethnic conflict have never ceased there for over hundreds of years, which was even before the creation of the nation. Nevertheless, Eriksen is right to say that identity is not chosen by personal will. It just happens while integrating with a new culture and society with many different people groups and culture, creating a new form of culture, ethnicity, and identity: "Israelity."

In June 2015, Israeli President Reuven Rivlin defined "four major identity groups" in Israel during his inaugural address: ultra-Orthodox (Haredi) Jews, National Religious (a.k.a. modern Orthodox) Jews, secular

---

38. Erikson, "Ethnic Identity, National Identity," 50.

Jews, and Arabs.[39] In simple terms, there are the extremely religious, conservative, and secular among Jews. So, what are the basic elements shaping those three Israeli cultural groups? Ben-Rafael, Ben-Chaim, and Yedidia Stern see them as religion, a community they belong to socially (culture and identity), and political position.[40]

As mentioned in a previous section, religion is a crucial element for the development of multiple modernities. According to Ben-Rafael and Ben-Chaim's classification, seculars can be categorized in three groups—Russian, Reconstructionist, and Canaanite—by social symptoms.[41] Religion is in every corner of the cultures of each identity group. Some of them, like Reconstructionists and some Canaanites, reject any religious element in their life and culture. Nevertheless, they are all ready to become "Jewish" whenever they need.

However, according to Stern, there are only two main cultures in Israel: religious and secular, which he calls "cultural duality."[42] These dual cultures are woven deeply within each other and cannot be separated, but they hate each other to death. It is more like a cultural symbiosis. Stern describes this Jewish cultural symbiosis in Israel.

> Many Jews in Israel live a life of cultural duality. They have two cultural foundations: Western-liberal culture and traditional Jewish culture [religious culture]. Presenting these two cultures as distinct alternatives is somewhat artificial; they are interlocked and nourish each other, and each is an organic part of the other.[43]

Most Israelis live a fully Western lifestyle (secular) with an Oriental mentality (traditional and conservative). Both types of cultures in the East and West mingle in the Israeli society. This dual lifestyle is noticeable in the modern Orthodox group. As Stern describes,

> When national religious Jews study the Torah, engage in education, and contemplate contemporary dilemmas, they fill the "Jewish drawer." When they learn a trade, engage in work, read literature, enjoy entertainment, go to the market, and go about

---

39. Stern, *Religion, State*, 3.
40. Ben-Rafael and Ben-Chaim, *Jewish Identities*, 12–15; 348–50.
41. Ben-Rafael and Ben-Chaim, *Jewish Identities*, 348.
42. Stern, *Religion, State*, 4.
43. Stern, *Religion, State*, 4.

their everyday lives, they close the Jewish drawer and open the "Western-liberal drawer" instead.[44]

In fact, among the younger generation, they call their dual culture Israelity, which has a completely Oriental content in a Western form. Many new immigrants are trying to learn how to put on Israelity as their cultural outfit as quickly as they can, although the native culture is still alive on the inner side of life. However, most of the second generations quit their mother culture and transfer to Israelity just to survive in Israel, where their true home is. Nevertheless, that unique Israelity is not identical for all Israelis. It takes shape differently, depending on what kind of ethnicity and religious group they belong to. Those distinctive groups usually do not interact with each other if there is no necessity. For instance, marrying between two different ethnicities, like between Ashkenazic and Sephardic, or between European Orthodox and Ethiopian, is even now an unimaginable issue. Ben-Rafael analyzes this phenomenon precisely. He presents the relationship between different collective identity groups with a map (fig. 1).[45] These collective identity groups are each forming a multiple modernity in a different area and section of society, but they are not integrated with each other, although they have a superficial link through their kin with "traditional Judaism" and "Jewishness." Ben-Rafael defines the characteristics of a few groups.[46]

2.3.1. Ultra-Orthodox

This group is characterized as "different." They have different values of ethnicity and culture than any other Israeli group, like setting their own school and life system. They do not serve in the army, because they think serving in the army jeopardizes their Haredi (ultra-Orthodox) identity. For the ultra-Orthodox, keeping their Haredi identity is more important than keeping their nation safe. Therefore, they made a special arrangement with the Israeli government to receive deferrals for military service from the very beginning of the founding of the nation.[47] The characteristics of those Haredi are:

---

44. Stern, *Religion, State*, 4.
45. Stern, *Religion, State*, 238.
46. Stern, *Religion, State*, 239–40. See also fig. 2 in appendix.
47. Stern, *Religion, State*, 15.

Missiological Application of God's Radical Love and *Missio Dei*

A. Closed and estranged community

B. Mostly extremely poor[48]

C. Separation from every other community and society

D. A firm belief in their duty: "bringing all cursed Israelis to repent their sin"[49]

E. Being hated to death by all other groups[50]

F. Fighting against "anti-Semitism by other Jews"[51]

What the ultra-Orthodox group does is "stay away" from sin and sinful secular-Zionist groups to preserve their קדושה (*kedusha*). Stern states about this group, "The ultra-orthodox alienation reflects that community's estrangement from the Zionist enterprises and the state."[52] In the eyes of the ultra-Orthodox Jews, the motivation for founding the state of Israel was not clean because it was deeply rooted in the secular Spinoza, who was a betrayer of Jewish people and led many Jews to God's judgment, according to the perspective of the ultra-Orthodox.

2.3.2. National Religious

This group is culturally and politically one of the dominant groups in Israel. At the same time, it is also the most problematic group, because they are leading in society and politics.[53] Stern paints a picture of this group, relating them to the "dual cultural system." "The members of the National Religious camp responded by adopting and perfecting a technique of compartmentalization and avoidance of decision."[54] For them, the dual commitment to

---

48. Because their profession is described as "studying Torah" by the authority, the Israeli government spends over a billion dollars just to support their lives (Stern, *Religion, State*, 10–20.)

49. Ben-Rafael and Ben-Chaim, *Jewish Identities*, 239.

50. Because Haredi were considered "blood suckers" due to not paying a penny of tax but getting all the social benefits and support from people's taxes due to their profession, "studying Torah" (Ben-Rafael and Ben-Chaim, *Jewish Identities*, 239).

51. Haredi always fight seriously when other groups are trying to settle equal civil rights of military service and cut funds to support the Haredi. Sometimes, it rises to an almost civil-war level (Ben-Rafael and Ben-Chaim, *Jewish Identities*, 239).

52. Stern, *Religion, State*, 15.

53. Ben-Rafael and Ben-Chaim, *Jewish Identities*, 239.

54. Stern, *Religion, State*, 5.

their culture is just two different ways of life. They choose each one as they need, as mentioned above.

They have their own agenda but don't care much for other groups such as seculars. They often push their agenda to all citizens whether they agree or not, such as a religious marriage-divorce law. However, they serve in the army and have a strong support for Zionism. They have a great passion for the land of Israel.[55] On the other hand, they are very aggressive to the Christian mission, and most members of the anti-missionary group (Yad L'Achim) belong to this group. They are also very active in persecuting local Messianic Jewish congregations in Israel, because they view Christian missionaries as "Jewish soul thieves." They are very into Israelity and keep a stereotype of Israeli cultures and identity. Ben-Rafael and Ben-Chaim's diagram shows that National Religious people are not so far from Haredi. For evangelism, it is a "mission impossible" to approach them because of their extremely closed community. Nevertheless, the author has seen that God works among them and lets them find Jesus through their Torah study. Culturally, they are more open minded about the gospel than Haredi are. But one should be aware of the danger of being attacked during evangelism. For most of the religious Jews, Nazi and Jesus are synonyms.

2.3.3. *Sephardic*

As with the National Religious group, this is another dominant group in Israel.[56] They mostly came from Spain or Arab countries and formed another typical cultural form in Israel. In the beginning, they were not the ruling group and had serious conflict with the ruling group (Ashkenazi). This conflict has created many literatures and its own cultures, and it has finally been deeply embedded in Israelity. Their social level has significantly improved, but it is still lower than Ashkenazi. Some of the Sephardic Jews have mixed well with the National Religious people, but others became secular. After the political success of the Shas (ש״ס) Party, which is representative of the Sephardic Jewish population in Israel, they have driven for a more religious cultural agenda in the Israeli society. For evangelism, the response on the gospel varies, depending on what belief the person has. They are mostly resistant to the gospel, but one can often find a Sephardi

---

55. Ben-Rafael and Ben-Chaim, *Jewish Identities*, 238.
56. Ben-Rafael and Ben-Chaim, *Jewish Identities*, 240.

who is very open to the gospel. When they become believers in Jesus, they become really solid Messianic Jews.

2.3.4. Russian

These people arrived with a massive immigration in the 1990s. As mentioned above, over one-and-a-half-million Russian Jews moved to Israel due to Gorbachev's perestroika. Because of the gigantic size of the population, they shifted the whole culture and society in Israel to a different form in a very short time. They quickly became a "dominant" cultural group in Israel and took over most of the high ranks of society because many of them were very intellectual and had been highly ranked in the former Soviet Union, such as doctors, professors, scientists, and successful businessmen. The cultural level of Israeli society quickly leveled up through Russian musicians, professors, and scientists. In addition, they were all seculars who had been brainwashed by communism in the former Soviet Union. They also rapidly took over the political positions and formed a political party. The number two in Israeli government is currently a Russian émigré. These Russians are very open to literally everything: learning the Hebrew language, culture, and even the gospel. According to a survey by Ben-Rafael and Ben-Chaim, over 16 percent of Russian émigrés are very open to the gospel.[57] In fact, in all the Messianic Jewish congregations in Israel, more than half of their members are Russian émigrés. Actually, many Russian émigrés are not Jewish but the spouses of Jews. So, those new Russian immigrants have always been great subjects for evangelism in Israel. There are especially a great number of new immigrants from Ukraine because of the war with Russia in the Donetsk and Luhansk provinces. Many Messianic Jewish congregations work hard to help them settle down and to share the gospel. They were mostly well educated and established in Ukraine, but they lost everything when they fled to Israel for life.

2.3.5. Secular

Over 50 percent of the Jewish population in Israel is secular. Many of them don't want to be a part of any religious sector. Stern describes the secular Jews, saying,

---

57. Ben-Rafael and Ben-Chaim, *Jewish Identities*, 302.

What does the secular public do? Rather than compartmentalization or alienation, secular Jews practice withdrawal from Jewish tradition. Israel's founding generation, led by David Ben-Gurion, declared a "holy rebellion" against the works of Jewish tradition and saw the classics of the "Jewish bookshelf" as an exilic millstone around the national movement's neck. The second generation of Israelis that followed them grew up in Jewish textual ignorance. Consequently, secular Israeli culture—as reflected in the education system, arts, philosophy, ethics, economy, law, media and politics—bears no significant traces of Jewish cultural heritage. Secular Jews have renounced aspects of traditional Jewish life as preserved in the Jewish cultural heritage, secular Israelis experience their Jewishness tangibly, in ways that do not exist in the diaspora. Those included the use of the Hebrew language, the use of the Hebrew calendar, the symbols of the state, and so on.[58]

Many Russians are included in this group too. Therefore, their culture is dominant through their population's number in Israel. Nevertheless, their Jewishness is concealed under their consciousness. No matter what identity an Israeli Jew describes, Judaism is hidden in their genes. Especially, whenever they encounter an "evil missionary," their Jewish genes suddenly become active and resist the missionary by saying, "Sorry, I am Jewish!," whether they have ever been in a synagogue or ever believed in God's existence. They are completely secular, atheists, or half-believing in Judaism as a tradition. They create the basic cultural platform in Israel. They are mostly religion haters. In particular, the gap and conflict between Orthodox Jews and secular Jews worsened in 1995 due to the assassination of Prime Minister Yitzhak Rabin. The assassin was a National Religious Jew. Prior to 1995, many secular Jews had thought of Judaism as the fundamental foundation of the Jewish soul and nation. There weren't many questions of Judaism as the foundation of Israeli identity. Then, in 1990, a mass immigration from Russia shook Israeli society, and then the assassination of the prime minister by an Orthodox man demolished the foundation of religious identity in Israeli society. Most seculars had lost their hope in Judaism by then. This is the point when secularization in Israel started speeding up. However, evangelizing in Israel also started speeding up from this point. Since many seculars and even religious people began questioning Judaism, they opened their hearts more easily to hear the gospel.[59]

58. Stern, *Religion, State*, 6.
59. Kai and Bodil, *Facts and Myths*, 12–14.

In sum, the diversity of ethnicity, culture, and Jewish identity is very unique in Israel and has formed in a very short period compared to other countries. This causes a serious cultural and religious war among the groups of people. At the same time, they build their identity from both sides, religious and secular, as Stern mentions:

> All Jews in Israel build their identity using fundamental components from both cultures, we might have expected that none of the three groups (Ultra-Orthodox Jews, National Religious Jews, Secular Jews) would reject either culture as an "other" whose influence must be silenced or suppressed: we might have expected there to be open dialogue marked by mutual respect between the two cultures.[60]

Although what Stern requests is tough to make happen, it happens anyway through cultural synthesization in the subconsciousness because of media. This cultural synthesization will be discussed in the next section. It is interesting to see that both sides, religious and secular Jews, are well united against their enemies, Arab terrorists and missionaries, who would destroy the existence of the Jewish nation and Jewish identity (in their perspective). Nevertheless, God has prepared a great door for the gospel through diversity and conflict.

3. How to Carry Out *Missio Dei* in Israel

3.1. Evaluating the Possibility

3.1.1. *Indigenization and Contextualization*

After a study of contextualization in Israel's history and views, the author has found a few obstacles in its application to the Israeli context, as revealed in the conclusion of the chapter:

A. The current contextualization methodology should be reconsidered in the Israeli context, because:

    a. The whole biblical culture is Jewish, and Israeli Jews learn the OT from preschool until graduation from high school. The OT is literally in their consciousness, although they become very secularized. Therefore, contextualization might work in the Israeli Jewish

---

60. Stern, *Religion, State*, 5.

context, but the author will try to find a better methodology in the cultural context.

b. Globalization has made contextualization outdated. The whole globe becomes homogenized by the globalizing force through media and internet. The world is under the force of "Hellenistic synthesization,"[61] regardless of cultural colonialism. The Jews are in the core of the global Hellenization.

c. Contextualization is a process to proselytize gentiles. However, when a Jew becomes a Christian, he/she is considered no longer a Jew from both sides of the perspective: Jewish and Christian. Both sides acknowledge that the opposite of a Jew is Christian, and they cannot go together. When a Jew claims to be a Christian, he/she is excommunicated from the Jewish community, which should not happen. When a Jew believes in Jesus, he/she becomes biblically Jewish, as Jesus is Jewish.

B. In the extreme "multiple modern society" in Israel, it is inevitable to find syncretism with an extreme pluralism.

C. God's word and God's Radical Love are supra-cultural and cross-cultural. Thus, they cannot be limited in human culture.

Contextualization is adjusting the gospel message into a different cultural context than the Western one. The Western culture was built on a Hebrew cultural foundation, with a mixture of Hellenism. Therefore, the term *contextualizing* doesn't fit in the concept of *missio Dei* with God's Radical Love, because God's Radical Love doesn't require contextualization but needs a common ground to be injected. Besides, the Internet speed is extremely fast now, and cultures in the world mingle and are synthesized every second. The contextualization process can never catch up to the speed of cultural changes.

The world is moving to extreme plural cultures and identities. Israel is far ahead in this movement, because of their highly developed technology of communication. Furthermore, Israel represents a mini global village.

---

61. Hellenistic synthesization is also known as Hellenization. However, the term here is not in the historical context, but is about a social phenomenon. Therefore, to differ from a historical event, here the term *Hellenistic synthesization* is used. When Alexander the Great conquered the world, he also planted Hellenistic culture in the colonies he took over. Then, the Hellenistic culture became the main cultural force to transform every Greek colony, mentally and culturally (Puchala, *Theory and History*, 147–49).

Therefore, there is no core target culture to contextualize the gospel in Israel, as the above survey of Israeli's multicultural society proves.

Finally, God's Radical Love is universal and supra-cultural, and at the same time it is cross-cultural too. There is no cultural bound or form that can limit God's Radical Love in God's creation, as with God's *missio Dei* through the Holy Spirit. As the Creator, God is in the culture, above the culture, and the absolute reality of which no human can determine what he does among his creation. The word is the sword of the Holy Spirit (Eph 6:17) and can penetrate every heart when the Holy Spirit works.

Consequently, contextualization might work in the context of Israeli Jewish culture, but there might be a better strategy for Israeli Jews based on the perspective of God's Radical Love. The following section will make a survey for the alternative methodology with which to carry out *missio Dei* in Israel.

3.1.2 Tools for Carrying Out Missio Dei in Israel

Through this study of God's Radical Love, it has become clear that God's Radical Love forms the foundation and initial motivation for *missio Dei*. Therefore, God's Radical Love is the most powerful and universal platform for evangelism that God has given us to use. There will be no objection among missiologists and theologians that the mission of God is fundamentally based on God's Radical Love. Without God's Radical Love, there would be no Christian mission or *missio Dei*.

3.2. What to Do

Before figuring out how to carry out *missio Dei* with God's Radical Love in Israel, there are some premises to clarify, which will form the foundation of the road map for *missio Dei*.

1. God is the Creator and Preserver of creation. So, God is supra-cultural, transcultural, and cross-cultural.
2. Therefore, God is absolute or ultra-reality who never receives any impact from human determination. God has created humans, not vice versa.

3. God is in history and runs history (*Heilsgeschichte*), regardless of human activities in history and culture.

4. God is not anti-culture, but anti-sin in culture.

Based on these premises, a proposal of mission strategy that would fit into the current context in Israel will be presented here. The author calls it "the radical cultural synthesization for *missio Dei* (or gospel)." Simply put, it is a process to transform specific people, communities, and cultures by injecting the gospel, which is the agent of transformation, through God's Radical Love. Therefore, the "radical cultural synthesization for the gospel" is a missional communication platform for individual evangelizing activity, to make a movement to transform society in Israel by using every means of Jesus-centered cultural breakthroughs. This transformational force should be created by transforming the major globalization forces: Davos, Faculty, and McDonald's.[62]

3.3. What Is Cultural Synthesization?

It is as difficult to determine what cultural synthesization is as it is to define what culture is. If one takes just the word *synthesis*, the *Merriam-Webster Learner's Dictionary* defines it as "something that is made by combining different things." Thus, *synthesize* means "to make (something) by combining different things" or "to combine (things) in order to make something new." Therefore, the literal meaning of cultural synthesization is simply a process of combining two or more cultures. However, the reality is not at all that easy, because so many different social and anthropological phenomena occur when multiple cultures encounter each other. Nevertheless, the clashing of multiple cultures in every corner of the world is truly inevitable now because of globalization. Cultural synthesis began far before globalization. However, it might be necessary to define the term first in order to move to the next step of the discussion on cultural synthesization.

The author could not find any clear definition of cultural synthesization, especially in the missiological field, where not even a single work related to cultural synthesization has been found so far. In fact, the author was surprised to find that there has been no conceptualization of cultural synthesization for the gospel even in the globalization research of the mission in the twenty-first century. The issue of globalization in the twenty-first

---

62. Berger and Huntington, *Many Globalizations*, 3–8.

century has been the hottest topic in missiology. After a lengthy time of searching, however, the author has come to the conclusion that cultural synthesization for the gospel is not yet formulated and conceptualized in the missiological world.

A number of Internet sites were found mentioning cultural synthesis, not cultural synthesization. One of the sites defined *synthesis*:

> Connecting single parts or elements into a unity or entity in contrast to ANALYSIS or dissection. Georg Wilhelm Friedrich Hegel (German philosopher, 1770–1831) described synthesis as a balance between opposites (or thesis and antithesis) into something higher by uniting contrasts, followed by creation of something new.[63]

This site also clarifies, "Therefore, synthesis is a collecting and uniting method." The author agrees to some degree with this definition of synthesis, because it brings complete unity after the combination and creates a new form with new content. However, the author cannot agree with Hegel, whom the site quotes, because synthesis does not always bring a "balance," especially in the context of culture. Cultures are usually replaced by a stronger force of synthesis, or coexist without synthesis for a while, and then gradually become isolated from the local culture.[64]

A website on early childhood development goes into detail about cultural synthesis in the areas of children's education, specifically for children who grow up in a globalized multicultural environment.[65] The site explains how etic and emic frameworks become set in those children's multicultural education. It then expounds on how to deal with those multicultural immigrant kids. One crucial note is that the teacher should learn the local culture of where the child came from, so that the teacher can communicate with the child better and know how to lead the child in education. Consequently, the immigrant children "can be enhanced through self-esteem boosts" by learning how to synthesize both cultures in their lives. There is no doubt that the host culture will be dominant in their life after a decade of education and life in the country to which they immigrated.

What then is radical cultural synthesization for the gospel? To avoid misunderstanding, it is not radical cultural synthesization *of* the gospel

---

63. See https://www.peace-through-culture.org/en/spiritual_culture/cont/synthesis.html (accessed Feb. 10, 2018).

64. Hsiao, "Coexistence and Synthesis."

65. Encyclopedia on Early Childhood Development, "Synthesis."

but radical cultural synthesization *for* the gospel, because the author believes that culture should be synthesized into the gospel according to the principle of the word, not vice versa. This is because the gospel is absolute ultra-reality that is the criterion of all human cultural values in the world. There can be no exception for any culture on this issue because God is the Creator, not a human.

It is also radical synthesization, because God's love should be the core of the synthesization process, and it is radical. Therefore, the process of cultural transformation of a target culture of an ethnic group by injection of the gospel can be radical. After being transformed, there might be a radical shift of culture, mentality, and lifestyle.

As the author is in just the beginning stage of solidifying the concept of radical cultural synthesization for the gospel, it is not easy to make a clear shape yet. Nevertheless, the author determines:

A. The radical cultural synthesization for the gospel is a process of transformation of humanity in a target area of *missio Dei* by injecting the gospel through a common ground of the cross-cultural environment, until the Jesus-centered culture and life become the dominant ones through the witness of Christians living in God's Radical Love.

B. The radical cultural synthesization for the gospel takes God's word as the absolute criterion of all human culture and life, and synthesizes them to God's word, which is "cosmos" and "ultimate reality."[66] Therefore, there will be no possibility of modification of the gospel in this process.

C. The radical cultural synthesization for the gospel takes culture as a "precarious reality."[67] The gospel should be the backbone of such a "precarious reality," because the gospel is the ultimate reality.

D. The radical cultural synthesization for the gospel should be carried out through Christians' kerygma, koinonia, and *diakonia*, which are missional actions. These actions are rooted in a life witnessing God's Radical Love.

---

66. Berger, *Sacred Canopy*, 31. Berger explains, "All legitimation maintains socially defined reality. Religion legitimates so effectively because it relates the precarious reality constructions of empirical societies with ultimate reality." The nature of culture is always precarious.

67. Berger, *Sacred Canopy*, 31.

E. The radical cultural synthesization for the gospel transforms the gospel information from a thin level of culture to a thick level.

F. The author believes that the radical cultural synthesization for the gospel can be processed through externalization, objectivities, and then internalization, until it forms a nomos with Jesus as its core.

Cultural synthesization has happened in human history all the time, even now, and it has two faces all the time: an angelic one and an evil one. The culture that has the power to be dominant swallows the other one. Hellenization is one of the best examples. When Alexander the Great conquered lands, he planted Hellenistic culture and knowledge. Some time later, Hellenization in the parts Alexander conquered processed itself without any force from the emperor. Puchala defines Hellenization as a "native adopting the Greek ways of life."[68] Some extreme cases can be found in India. It is quite well known that the east part of India has been synthesized with Hellenistic culture.[69]

One significant story of cultural synthesization in the NT is about the "God fearers" (Acts 17:4) and "Judaizers" (Gal 2:14). These were not Jews but Greeks converted to Judaism or advocates of Judaism. This is one case showing that radical cultural synthesization can work in any heathen country.

In the book of Daniel, there is another case of cultural synthesization. Chapter 6 explains the story of King Darius. This is not exactly the full scenario of cultural synthesization, but it presents a possibility on how the "Protestant" culture can impact the "Davos" power.[70]

3.4. Components of Cultural Synthesization

3.4.1. Cultural Common Ground

Most anthropologists agree that there are human commonalities in culture. Donald Brown published his book *Human Universals* in 1991, and he lists all of the human commonalities. In fact, the categories of human

---

68. Puchala, *Theory and History*, 147.
69. Sengupta, *Art of Terracotta*, 1–18.
70. Berger, *Sacred Canopy*, 7–8.

commonality in cultures are far beyond one's imagination. Kraft quotes from Nida: "Nida suggests that such evidence indicates that the similarities that unite mankind as a cultural species are much greater than the differences that separate."[71] Additionally, Kraft classifies four areas of human commonalities:

1. Human beings are biologically similar.
2. They are also psychologically alike.
3. Human beings also share common spiritual characteristics.
4. Those commonalities are expressed socioculturally.[72]

Basically, what Kraft describes is that all human beings are biologically the same, except male and female. All have the same red blood and live in the same way: eat, breathe, work, sleep. This is same in psychological issues. All humans have the same emotions, although sometimes they take different cultural expressions. Spiritually, all humans, even atheists, seek some supernatural symbol in order to have peace and spiritual comfort, such as meditation or yoga.

It is a great strategy to use a cultural common ground to inject God's Radical Love and the gospel, because finding common ground in a cross-cultural environment is a quick process. The easiest topics with which to initiate conversation are the weather or introducing the native countries. While getting acquainted with each other, the evangelist tries to find another common ground to step on for the gospel message. Therefore, common ground is the very first step for the radical cultural synthesization for the gospel. It is the first door in penetrating the target's thin culture.

3.4.2. *Thin and Thick Culture*

The concept of thin and thick culture in psychology and sociology is popular among anthropologists such as Geertz. As a symbolistic anthropologist, Geertz borrows the concept of thick and thin from Gilbert Ryle, and Geertz states that a thick description provides a cultural context with meaning through language, behavior, and symbols. Contrastingly, he describes thin culture as a simple culture with no need of interpretation. Geertz classifies four elements of the thick culture: interpretation of symbols, context

---

71. Kraft, *Christianity in Culture*, 67.
72. Kraft, *Christianity in Culture*, 68–69.

of social disclosure, what is being spoken, and microscopic. As a cultural symbolist, he focuses on how to decode all the symbols from words, actions, and things. The thick description for Geertz is all words, actions, and things that come out, with consciousness and without.[73] However, there are various different understandings and usages of the thick and thin concept, depending on the area to which the scholar applies the theory. An art critic, Roberta Green Ahmanson, uses thick culture in her own way.

> A thick culture, in other words, provides a foundation for the challenges of our lives: for building friendships, marriages, and commitments, for facing loss, suffering, and even death. The art on display at these two London museums shows clearly the different worlds created by thin and thick cultures.[74]

Toyohiro Kono and Stewart Clegg have a different perception than Ahmanson on the thick and thin concept. They determine that there are three elements of thick culture: value and pattern of decision-making, above-average values for the dimensions of culture, and crystallization.[75] This means that people in one society or organization with a thick culture share the same orientation of a formal goal, and they work hard together to achieve the goal because they share a social value or commitment for the task.

Kono and Clegg explain that in thin culture, one does not share the same values as other members.

> Thin culture means the members do not share common values with respect to the goals of the organization or group. Thin culture is associated with either a stagnant or a vitalized culture.[76]

William Mishler and Detlef Pollack explain thick and thin culture in the context of a political culture. They see the thick and thin system as part of cultural synthesization. They summarize the assumptions of thick culture as the following:

1. Thick culture is essential; it is real, and it matters.
2. Thick culture is fundamental if not primordial.
3. Thick culture is exogenous.

---

73. Geertz, *Interpretation of Cultures*, 6–10.
74. Ahmanson, "Art through Thick and Thin," para. 4.
75. Kono and Clegg, *Transformations of Corporate Culture*, 67–69.
76. Kono and Clegg, *Transformations of Corporate Culture*, 69.

4. Thick culture is holistic.
5. Thick culture is externally bounded and internally homogenous.
6. Thick culture is a coherent cluster of orientations.
7. Thick culture is durable.[77]

In fact, Mishler and Pollack share a similar perspective as Kono and Clegg on thick and thin culture. Thick culture is essential because one shares the same community or societal value. In the sociological terms of Peter Berger, it is internalized and turns into a norm or tradition. People will live with it, and their descendants will be born into it. It becomes a social platform for every member of the community. Therefore, it is fundamental, holistic, and "externally bounded and internally homogenous." This is how "America's melting pot" educational system works. It doesn't allow a parallel or coexistence. An émigré must be melted into the hosting American culture and spirit to be a good citizen of the United States. All good American citizens must synthesize into the American thick culture.

However, the melting pot system doesn't always work as the system is designed to. There are always people with thin culture. Mishler and Pollack explain thin culture as the following:

1. Thin culture is empirical; it may (or may not) matter.
2. Thin culture is constructivist and rational.
3. Thin culture is endogenous.
4. Thin culture is individualist.
5. Thin culture is relatively unbounded and diverse.
6. Thin culture is as a rule heterogeneous and ambivalent.
7. Thin culture is dynamic.[78]

Puchala explains that Hellenization in certain areas could penetrate only the surface level of culture. Puchala quotes from Avi-Yonah, saying that

> the Hellenized elements of the subject populates constituted only a "thin Greek veneer" on their society, and perhaps also that

---

77. Mishler and Pollack, "On Culture."
78. Mishler and Pollack, "On Culture."

Greekness constituted only a thin veneer over the thinking and behavior of the Hellenized individuals themselves.[79]

Therefore, various cultures always come and go and are mixed up in globalization, but not all of them infiltrate to the bottom of people's spirits. Many émigrés of society choose not to synthesize into the host thick culture and become alienated. Peter Berger expounds on alienation:

> It is important to emphasize that this estrangement is given in the sociality of man, in other words, that it is anthropologically necessary. There are, however, two ways in which it may proceed—one, in which the strangeness of world and self can be reappropriated (*zurueckgeholt*) by the "recollection" that both world and self are products of one's own activity—the other, in which such reappropriation is no longer possible, and in which social world and socialized self-confront the individual as inexorable facticities analogous to the facticities of nature. The latter process may be called alienation.[80]

In terms of the thick and thin cultural context, one fails to transform himself with the local thick culture and becomes an outcast. Or rather, one rejects synthesizing his own thick culture with the host one.

Accordingly, this research matches with Kono and Clegg's perspective. A good thing is that the thick and thin culture is not an "ultimate reality" but "precarious"[81] since it is still a human-made culture. Therefore, when one finds a common ground with a heathen culture and injects the gospel in the thin culture with the help of the Holy Spirit, the Holy Spirit will make the seed of the gospel grow. The target person to be evangelized must come into the community of people who live, serve, witness, and multiply in the Radical Love of God, so that the target person can undergo the process of radical cultural synthesization through the gospel.

3.4.3. *Supra-Cultural, Countercultural, and Cross-Cultural*

In the modern missiological world, the term *cross-cultural* has dominated. While the author studied at Fuller Theological Seminary for three years, the author never heard of other terms such as *super-cultural, supra-cultural,*

---

79. Puchala, *Theory and History*, 147.
80. Berger, *Sacred Canopy*, 85.
81. Berger, *Sacred Canopy*, 31.

transcultural, and *countercultural*. The reality is, however, that God is not always cross-cultural. In fact, there are more cases in which God is countercultural and supra-cultural, as Kraft has mentioned.[82] However, the author mostly does not agree with Kraft about the understanding of the term *supra-cultural*.

In this chapter, the author's position on the relationship between culture and God has been mentioned: "God created the universe and humankind, and humankind created culture." "Since culture is created by sinful humanity, the nature of culture is also sinful." "God is not anti-cultural but is anti-sin in the human culture." "God is omnipresent." Therefore, God is in, out of, and above culture. Human culture cannot define or limit where he is in culture.

Modern missiologists have worked hard to surpass cultural barriers and communicate with people in different cultures, in order to share the gospel of Jesus. This is the motivation and initiation for creating the concept of contextualization. However, the grave mistake of those missiologists, which made all efforts become vain, is that they could not overcome cultural barriers after decades of hard work. Furthermore, they never will, because they have missed two crucial facts: First, culture is water. It just flows, and humans are floating on it. No one knows where the water stream will move those people, especially in the stream to the globalization waterfall. No one can make such a quick contextualization at the fast speed of cultural transformation and bear fruit. Second, the power source of *missio Dei* is the Holy Spirit. The Christians sow the seed, the Holy Spirit makes it grow, and the word is the sword of the Holy Spirit. Most missionaries and missiologists confess that they want to do mission in God's way. That is great. Nevertheless, human plans are often completed faster than God's plan in the field. This often creates conflict and error.

Throughout the Bible and in this research, God is cosmic reality. He is supra-cultural. However, he is not in the supra-position that Kraft has described in his book.[83] If God is omnipresent, then why can he be only either above all or "penetrating" through a culture? Why can he not do both? Does "omnipresent" mean that he is limited to not being among evil or human sins? Then, is God only transcendent, not economic, in the sinful human life? If he is, what does his incarnation in Jesus mean? What about the meaning of the humiliation and suffering of God? One thing that is

---

82. See Kraft, *Christianity in Culture*.

83. Kraft, *Christianity in Culture*, 95; see also fig. 7.1.

clear here is that God is God, no matter what and where he is. Therefore, the term *supra-cultural* by Kraft sounds great, but it has a grave fallacy in the issue of God's omnipresence.

God is simultaneously supra-cultural, countercultural, and cross-cultural, because there is no cultural barrier that the Holy Spirit cannot go through. God is supra-cultural, because he did not create human culture and is not bound to it. He is countercultural, because he can cure a sinful human culture by injecting his word and the Holy Spirit, and then transform it into a Jesus-centered culture. God is also cross-cultural, because his word can be understood based on common grounds of universal human life.

To go in-depth with this section, one would need another research project to write a book on this theme. Therefore, this theme should be put into the further research section for next time.

3.4.4. *Globalization*

This section will discuss globalization as a process of radical cultural synthesization for the gospel, mainly based on Peter Berger's theory. It is crucial to understand how to carry out *missio Dei* in the stream of globalization in the twenty-first century. This section cannot provide the full portrait of it. Nevertheless, this section will try to present at least some picture of it.

Globalization is a major paradigm shifter of worldwide Christian missions in the twenty-first century. In fact, globalization has occurred because of a huge tear in the innovation of technology. Jim Sutherland writes,

> Globalization can be defined as the breakdown of social and technological barriers across the planet toward the creation of a one-world grid of increasing connection, interdependency, and homogeneity.[84]

Then, a question that should be asked is "Who runs the globalization dynamics?" Antonio Rappa clarifies this question in his book:

> Modern America's search for global control since World War I has demonstrated the extent of its global reach. Yet, despite the international prominence of America, the greatest impact that America has had for the past 200 years is on its own domestic politics. While the trend is for America to think of itself more often than it

---

84. Sutherland, "Globalization and Christian Missions," 1.

thinks of the rest of the world, it is also true that America thinks of itself by "out-thinking" the rest of the world. For this we need to understand its domestic politics because American domestic policies influence the nature of America's response to globalization and the world.[85]

What Rappa means is that globalization is run purely by capitalism. He is accusing Americans of controlling capitalistic globalization. He is right. America took over the world markets long before European giants, like Mercedes-Benz or Siemens, could do so in America. Ford was the first company in the world that made mass production of automobiles possible. Ford globalized the world's automobile market long before any European company could. The issue here is not who did what. The key issue here is the greediness of the nature of the world enterprise, which always wants a bigger market to sell more products. The richer they become, the more powerful they are. The enterprise wants to sell more of their products, and faster. Therefore, the globalization of the market brought the globalization of the world culturally, politically, and socially.

Peter Berger and Samuel Huntington published a book on globalization in 2002. They categorize the force of globalization in four groups: Davos, Faculty, McDonald's, and Protestantism.[86] Berger presents the Davos group for globalization as an international business culture. The Faculty Club international culture is a world intellectual culture. The McDonald's culture is a global pop culture, which is mainly run by Hollywood. The last one is Protestantism, which provides for the spiritual needs of all the other groups. These groups are not separated but are related to each other, and they often work together for their common interests in markets of other needs. In an article written in 1997, Berger also clarifies four results of these groups' interactions: replacement, coexistence, synthesis, and rejection.[87]

According to Berger, Davos is a major powerhouse of globalization. "This culture is globalized as a direct accompaniment of global economic processes."[88] They know the "how-to" of globalizing and of dealing with it. They are an elite group, all speaking English like natives, and have Western cultural traits. Whether they are Western Caucasians or not, they copy lifestyles from each other. So, they think and act like other Davos members.

---

85. Rappa, *Globalization*, 10.
86. Berger and Huntington, *Many Globalizations*.
87. Berger, "Four Faces," 23–27.
88. Berger, "Four Faces," 24.

In fact, their motivation for life is more than about surviving. It is about controlling or being controlled. The dominant one will survive while others die out, as it is with globalization. But these people often "may lead to the emergence of a nationalist or religious counter-elite."[89] In fact, none of these globalization groups can survive by themselves. They must have interactions between these cultural groups for their spiritual, personal, or business needs. They are all interacting and interdependent to a certain degree. An explanation comes at the last part of this section.

The Faculty Club culture is as international as Davos is. Berger defines it as "the globalization of the Western intelligentsia."[90] It has a network of academics, NGOs, foundations, and some government agencies around the world. These members are globalized, but the main theories and intellectual ideas to market are mainly "invented by Western-Americans."[91] If some members are not Western, they must synthesize their ways of thinking and behaving from the Faculty Club members, as Berger mentions. Whether one agrees or not, it is clear that the dominant culture of the Faculty Club is Western, and that globalization is synthesizing the Faculty Club culture in the world with acceptance or rejection. The Davos and Faculty Club cultures are interdependent. Berger says,

> It is intriguing to look at the two elite cultures in the light of the old neo-Marxist dependency theory. The Davos and the faculty club cultures have their "metropolitan" centers, with a "periphery" dependent of them.[92]

The McDonald's culture is "popular culture." Berger states, "It is propagated by business enterprises of all sorts (such as Adidas, McDonald's, Disney, MTV, and so on)."[93] The main power of the McDonald's globalization is fully based on technology. Before the Internet came out, children played in the yard or on a playground. They read books and chatted with friends for hours. However, books and playgrounds have moved into smartphones. Davos uses the McDonald's culture to convey the cultural content that Davos wants to spread out in the world market, such as eating hamburgers

---

89. Berger, "Four Faces," 25.
90. Berger 2004, 4.
91. Berger 2004, 4.
92. Berger 2004, 5.
93. Berger 2004, 6.

and watching Disney or Hollywood movies. The young generations in the global area are being brainwashed by these dominant American cultures.

The last cultural globalization force is Evangelical Protestantism. Berger has especially pointed out American Pentecostalism.[94] He has noticed how fast the Pentecostals have spread out in the world and have been globalized. It is interesting to note Berger's observation on this group. Evangelical Protestantism began in America and has spread out in the world. People in this culture do not speak English nor live in the American way. Most forms of this culture have been indigenized in each local area. But, they worship in the American "spirit"[95] with Oral Roberts's theology. Berger explains that "that (spirit) is expressed here with unmistakably Anglo-Saxon traits, especially in its powerful combination of individualistic self-expression, egalitarianism (especially between men and women), and the capacity for creating voluntary associations."[96]

It is true that this Evangelical Protestantism has been globalized. Saddleback Churches has spread out its branches around the world with its brand name.[97] The same has happened with the international Hillsong Church from Australia.

What is interesting in the globalization of Evangelical Protestantism is its interaction with other groups. Many Davos cultural CEOs are serving as elders or deacons of those megachurches. They form a Davos group in the church and cooperate with the church for marketing by using McDonald's cultural groups—the so-called "Christian entertainers or artists." Or rather, by using the TV or Internet, they market their Evangelical Protestantism. Today, many Christians are listening to sermons from their favorite preachers in America on their smartphones through YouTube channels. Actually, many of those cultural groups are linked to a religious or spiritual group and are volunteering as members. One prominent phenomenon of Evangelical Protestantism is using every means of the Davos, Faculty Club, and McDonald's cultural impact to promote their influence in the global areas.

Therefore, these four globalization forces are interactive, interwoven, and interdependent. Berger describes these four forces of globalization, which he calls the "four faces of globalization":

---

94. Berger 2004, 8.
95. Berger 2004, 8.
96. Berger 2004, 8.
97. Weissmann, "Rick Warren Goes Global."

Each is distinctive, each relates to the other three in complex ways. Yet they have important common features. The two perhaps most important features have already been mentioned—their Western, principally American, provenance, and related to this, their relation to the English language.[98]

Although people in Third World countries accuse Americans of being "cultural imperialists" or "Western colonialists," they themselves cannot escape from this globalization, whether they want to or not. Fig. 3 in the appendix shows how those four forces have linked to each other.

Then, the question this research might ask here is "How can these globalization forces be led to carry out *missio Dei* with God's Radical Love?" The answer will be found in the following section. The process should be through the radical synthesization of culture for the gospel. Hopefully, this synthesization can transform the globalization form, as fig. 4 shows. By using any means for evangelism with the work of the Holy Spirit, these four forces must be transformed to Jesus-centered forces, without the human greediness of power and money.

3.4.5. Peter Berger's World-Making Theory

Berger published his magnum opus, *The Sacred Canopy*, in 1966. The book is about the so-called "sociology of knowledge." Berger explains how humans constructed society and how society shaped humanity. The book also explains how a religion functions in the process of world construction. The author believes that the radical cultural synthesization for the gospel can be done through Berger's theory of world construction.

Berger interprets the role of religion in human society from a sociological perspective. He begins his interpretation by recognizing each human as an "unfinished" character. "Becoming man" is a process of completing "man's development" by way of society. "Man" becomes complete through his life in his society. Therefore, human society is the building process of a world by human who themselves are products of society. In this "finishing" process of human development, there are social processes that Berger calls the "dialectic process of world building." This consists of "externalization, objectivation, and internalization."[99]

---

98. Berger, "Four Faces," 29.
99. Berger, *Sacred Canopy*, 4.

Externalization is "an outpouring or expression." This includes all human acts and doings. "Every time we externalize, we impact the environment."[100] This may create a new set of choices to be faced. Since the relationship between self and world is always changing, humans are always "off balance."[101] However, a world, or nomos, is socially built through the "ordering of human experience," which provides meaning.[102] Therefore, a nomos is a relative perspective of the cosmos, which is "absolute reality."[103] This understanding makes clear what Berger has described as nomos. "A meaningful order, or nomos, is imposed upon the discrete experience and meanings of individuals."[104] Nomos is a relative and subjective standpoint. The Bible is a cosmic or absolute reality, but a denominational interpretation of Scripture is anomic reality. Externalizing is the beginning of the world-building process. Kerygma is the beginning of world building and externalizing. Externalization is in thin culture.

A society tends to be stable and to resist any threat to shake its stability. Society, therefore, creates a sense of stability, establishing and maintaining a nomos. A nomos is, in fact, always a partial representation, which becomes a subjective and relative projection of an absolute reality. Society does this by objectivating (society becomes an object), which means teaching people (especially when they are children) to make the same choices over and over again as they externalize themselves. Then, people come to believe whether the nomos is the right or wrong projection. Society wants people to act as if something were necessary and inevitable, as if that thing were an objective reality beyond their ability to change. The process of learning these roles is called *socialization*.[105] In order for socialization to work effectively, people must also feel that their inner identity depends on playing those roles. This is a process that transforms the culture from thin consciousness to thick.

Objectivation is the objective reality that humans produced by externalization.[106] Culture and society are the objective reality. Culture and society exist even though they are humans' productions. They cannot go back to where they have come. They have spread out since they were produced,

---

100. Berger, *Sacred Canopy*, 4.
101. Berger, *Sacred Canopy*, 5.
102. Berger, *Sacred Canopy*, 19.
103. Berger, *Sacred Canopy*, 56.
104. Berger, *Sacred Canopy*, 19.
105. Berger, *Sacred Canopy*, 7.
106. Berger, *Sacred Canopy*, 11–13.

Missiological Application of God's Radical Love and *Missio Dei*

whether the producer has intended them to or not, like slang on the Internet or emoticons on SMS. The objective reality has coercive power over individuals and shapes them by its own power. "Society directs, sanctions controls, and punishes individual conduct. In its most powerful apotheosis, society may even destroy the individual."[107] However, this confrontation of social and cultural objectivation is not internalization yet. Berger explains, "Internalization is rather the reabsorption into the consciousness of the objectivated world in such a way that the structures of this world come to determine the subjective structures of consciousness itself."[108]

An Israeli young man accepts Jesus as his Lord and is baptized after a few months of learning the Scriptures and Messianic Jewish life. However, his lifestyle as a secular person does not change, and he is still confused after learning the Scriptures for more than half a year. For him, the gospel is still in his thin consciousness and is in the process of objectivation. But it is not internalized in him yet.

Objectivation should be processed by koinonia and *diakonia*, which are included in Scripture study and prayer. Koinonia is a spiritual socializing process with God's Radical Love. These themes are too big to describe in detail, and the theological explanation would not be relevant here. As humans are born "incomplete," they are in the "caretaking" of society and becomes "complete" in society. Koinonia and *diakonia* are the first steps after externalization, which is kerygma, to bring a newborn spiritual child to be taken care of with God's Radical Love. A sinner becomes a citizen in the kingdom of God by the blood of Jesus, and he or she will be grown as a work of *missio Dei* through koinonia, *diakonia*, and kerygma.

In Berger's terms, one must "internalize" the object-like realities that society imposes upon him or her. Society's reality becomes one's reality. Most Jewish people believe that if they eat meat with dairy, it can cause the stomach to be upset, even though they are not religious people at all. Some people really get an upset stomach after breaking the kosher rule. Believing in Jesus is a national sin for Jewish people because of their history of persecution by gentiles Christians. That prejudice against Christianity has been internalized among the Jewish people and has become a pattern of their thinking against Jesus. To denote the sum total of all the patterns that a particular society objectivates and wants individuals to internalize, Berger uses the term *nomos*. The nomos is made up of the society's worldview and

---

107. Berger, *Sacred Canopy*, 11.
108. Berger, *Sacred Canopy*, 15.

its ethos, which provides for its members a sense of meaning. The nomos is the product of a long series of human choices, all of which could have been made differently.

When a new believer has been in the fellowship with "caretaking" through koinonia and *diakonia*, the person grows up after a while and then becomes an adult who can have his or her own family. It means that the adult can externalize and bring in some nonbelievers. Then, through caretaking through koinonia and *diakonia* (objectivation), the adult builds his or her own family (nomos) through internalization. This process can be shaky because until the new child has grown up, the gospel and God's Radical Love are still in the thin level or on the way to the thick consciousness.

The nomos is sometimes threatened by unusual experiences—for example, dreams, confusion with liberalism, or encounters with death. Those threats raise the possibility of a situation without a nomos (leaving the faith). Berger calls this threat *anomy*. Since anomy is always a possibility, society wants to strengthen its nomos as much as possible. According to Berger, this is where religion steps in for society. Religion is based on the claim that the particular nomos of a given society is not merely one among many possible choices. Rather, religion professes, the nomos is entrenched in the cosmos itself because of the Holy Spirit's work. Therefore, religion functions to make its believers sure that the universe and the individual's, as well as the group's, life in the universe are all based on the same unified and orderly pattern.

A nomos is always fragile and uncertain, which makes a society unstable, because nomos is a human product. As a result, every society tries to present itself as a permanent order, which is, in fact, absolutely impossible. According to Berger, when a religion equates a nomos with the cosmic, it provides its adherents with a sense of the eternal. This religious persuasion gives people no choice to find other options, which implies religious monopoly. This is a point where the author disagrees with Berger. On one hand, if one considers "religion" as only a human-made nomos, Berger's theory can be justified. On the other hand, God never created any religion but a "relationship" with his children. So, Berger's human-made theory of religion cannot fit in with the missiological application and context of God's Radical Love, because God's Radical Love is not a human-made nomos. Therefore, the author rejects Berger's theory of religion in the process of world construction, although it makes sense in the socioreligious context

MISSIOLOGICAL APPLICATION OF GOD'S RADICAL LOVE AND *MISSIO DEI*

of humanity. Unfortunately, this is the limitation for missiology in applying a sociological theory to the mission field.

3.5. Assembling the Cultural Synthesization Components

As was mentioned in section 3.3, cultural synthesization is not a new phenomenon or invention. It has always occurred in human history. However, depending on who runs the dynamics of cultural synthesization, the outcome can be different, as we see in Hellenization by Alexander the Great or the Enlightenment movement by laity. Consequently, the dominant power of cultural synthesization has always led the momentum of the transformation. The liberal groups of progressivism in the twenty-first century have acknowledged this synthesization very well, and they have taken over the synthesization dynamics with the great support of Obama (Davos and Faculty Club).[109] They know how to play with it. The progressive teams of cultural synthesization managed to drive all four globalization powerhouses in order to globalize progressivism and to make the etymological shift from thin to thick culture. They have greatly succeeded so far.

There is no doubt for the author that Christian evangelical groups can use the same tactics as progressivism to change society. The Christian can rebuild God's kingdom again through radical cultural synthesization. In this social context of the twenty-first century, Berger's theology of world construction is very useful for missiological application, apart from the obvious problems that should have further study in the missiological application of his theory.

Furthermore, when other components of cultural synthesization are assembled together with the help of the Holy Spirit, there is a great possibility of turning around the huge ship of cultural synthesization from secularism to evangelicalism again. Christians have always believed that God is greater than any human, and he is the Creator of the universe. As God said to Job, God will make his children great in the end, "and though your beginning was small, your latter days will be very great" (Job 8:9).

Now, how do the components of cultural synthesization work for world evangelism? This functionality of cultural synthesization is mainly based on four premises: 1) God is the creator of the universe and is omnipresent, omnipotent, and omniscient. 2) As Berger defines, "man is unfinished

---

109. See the previous sections on globalization for the explanation of these terms, or see Berger, "Four Faces."

at birth," and he needs to be "finished" in the process of socialization.[110] 3) Human socialization, which forms culture or social norms, can never be completed, as Berger mentions: "It must be an ongoing process throughout the lifetime of the individual."[111] 4) God's Radical Love is the foundation of mission to Jews and gentiles.

Given these premises, how can conservative, evangelical Christians take over the dynamics of cultural synthesization in the extremely pluralistic and secular society of the twenty-first century? Basically, the form and process of cultural synthesization has not changed throughout human history. It has always occurred through the process of externalization, objectivation, and internalization, until a nomos of a society has been set up. There is always some way to penetrate the cultural or social barriers in human society, because it has never been complete, as Berger has stated above. The twenty-first century is not so different from the era of the Roman Empire. Nevertheless, the gospel has penetrated the Roman and Hellenistic cultural wall with God's Radical Love and martyrdom. We can take the same social transformation tactics as liberals did, but with completely different content: the word of God's Radical Love. There is nothing in the universe that can block the breakthrough of God's Radical Love.

What must be clarified here are the functions of each component and the synthesization process. The common ground is the initial contact point of kerygma. This is the door that can be opened for the gospel, with the help of the Holy Spirit (see fig. 5). However, this is the stage that requires great sensitivity of the target culture, to not commit any taboos nor cross the boundaries of the culture. Until the first seed of the gospel has been planted in the thin consciousness, the common ground must keep opening through conversation. Berger mentions,

> The world is built up in the consciousness of the individual by conversation with significant others (such as parents, teachers, "peers"). The world is maintained as subjective reality by the same sort of conversation, be it with the same or with new significant others (such as spouses, friends, or other associates). If such conversation is disrupted (the spouse dies, the friends disappear, or one comes to leave one's original social milieu), the world begins to totter, to lose its subjective plausibility. In other words,

---

110. Berger, *Sacred Canopy*, 4.
111. Berger, *Sacred Canopy*, 16.

Missiological Application of God's Radical Love and *Missio Dei*

the subjective reality of the world hangs on the thin thread of conversation.[112]

In fact, when the "subjective plausibility" becomes shaky, that is the best time to inject the cure, the gospel. The concept of thin and thick culture is about the process of etymological shift. It is also about worldview and social mentality. Moving from a thin culture of Christianity to thick is the final goal of the radical cultural synthesization for the gospel. This goal will be reached by repeating the process of Berger's four faces of globalization and world-building theories. Three of the four faces (Davos, McDonald's, Faculty Club) of globalization must be converted to become powerhouses (agents) for the globalization of the evangelical gospel. The other one, Protestantism, should be an intermediate and link between the work of the Holy Spirit and the three dynamics of kingdom building. Then, the three steps for the world-building process become the four stages of God's kingdom-building process.

The process of radical cultural synthesization for the gospel has occurred in many places through a community or individual who is living in God's Radical Love. The process begins with contacting or encountering a person or a people group. Then the search for a common ground begins, where the gospel can be injected and where it can be planted in the thin culture. This is externalization.

Then, through koinonia and *diakonia* of the believers' community (churches and disciple groups), the word of God penetrates deeper with the help of the Holy Spirit. People can hear of the Christian faith more often in public. There is a very long process of objectivation. This process is what Paul Hiebert calls "cognitive process."[113] Hiebert specifies four levels of how human consciousness is constructed.[114] The first level is the gathering of data and theories, which is externalization in Berger's terms. Then, that data "is embedded in higher level systems of knowledge."[115] This is the objectivation process. The seed of God's Radical Love is sown in an individual, and it starts growing.

Objectivation usually takes a very long time, and it is an unlimited repeating process, often for more than a generation. For Christianity to become objectivated took more than three centuries. However, today is quite

---

112. Berger, *Sacred Canopy*, 16–17.
113. Hiebert, *Missiological Implications*, 81.
114. Hiebert, *Missiological Implications*, 82.
115. Hiebert, *Missiological Implications*, 82.

different because of technology. Many things change after even a year. At this point, all four agents of the globalization dynamics need full horsepower to run the globalization of God's word and his Radical Love in a society, according to the leading of the Holy Spirit through the word of God. At this stage, the gospel changes people's beliefs and knowledge system as Hiebert describes.[116]

As the final stage of cultural synthesization, the gospel creates a social norm through internalization. Then, the gospel in thin culture shifts to thick.

Hiebert explains, "A number of research traditions and a great deal of common sense knowledge are loosely integrated in a larger worldview."[117] Berger illustrates internalization in a similar way:

> Internalization, then, implies that the objective facticity of the social world becomes a subjective facticity as well. The individual encounters the institutions as data of the objective world outside himself, but they are now data of his own consciousness as well. The institutional programs set up by society are subjectively real as attitudes, motives and life projects. The reality of the institutions is appropriated by the individual along with his roles and his identity.[118]

However, there might always be the enemy's attacks on *missio Dei*. The enemy works hard to create anomy, which causes "radical separation from the social world."[119] Anomy means "not only that the individual loses emotionally satisfying ties in such cases. He loses his orientation in experience. In extreme cases, he loses his sense of reality and identity. He becomes anomic in the sense of becoming world-less."[120] This is the point when one must go back to the word to find any error in the synthesization process in order to fix the anomy, which can open a door for the enemy to penetrate into the new norm with the word, because anomy can be used for Satan to enter the new norm of the kingdom of God.

To conclude, no matter what, the human way always has a limitation. Cultural synthesization cannot finish building God's kingdom without

---

116. Hiebert, *Missiological Implications*, 83, fig. 12.
117. Hiebert, *Missiological Implications*, 84.
118. Berger, *Sacred Canopy*, 17.
119. Berger, *Sacred Canopy*, 21.
120. Berger, *Sacred Canopy*, 21.

Missiological Application of God's Radical Love and *Missio Dei*

God's Radical Love, the word, and the Holy Spirit. However, it is wise to use every means of evangelism existing in society.

Chapter Eight

Conclusion

THE RESEARCH OF THIS book began with the following hypothesis: *John 3:16 reveals that, motivated by his radical (אמת, חסד, רחם) and self-giving love, the* missio Dei *is the Triune God's eternal salvific action and plan to bring humanity to eternity, which is fully from his free will as the Creator.*

Throughout the philological study of the Hebrew terms for God's love, it became clear that the first phrase of John 3:16, Οὕτως γὰρ ἠγάπησεν ὁ θεὸς τὸν κόσμον, is a true description of God's fundamental motivation for *missio Dei*.

Chapter 3 demonstrated the original meaning of God's Radical Love in Hebrew through the philological study of רחם, נחם, אמת, חסד, and חנן. The research shows how translations of the Bible in foreign languages miss the true meaning of God's Radical Love. God's Radical Love is really the foundation of *missio Dei*. Without God's Radical Love, there would be no *missio Dei* and no existence of churches and Christians, because God's Radical Love is the backbone of the entire Bible and the Christian faith. Churches and Christians are products of God's Radical Love. Therefore, all Christians *must* live in it to be lights for all sinners. James 2:17 says, "So also faith by itself, if it does not have works, is dead."

Chapter 4 confirmed that God's Radical Love created the churches, and showed what God did and is doing in his creation. This chapter revealed that ὥστε τὸν υἱὸν τὸν μονογενῆ ἔδωκεν, ἵνα πᾶς ὁ πιστεύων εἰς αὐτὸν μὴ ἀπόληται ἀλλὰ ἔχῃ ζωὴν αἰώνιον in John 3:16 is a blueprint of *missio Dei* through Jesus and his disciples. The Greek word ὥστε shows that this phrase is a result of the preceding one, which is Οὕτως γὰρ ἠγάπησεν ὁ θεὸς τὸν κόσμον. The concept of God's suffering, humiliation, and self-giving

Conclusion

love is the process for the salvation of and reconciliation with the entire humanity.

Chapter 5 summarized God's Radical Love in the missiological context and presented the author's definition of *missio Dei* based on God's Radical Love. Missiologically, there is no boundary or cultural limitation for God's Radical Love. It is universal, as God is. The author's definition of *missio Dei* and its functionality in chapter 5 showed why God is doing his mission and what he is doing for humanity.

Based on the study from chapters 3 to 5, the ultimate principle of Christian mission has become clear. All Christians and churches exist to carry out *missio Dei* with God's Radical Love. There are no "tasks" or "jobs" to achieve something in *missio Dei*, but only sacred duties to restore God's kingdom through the blood of Jesus on the cross. The duty for humans is doing and living in *missio Dei*. Humans should be ready to give everything to the Lord with Radical Love, since God has done so, including even his life. Nothing but *missio Dei* can be the ultimate goal of Christians' lives. No other way but God's Radical Love can be the way of Christian life. Since God's Radical Love is universal, all Christians around the world should take it as the absolute nomos, regardless of cultural or ethnic differences.

Finally, chapter 6 made a suggestion of a mission strategy for the Jewish population in Israel. Jewish people are as unique as any other gentile ethnic groups, in many ways: in history, ethnicity, culture, and so on. The most prominent way is what St. Paul points out in Rom 9:4–5: "They are Israelites, and to them belong the adoption, the glory, the covenants, the giving of the law, the worship, and the promises. To them belong the patriarchs, and from their race, according to the flesh, is the Christ, who is God over all, blessed forever."

According to the modern Messianic Jewish (or Hebrew Christian) belief, God was initially called God of Israel to be the light of the gentiles (Isa 49:6). Our "Christ has been born as a Jew."[1] This is not about their particularity but about a different role in *missio Dei*.[2] Therefore, Jewish people don't need to convert, since they believe in the same God of Israel as all

---

1. *LW* 45:197.

2. The role of Israel in *missio Dei* was as a passive witness of God, as mentioned in ch. 2. God has chosen Israel as a sample of sinful humanity and used them in a pedagogical role to teach the gentiles about God, his love, and his promise. All Messianic Jews believe that all humans (including Jews) are sinful creatures in front of God. There shouldn't be any ethnic particularity. See more in Rudolph and Willitts, *Introduction to Messianic Judaism*.

Christians do. But they need to open their eyes to repent and to accept that Jesus is the Jewish Messiah, whom God promised in Scripture to give to the Jewish people and to all nations. This is because the term *conversion* in the Jewish perspective means the person who converted to Christianity has lost his/her Jewishness. Keeping Jewishness is a key issue when being a witness of Jesus in the Jewish community.

Despite such uniqueness of the Jewish people, *missio Dei* should be active among them through God's Radical Love. It does not matter if it is in a gentile Christian way, contextualization, or synthesization, since the Holy Spirit uses every means to spread out the gospel of Jesus (Phil 1:15). If there is any way to find a common ground among Jews in which to inject the gospel with God's Radical Love, the Holy Spirit will transform the Jews by giving a "new heart and new spirit." God's Radical Love does not have anything that can stop it, because it can break through any barrier. God's workers should let the gospel work by itself if they believe in the power of God Almighty and the power of God's Radical Love.

The radical cultural synthesization for the gospel is a proposal as a mission strategy in Israel. Even though the author does not believe that this is the absolute way for evangelizing Israeli Jews in Israel, he hopes it becomes an alternative and more effective way. Due to the history of Christian persecution of Jewish people and anti-Semitism, delivering the good news to Jewish people is extremely hard. However, the Holy Spirit is changing the situation and opening more and more doors. The ultimate goal of the radical cultural synthesization for the gospel is to transform the entire Israeli culture and lifestyle through Jesus. It looks like a mission impossible, but nothing is impossible for God, because he has promised the restoration of Israel (Jer 23:5–8). Radical cultural synthesization begins with a personal conversation between two or more individuals. In fact, all of human history begins with a personal conversation. The methodology of connecting people through a cultural common ground is the initial point of the radical cultural synthesization. Using a cultural common ground is the initial communicative way to deliver the gospel message cross-culturally. One of the basic principles of communication using cultural common ground is that the gospel is supra-cultural, countercultural, and also cross-cultural. Another principle is that God is cosmos (absolute reality), which humans cannot modify. Therefore, the gospel will transform a sinful culture to a Jesus-centered culture, regardless of people's intentions or different cultural contexts, since the word of God is the sword of the Holy Spirit (Eph 6:17).

Conclusion

The mission for all Christians is clear now: "For God so loved Israel and the world with his Radical Love, that he gave his only Son, that whoever among Jews believes in him should not perish but have eternal life with all gentiles believers together." Accordingly, all Messianic Jewish communities should take God's Radical Love as their foundation of life principle and make a life commitment to be tools for *missio Dei* until God restores Israel. All Christians are obliged to make Israel "jealous" through God's Radical Love (Rom 11:11).

Further Need of Research

THIS BOOK WAS DESIGNED to provide a road map for carrying out *missio Dei* in Israel. This might be the first missiological work in Israel to provide a foundation of mission theology, missiological analysis, and mission strategy. Therefore, there were enormous barriers in research due to the lack of materials. Nevertheless, this research is supposed to be done for the future of evangelism in Israel, no matter by whom it is done. Due to many reasons, there are some issues that this research could not include.

The first is the difference of the doctrinal understanding of Israel. Understanding of the nation of Israel, election of Israel, the ברית, and eschatological understanding of the role of Israel varies among different denominational doctrines. Therefore, the research had to omit the chapter of God's election of Israel, in order to avoid doctrinal confusion. Therefore, ברית and God's election of Israel in relation to God's Radical Love should be investigated in further research later.

Second, no previous missiological research on the Messianic Jewish mission in Israel has been done until today because the terms *mission* and *missiology* have a negative connotation for Jewish people, and missions is also considered an activity for gentiles. Therefore, the missiology for the Messianic Jewish community must be developed further and deeper later. This thesis is just the first stepping stone for initiating other Messianic Jewish scholars to shape the Messianic Jewish missiology further and better.

Third, God's Radical Love is the platform for Messianic Jews, Christians, and churches to carry out *missio Dei*. All missions for God should take this to the bottom of their hearts before taking action. However, God's Radical Love should be performed through kerygma, koinonia, and *diakonia* with the hope of the eschaton. Thus, there is a great need for further study on how people can operate from God's Radical Love as the foundation of missions.

Finally, the communication method through cultural common ground and the radical cultural synthesization should be revisited by many other scholars and should be further discussed to sharpen the strategy in action. As the first proposal for the communication method through cultural common ground and the radical cultural synthesization for the gospel, this book could not go deeply enough into this issue. As the concept of contextualization has been developed and tested in the field for over four decades, the same should be done for radical cultural synthesization for the gospel.

Appendix

Table 1. Greek Words used for Translations of God's Radical Love

	חסד	רחם	אמת
Greek (based on *DBL*)	φιλέω; φιλία, φιλαδελφία, φιλανθρωπία, φιλότεκνος, ἀγαπάω, ζηλόω, ἐπιποθέω, σπλαγχνίζομαι, εὔσπλαγχνος, πολύσπλαγχνος, πλατύνω τὴν καρδίαν, συμπαθέω	Φιλέω, ἱλάσκομαι, ἐλεάω, ἵλεως, ἐλεεινός, οἰκτίρω	Πείθω, πεποίθμσις, εως, ἐπαναπαύομαι, ὑπόστασις, εως, πιστεύω, ἀπιστία, βέβαιος, ἑδραῖος, θεμελιόω, ἀληθής, παρίστημι, ἐπιδείκνυμι, ἀληθής
English (based on BDB)	Kindness of humans towards humans, lovingkindness, mercies, deeds of kindness	Compassion, love	Reliability, sureness, stability, continuance, faithfulness, truth

Appendix

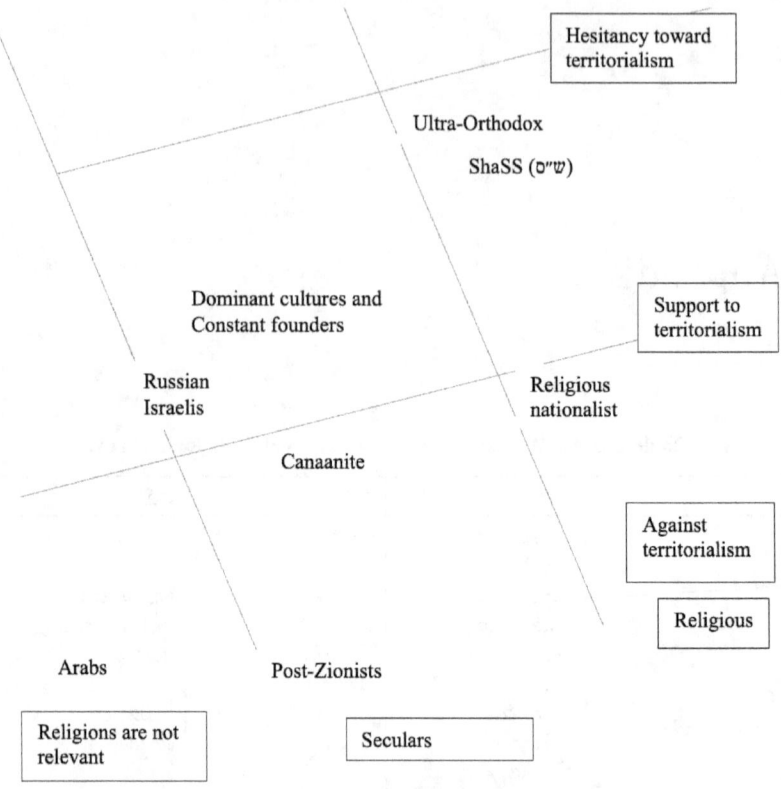

Fig. 1. Social Group Relation (Closeness-Distance) Map (from Ben-Rafael and Ben-Chaim, *Jewish Identities*, 238)

Appendix

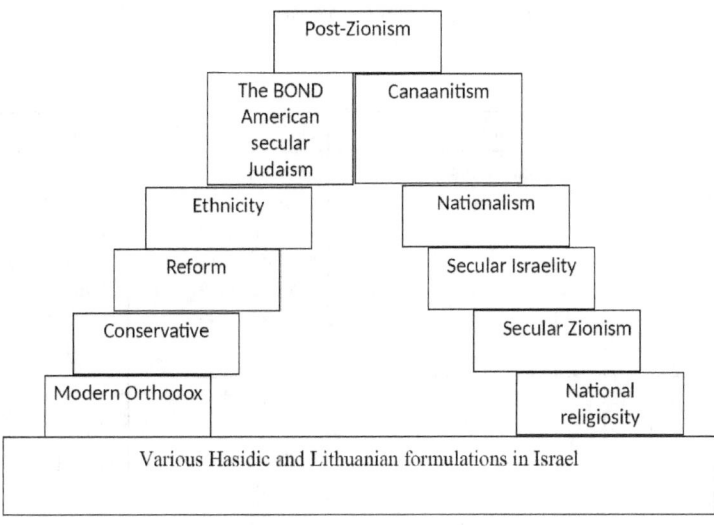

Fig 2. The Importance of the God of Israel's Torah (from Ben-Rafael and Ben-Chaim, *Jewish Identities*, 350)

Appendix

Table 2. Collective Identity in Israel (from Ben-Rafael and Ben-Chaim, *Jewish Identities*, 237)

	Commitment Group	Uniqueness	"Others"
Dominant Culture (DC) in General Way	Nationalist Jewish Eretz-Israeli	Territorialism—people in the land, secular Judaism, multiple Jewish icons, collectivism	The aspiration to engage in the Middle East alongside the preservation of Jewish uniqueness and solidarity with the diaspora
DC in the Settlement Time	Nationalist Eretz-Israeli	General characteristic DC + Israeli icons + native elitism	Emphasizing the Middle Eastern while preserving uniqueness
DC Today	Nationalist Eretz-Israeli	General characteristic DC + Western icons + individualism	Emphasizing the Western—no Middle Eastern
Shas (ש״ס: A religious political party in Israel)	Nationalist Israeli Jews	"Israelity" + ethno-religious heritage + mostly Sephardic heritage	Compartmentalization: full of Jews in the area. Partially no Sephardic Jews. Mostly in diaspora.
Religious Nationalist	Nationalist Israeli	"Israelity" + religiosity	Compartmentalization: full of Jews, including Arabs, partially Jews from diaspora
Russian Émigrés	Jewish Russian + Nationalist Israeli, Jewish	Russian language and culture + Israeli perspective	Compartmentalization: Partially old-timer Israelis

APPENDIX

Orthodox	Jews in general	Israeli religion + "Israelity" elements (i.e., Hebrew)	Compartmentalization: full of Jews, including Arabs in Israel and in areas. Some of them secular Jews.
Canaanite	Israeli Jews (Hebrews)	Hebrew culture, Middle Eastern	Compartmentalization: Israelis, no Jewish and partially Western Israelis
Post-Zionist	Just Israeli in general	A state for all its citizens (regardless of religions or political beliefs), local Hebrew and Arab culture	Compartmentalization: from Zionist Jews
Israeli Arab	Israeli Arab, Palestinians, Arabs in the area	Arab-Palestinian culture and all-Israeli perspective (Hebrew, etc.)	Compartmentalization: partially from Jewish Israelis

Table 3. Jewish Identity at the Beginning of the Twenty-First Century (from Ben-Rafael and Ben-Chaim, *Jewish Identities*, 348)

Three Syndromes and Their Models	Collective obligations: people of Israel (לארשי סע)	Perception of collective uniqueness: God of Israel and Torah	Collective location image: land of Israel
Cassette Syndrome	Adhering to a traditional lifestyle and the desire to return the people to the "beneficiary"	Observing the faith as a central component of Judaism	Faith in the messianic return to Zion; halakic derashot from Israel
American Model			This concept may also refer to any place where the Torah is observed.

APPENDIX

Israeli Model: Ashkenazim	Involvement in public life	Hebrew as the main language of the community	
Israeli Model: Sparadim	Emphasis on integration in "Am Yisrael"	Emphasis on the Sephardic worship style	
Ethno-Cultural Perception	Peoplehood as the central concept	Various relations to a process, and a positive attitude toward adaptation to modern secular society	Metaphorical reference to the concept and acceptance of a pan-social national identity
American Model		Pluralism of cultural-religious communities	
French Model	Jewishness as a feature of individuals does not mean much community	Religious-cultural approach	
Argentinian Model			A desire to bridge between a particular and national identity
Russian Model	Judaism as identification		
Modern Orthodox		Acceptance of halakah and modernity	
Conservative		Selectivity towards halakah	
Reconstructionist	Community as the center of religious life		
Reform		Religiosity without halakah, and emphasis on universal value	

Appendix

Secular Humanist			
Israeli Post-Zionist	Israeli Jews as an ethnic group	Israeli culture and Israeli-Jewish	Israel as a state of all its citizens
National Symptoms	Decomposition of the Jewish world	Secularization of traditional symbols	The main component
(1) National religious		Faith as the foundation of the national politics	
(2) Russian Jews in Israel	Cultural ethnicity in the nation	Preserving the original culture too	Keep the relations to original country
(3) Canaanite	Separation of the Israeli nation from the Jewish people in the diaspora	Emphasizing Israeli culture	Exclusive link to territory

Table 4. Formulations of Modern Jewish Identity (from Ben-Rafael and Ben-Chaim, *Jewish Identities*, 338)

Formulas	Collective obligation: people of Israel	Perception of collective uniqueness: God of Israel and Torah	Collective location image: land of Israel
Ultra-Orthodox	Jewish solidarity, but first of all by the ultra-Orthodox themselves	Adhering to a traditional lifestyle and the desire to return the people to the "beneficiary"	Faith in the messianic return to Zion; halakic derashot from Israel.
Modern Orthodox	Adherence to general Jewish solidarity	Uphold the covenant with the aim of restoring the people "to the best"	Faith in the messianic return to Zion

APPENDIX

Prediction	Cultural community based on loyalty to symbols	Connection to halakah, while also willing to adopt a general culture	Postponing until the idea of establishing a national-cultural center developed
Reform	Central, but in terms of "believers community"	Selectiveness and symbols of tradition and universal content prominence	Metaphoric-symbolic, meaning, more than geographic, territorial
	A cultural community dimension, especially in reconstructionalism	Selectivity is less halakic than that of the reform: religious life as cultural uniqueness	Not only a moral-theological ideal, but also positive relation to Zionist project
The BOND	In terms of "proletarian Jews"	Yiddish culture, while attributing ideas to the values of Jewish justice	Cultural autonomy in the socialistic society that will rise
Zionism	For the sake of dispersed kibbutz and building a nation	National modern ideology that absorbs traditional symbols	Central dimension of identity

Fig. 3. Globalization Model (based on Berger and Huntington, *Many Globalizations*)

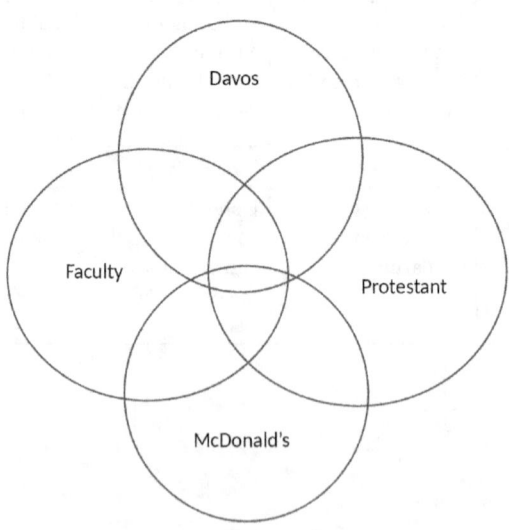

Appendix

Fig. 4. The Goal of Globalization through Radical Cultural Synthesization for the Gospel (based on Berger and Huntington, *Many Globalizations*)

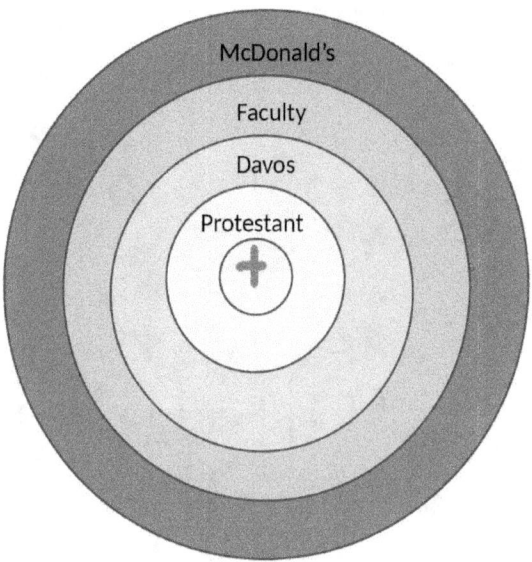

Appendix

Fig. 5. Radical Cultural Synthesization for the Gospel

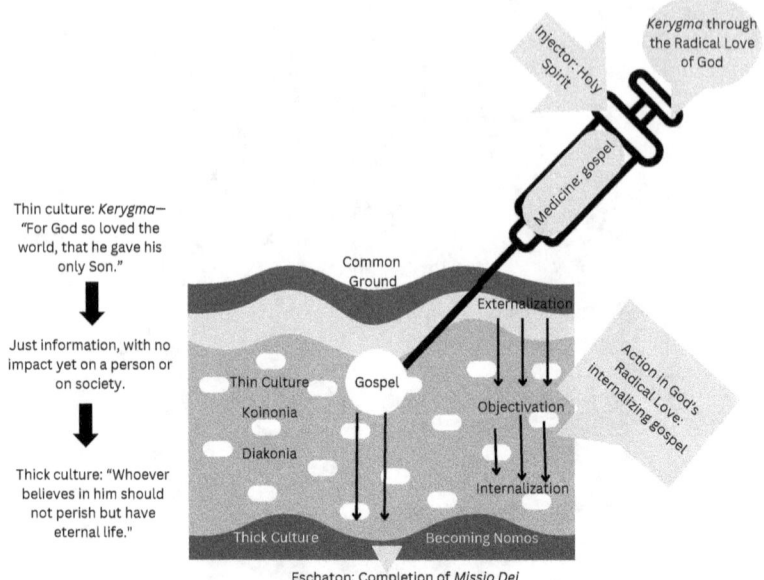

Fig. 6. Berger's Theory of Making a Society (based on Berger, *Sacred Canopy*, 25)

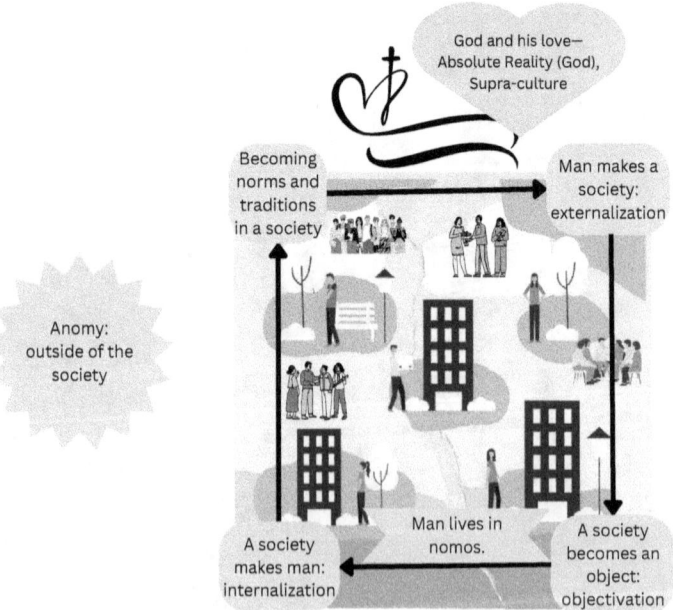

Bibliography

Abulafia, A. S. "Jews and Crusade." In *The Crusades: An Encyclopedia*, edited by Alan V. Murray, 2:679–82. Santa Barbara, CA: ABC-CLIO, 2006.
Adler, Jacob. "The Zionists and Spinoza." *Israel Studies Forum* 24 (2009) 3825–38.
Ad-Thomas, Bangor. "Some Aspects of the Root *Hnn* in the Old Testament." *Journal of Semitic Studies* 2 (1957) 128–48. https://doi.org/10.1093/jss/2.2.128.
Ahmanson, Roberta Green. "Art through Thick and Thin." *First Things*, Jan. 15, 2010. https://www.firstthings.com/web-exclusives/2010/01/art-through-thick-and-thin.
AJC. "5 Facts about the Jewish People's Ancestral Connection to the Land of Israel." AJC, Feb. 26, 2024. https://www.ajc.org/news/5-facts-about-the-jewish-peoples-ancestral-connection-to-the-land-of-israel.
Akhtar, Shamim. *Faith and Philosophy of Islam*. Indian Religions Series 2. Delhi: Kalpaz, 2009.
Aumann, Moshe, and Academic Committee on the Middle East. *Israel: Land Ownership in Palestine, 1880–1948*. [Jerusalem]: Israel Academic Committee on the Middle East, 1972.
Bachi, Roberto. *The Population of Israel*. CICRED Series. Jerusalem: Scientific Translations International, 1974. http://www.cicred.org/Eng/Publications/pdf/c-c26.pdf.
Baillie, D. M. *God Was in Christ*. New York: Scribner's Sons, 1948.
Becker, Matthew L. *The Self-Giving God and Salvation History: The Trinitarian Theology of Johannes Von Hofmann*. New York: A&C Black, 2004.
Beekes, Robert, with Lucien van Beek. *Etymological Dictionary of Greek*. 2 vols. Leiden Indo-European Etymological Dictionary. Boston: Brill, 2010.
Ben-Rafael, Eliezer, and Lior Ben-Chaim. *Jewish Identities in an Era of Multiple Modernities*. [In Hebrew.] Raanana: Open University of Israel Press, 2006.
Berger, Peter L. "Four Faces of Global Culture." *National Interest* 49 (1997) 23–30.
———. *The Sacred Canopy*. New York: Open Road Media, 2011.
Berger, Peter L., and Samuel P. Huntington, eds. *Many Globalizations: Cultural Diversity in the Contemporary World*. Oxford: Oxford University Press, 2002.
Beyerhaus, Peter. *Missions: Which Way? Humanization or Redemption*. Grand Rapids: Zondervan, 1971.
Bird, Phyllis A. *Missing Persons and Mistaken Identities: Women and Gender in Ancient Israel*. Overtures to Biblical Theology. Minneapolis: Fortress, 1997.
Bosch, David J. *Transforming Mission: Paradigm Shifts in Theology of Mission*. American Society of Missiology. Maryknoll, NY: Orbis, 1991.
Bowen, Boone M. "A Study of Chesed." PhD diss., Yale University, 1938.

Bibliography

Boyarin, Daniel. "Justin Martyr Invents Judaism." *Church History* 70 (2001) 427–61.

Briggman, Anthony. *Irenaeus of Lyons and the Theology of the Holy Spirit*. Oxford Early Christian Studies. Oxford: Oxford University Press, 2012.

Brønno, Einar. *Studien über hebräische Morphologie und Vokalismus: Auf Grundlage der mercatischen Fragmente der zweiten Kolumne der Hexapla des Origenes*. Repr., Nendeln, Licht.: Kraus, 1966.

Brown, Donald E. *Human Universals*. Boston: McGraw Hill Higher Education, 1991.

Bunkowske, Eugene W., ed. *The Lutherans in Mission: Essays in Honor of Won Yong Ji*. Lutheran Society for Missiology. Fort Wayne, IN: Fairway, 2000.

Calvin, John. *Commentary on the Gospel According to John*. Vol. 1. Edinburgh: Calvin Translation Society, 1847.

Chazan, Robert. "The Jewish in Europe and the Mediterranean Basin." In *New Cambridge Medieval History*, edited by David Luscombe and Jonathan Riley-Smith, 4:623–57. Cambridge: Cambridge University Press, 2000.

Cicero. "On Divination." University of Chicago, n.d. From *De Divinatione*, 1923. LCL. https://penelope.uchicago.edu/Thayer/E/Roman/Texts/Cicero/de_Divinatione/1*.html#ref3.

Clark, Gordon R. *The Word* Hesed *in the Hebrew Bible*. Sheffield, UK: JSOT, 1993.

CMJ USA. "Joseph Frey in America." CMJ USA, Feb. 15, 2022. https://www.cmj-usa.org/blog/joseph-frey-america.

Commission on Worship of The Lutheran Church—Missouri Synod, The. *Lutheran Service Book*. Saint Louis: Concordia, 2006.

Crombie, Kelvin. *A Jewish Bishop in Jerusalem: The Life Story of Michael Solomon Alexander*. Jerusalem: Nicolayson's, 2006.

Cullmann, Oscar. *Christ and Time: The Primitive Christian Conception of Time and History*. Philadelphia: Westminster, 1964.

Dahl, Nils Alstrup. *Jesus the Christ: The Historical Origins of Christological Doctrine*. Edited by Donald H. Juel. Minneapolis: Fortress, 1991.

Dahood, M. "Denominative *Riḥḥam*, 'to Conceive, Enwomb.'" *Biblica* 44 (1963) 204–5.

Dauermann, Stuart. *The Rabbi as a Surrogate Priest*. Eugene, OR: Pickwick, 2009.

Dumbrell, William J. *Covenant and Creation: An Old Testament Covenant Theology*. Exeter, UK: Paternoster, 2013.

Encyclopedia on Early Childhood Development. "Synthesis." EECD, n.d. http://www.child-encyclopedia.com/culture/synthesis.

Engelsviken, Tormod. "*Missio Dei*: The Understanding and Misunderstanding of a Theological Concept in European Churches and Missiology." *International Review of Mission* 92 (2003) 481–97.

Eriksen, Thomas Hylland. "Ethnic Identity, National Identity, and Intergroup Conflict." In *Social Identity, Intergroup Conflict, and Conflict Reduction*, edited by Richard D. Ashmore et al., 42–68. Rutgers Series on Self and Social Identity 3. New York: Oxford University Press, 2001.

Even-Shushan, Avraham. *Milon Hahadash Le Ivrit*. [In Hebrew.] 6 vols. Jerusalem: Kyriat Sefer, 1993.

Facts about Israel. "Aliyah—Immigration of Jews to Israel." Facts about Israel, n.d. http://www.factsaboutisrael.uk/aliyah-jewish-immigration-israel/.

Flett, John G. *The Witness of God: The Trinity, Missio Dei, Karl Barth, and the Nature of Christian Community*. Grand Rapids: Eerdmans, 2010.

Bibliography

Freeman, James M. *Handbook of Bible Manners and Customs*. New York: Nelson & Phillips, 1875.
Fretheim, Terence E. *The Suffering of God: An Old Testament Perspective*. Overtures to Biblical Theology 14. Philadelphia: Fortress, 1984.
Fruchtenbaum, Arnold G. *Messianic Christology*. San Antonio: Ariel Ministry, 1998.
Geertz, Clifford. *The Interpretation of Cultures: Selected Essays*. New York: Basic, 2008.
Gesenius, Wilhelm. *Gesenius' Hebrew Grammar*. Edited and enlarged by E. Kautzsch. Translated by A. E. Cowley. 2nd ed. Oxford: Clarendon, 1910.
——. *Gesenius's Hebrew and Chaldee Lexicon to the Old Testament Scriptures*. Edited and translated by Samuel Prideaux Tregelles. London: Bagster & Sons, 1857.
Gesenius, Wilhelm. *Gesenius' Hebrew Grammar*. 2nd ed. Oxford: Clarendon, 1910.
Glasser, Arthur F., with Charles E. Van Engen et al. *Announcing the Kingdom: The Story of God's Mission in the Bible*. Grand Rapids: Baker Academic, 2003.
Glueck, Nelson. *Hesed in the Bible*. Translated by Alfred Gottschalk. Cincinnati: Hebrew Union College Press, 1967.
Goldenberg, Gideon. *Semitic Languages: Features, Structures, Relations, Processes*. Oxford: Oxford University Press, 2013.
Goldman, Dan. "The Architecture of the Templers in Their Colonies in *Eretz*-Israel, 1868–1948, and Their Settlements in the United States, 1860–1925." PhD diss., Union Institute, Cincinnati, 2003.
Goodall, Norman. *Missions under the Cross*. London: Edinburgh, 1953.
Gordon, Cyrus H. *Ugaritic Textbook: Grammar, Texts in Transliteration, Cuneiform Selections, Glossary, Indices*. AnOr 38. Rome: Pontifical Biblical Institute Press, 1998.
Grisanti, Michael A. "Israel's Mission to the Nations in Isaiah 40–55: An Update." *Master's Seminary Journal* 9 (1998) 39–61.
Gruber, Daniel. *Rabbi Akiba's Messiah: The Origins of Rabbinic Authority*. Hanover, NH: Elijah, 1999.
Hess, Richard S. *Amarna Personal Names*. American Schools of Oriental Research Dissertation Series 9. Winona Lake, IN: Eisenbrauns, 1993.
Hiebert, Paul G. *The Missiological Implications of Epistemological Shifts: Affirming Truth in a Modern/Postmodern World*. Christian Mission and Modern Culture. Harrisburg, PA: Trinity International, 1999.
Hill, Sidney R. "The Servant of the Lord and His Servant People: A Study of a Prophetic Idea." *Int* 11 (1957) 19–32.
Hoekendijk, Johannes Christian. *The Church Inside Out*. Philadelphia: Westminster, 1966.
Hsiao, Hsin-Huang Michael. "Coexistence and Synthesis." In *Many Globalizations: Cultural Diversity in the Contemporary World*, edited by Peter L. Berger and Samuel P. Huntington, 48–67. New York: Oxford University Press, 2002.
Ibn Ezra, Abraham ben Meir. "Ibn Ezra on Isaiah 11:2." Sefaria, 1873. From *Commentary of Ibn Ezra on Isaiah*, translated by M. Friedlander. https://www.sefaria.org/Ibn_Ezra_on_Isaiah.11.2?lang=bi.
Jacob, Edmund. *Theology of the Old Testament*. Translated by Arthur W. Heathcote and Philip A. Allcock. London: Hodder & Stoughton, 1958.
Jewish Virtual Library. "The Kibbutz & Moshav: History & Overview." Jewish Virtual Library, n.d. http://www.jewishvirtuallibrary.org/history-and-overview-of-the-kibbutz-movement.
Jocz, Jakob. *The Covenant: A Theology of Human Destiny*. Grand Rapids: Eerdmans, 1968.

Bibliography

Kai, Kjaer-Hansen, and F. Skjøtt Bodil. *Facts and Myths about the Messianic Congregations in Israel 1998–1999*. Jerusalem: United Christian Council, 1999.

Kaiser, Walter C. *Mission in the Old Testament: Israel as a Light to the Nations*. Grand Rapids: Baker, 2000.

Kim, H. Edward. "The Radical Love: Exploring the Divine Motivation in God's Mission toward Humanity." PhD diss., Concordia Theological Seminary, 2018.

Kolb, Robert, and Timothy J. Wengert, eds. *The Book of Concord (New Translation): The Confessions of the Evangelical Lutheran Church*. Minneapolis: Fortress, 2000.

Kono, Toyohiro, and Stewart R. Clegg. *Transformations of Corporate Culture: Experiences of Japanese Enterprises*. De Gruyter Studies in Organization. New York: De Gruyter, 1998.

Köstenberger, Andreas J., and Peter T. O'Brien. *Salvation to the Ends of the Earth: A Biblical Theology of Mission*. New Studies in Biblical Theology 11. Downers Grove, IL: InterVarsity, 2001.

Kraft, Charles H. *Christianity in Culture: A Study in Dynamic Biblical Theologizing in Cross-Cultural Perspective*. Rev. 25th anniv. ed. Maryknoll, NY: Orbis, 2005.

Lamparter, Fritz H., ed. *Karl Hartenstein: Leben in Weltweitem Horizont; Beiträge zu Seinem 100. Geburtstag*. Mission Scripts 9. Bonn: Kultur und Wissenschaft, 1995

Levenson, Alan. "Missionary Protestants as Defenders and Detractors of Judaism: Franz Delitzsch and Hermann Strack." *Jewish Quarterly Review* 92 (2002) 383–420.

Levy, Avigdor. *Jews, Turks, Ottomans: A Shared History, Fifteenth through the Twentieth Century*. Modern Jewish History. Syracuse, NY: Syracuse University Press, 2002.

Lewis, Bernard. *The Jews of Islam*. Princeton, NJ: Princeton University Press, 1984.

Lillas, Rosmari. "Hendiadys in the Hebrew Bible: An Investigation of the Applications of the Term." DTh diss., University of Gothenburg, 2012.

Lindemann, James. *Covenant: The Blood Is the Life*. N.p.: Lulu, 2011.

Louw, Johannes P., and Eugene Albert Nida. *Greek-English Lexicon of the New Testament: Based on Semantic Domains*. New York: United Bible Societies, 1996.

Ma, Wonsuk. *Until the Spirit Comes: The Spirit of God in the Book of Isaiah*. Library of Hebrew Bible/Old Testament Studies. Sheffield, UK: Sheffield Academic, 1999.

Maier, Walter A., III. "Does God 'Repent' or Change His Mind?" *CTQ* 68 (2003) 127–43.

Mankowski, Paul V. *Akkadian Loanwords in Biblical Hebrew*. Harvard Semitic Studies 47. Winona Lake, IN: Eisenbrauns, 2000.

Masing, U. "Der Begriff *Hesed* im Alttestamentlichen Sprachgebrauch." *Charisteria Iohanni Kopp: Papers of the Estonian Theological Society in Exile* 7 (1954) 29–63.

Metz, Helen Chapin, ed. "The 'Who Is a Jew?' Controversy." From *Israel: A Country Study*. Washington, DC: GPO for the Library of Congress, 1988. https://countrystudies.us/israel/46.htm.

Mishler, William, and Detlef Pollack. "On Culture, Thick and Thin: Toward a Neo-Cultural Synthesis." In *Political Culture in Post-Communist Europe: Attitudes in New Democracies*, edited by Detlef Pollack et al., 221–40. Aldershot, Eng.: Ashgate, 2003.

Morris, Leon. *Testaments of Love: A Study of Love in the Bible*. Grand Rapids: Eerdmans, 1981.

Murray, Alan V., ed. *The Crusades: An Encyclopedia*. 4 vols. Santa Barbara, CA: ABC-CLIO, 2006.

Nemoy, Leon. "Karaite." In *Dictionary of the Middle Ages*, edited by J. R. Strayer, 209–11. New York: Scribner's Sons, 1986.

Bibliography

Nerel, Gershon. "Messianic Jews in *Eretz*-Israel (1917–1967): Trends and Changes in Shaping Self-Identity." [In Hebrew.] PhD diss., Hebrew University of Jerusalem, 1995.

Neusner, Jacob. *Genesis Rabbah: The Judaic Commentary to the Book of Genesis; A New American Translation*. 3 vols. Brown Judaic Studies 104–6. Atlanta: Scholars, 1985.

Ngien, Dennis. *The Suffering of God According to Martin Luther's "Theologia Crucis."* Eugene, OR: Wipf and Stock, 2001.

Öberg, Ingemar. *Luther and World Mission: A Historical and Systematic Study*. Translated by Dean Apel. St. Louis: Concordia, 2007.

Okoye, James Chukwuma. *Israel and the Nations: A Mission Theology of the Old Testament*. American Society of Missiology. Maryknoll, NY: Orbis, 2006.

Poluack, Meira, ed. *Karaite Judaism: A Guide to Its History and Literary Sources*. Handbook of Oriental Studies, Section 1: The Near and Middle East 73. Leiden Brill, 2003.

Puchala, Donald J. *Theory and History in International Relations*. New York: Routledge, 2003.

Qadari, Menaḥem. מילון העברית המקראית. אוצר לשון המקרא מאל״ף עד תי״ו [Dictionary of biblical Hebrew]. Ramat-Gan, Isr.: Hotza'at Universiṭat Bar-Ilan Press, 1968.

Qimron, Elisha. *Biblical Aramaic*. [In Hebrew.] 2nd expanded ed. Jerusalem: Bengurion University Press, 2002.

Rappa, Antonio L. *Globalization: Power, Authority, and Legitimacy in Late Modernity*. 2nd enlarged ed. Singapore: Institute of Southeast Asian Studies, 2011.

Rosin, H. H. *Missio Dei: An Examination of the Origin, Contents and Function of the Term in Protestant Missiological Discussion*. Leiden Interuniversity Institute for Missiological and Ecumenical Research, 1976.

Rudolph, David, and Joel Willitts, eds. *Introduction to Messianic Judaism: Its Ecclesial Context and Biblical Foundations*. Grand Rapids: Zondervan Academic, 2017.

Sabar, Yona. *A Jewish Neo-Aramaic Dictionary: Dialects of Amidya, Dihok, Nerwa and Zakho, Northwestern Iraq: Based on Old and New Manuscripts, Oral and Written Bible Translations, Folkloric Texts, and Diverse*. Wiesbaden: Harrassowitz, 2002.

Sakenfeld, Katharine D. "Studies in the Usage of the Hebrew Word *Hesed*: A Thesis." PhD diss., Harvard University, 1970.

Sakenfeld, Katharine Doob. *Faithfulness in Action: Loyalty in Biblical Perspective*. Overtures to Biblical Theology. Philadelphia: Fortress, 1985.

———. "Loyalty and Love: The Language of Human Interconnections in the Hebrew Bible." *Michigan Quarterly Review* 22 (1983) 190–203.

———. *The Meaning of* Hesed *in the Hebrew Bible: A New Inquiry*. Missoula, MT: Scholars, 1978.

Sauer, Christof. "Die Bedeutung von Leiden und Martyrium für die Mission nach Hartenstein." In *Karl Hartenstein: Leben in weltweitem Horizont*, edited by F. Lamparter, 96–111. Stuttgart: Kultur und Wissenschaft, Barsortiment Hanssler, 1995.

Scherer, James. "Luther on Mission: A Rich but Untested Potential." In *The Lutherans in Mission: Essays in Honor of Won Yong Ji*, edited by Eugene W. Bunkowske, 1–8. Lutheran Society for Missiology. Fort Wayne, IN: Fairway, 2000.

Schnabel, Eckhard J. *Early Christian Mission*. 2 vols. Downers Grove, IL: InterVarsity, 2004.

Schulz, Klaus Detlev. *Mission from the Cross: The Lutheran Theology of Mission*. St. Louis: Concordia, 2009.

———. "Tension in the Pneumatology of the Missio Dei Concept." *Concordia Journal* 23 (1997) 99–107.
Sengupta, Arputha Rani. *Art of Terracotta: Cult and Cultural Synthesis in India*. Delhi: Agam Kala Prakashan, 2005.
Soulen, R. Kendall. *The God of Israel and Christian Theology*. Minneapolis: Fortress, 1996.
Snaith, Norman. *The Distinctive Ideas of the Old Testament*. London: Epworth, 1944.
Starr, Ivan. "The *bārûtu*." *SAAB* 6 (1992) 45–53.
Stern, Yedidia Z. *Religion, State, and the Jewish Identity Crisis in Israel*. Washington, DC: Brookings Institution, 2017. https://www.brookings.edu/wp-content/uploads/2017/03/cmep_20170331_jewish-identity-crisis.pdf.
Stoebe, Hans Joachim. "Die Bedeutung des Wortes *Hasad* im Alten Testament." *Vetus Testamentum* 2 (1952) 244–54.
Sutherland, Jim. "Globalization and Christian Missions." Reconciliation Ministries Network, Sept. 2005. https://www.rmni.org/files/teaching_papers/Missions/Globalization-and-Christian-Missions.pdf.
Thomas, Norman E., ed. *Classic Texts in Mission and World Christianity*. Maryknoll, NY: Orbis, 1995.
Thompson, Marianne Meye. *The God of the Gospel of John*. Grand Rapids: Eerdmans, 2001.
Tolts, Mark. "Post-Soviet Jewish Diaspora: Latest Estimates." Paper presented at "Modern Russian-Speaking Jewish Diaspora" conference, Harvard University, Cambridge, MA, Nov. 13–15, 2011.
Van Engen, Charles, et al., eds. *The Good News of the Kingdom: Mission Theology for the Third Millennium*. Maryknoll, NY: Orbis, 1993.
Verkuyl, Johannes. "The Biblical Notion of Kingdom." In *The Good News of the Kingdom: Mission Theology for the Third Millennium*, edited by Charles Van Engen et al., 71–81. Maryknoll, NY: Orbis, 1993.
———. *Contemporary Missiology: An Introduction*. Edited and translated by Dale Cooper. Grand Rapids: Eerdmans, 1978.
Vicedom, Georg F. *The Mission of God: An Introduction to a Theology of Mission*. Translated by Gilbert A. Thiele and Dennis Hilgendorf. St. Louis: Concordia, 1965.
Waltke, Bruce. *An Introduction to Biblical Hebrew Syntax*. Winona Lake, IN: Eisenbrauns, 1990.
Weissmann, Dan. "Rick Warren Goes Global, for More Mega-Church Action." *Marketplace*, Apr. 23, 2014. https://www.marketplace.org/2014/04/23/business/rick-warren-goes-global-more-mega-church-action.
Wesley, John. *Wesley's Notes on the Bible*. Grand Rapids: Asbury, 1987.
Wight, Fred H. *Manners and Customs of Bible Lands*. Chicago: Moody, 1953.
Wright, Christopher J. H. *The Mission of God: Unlocking the Bible's Grand Narrative*. Downers Grove, IL: IVP Academic, 2013.
Wright, N. T. *The New Testament and the People of God*. Minneapolis: Fortress, 1992.

www.ingramcontent.com/pod-product-compliance
Lightning Source LLC
Chambersburg PA
CBHW062027220426

43662CB00010B/1512